TOLLAND

THE HISTORY OF AN OLD CONNECTICUT POST ROAD TOWN

D1484518

COMPILED BY HAROLD WEIGOLD
FOR
THE TOLLAND HISTORICAL SOCIETY, INC.

Globe
Pequot

Guilford, Connecticut

Published by Globe Pequot
An imprint of The Rowman & Littlefield Publishing Group, Inc.
4501 Forbes Boulevard, Suite 200, Lanham, Maryland 20706
www.rowman.com

Unit A, Whitacre Mews, 26-34 Stannary Street, London SE11 4AB

Distributed by NATIONAL BOOK NETWORK

British Library Cataloguing in Publication Information Available

Library of Congress Cataloging-in-Publication Data
The hardback edition of this book was previously cataloged by the Library of Congress as follows:

Library of Congress Catalog Card Number: 79-180543

ISBN 978-1-4930-3326-3 (paper : alk. paper)
ISBN 978-1-4930-3327-0 (electronic)

♾™ The paper used in this publication meets the minimum requirements of American National Standard for Information Sciences—Permanence of Paper for Printed Library Materials, ANSI/NISO Z39.48-1992.

Printed in the United States of America

Contents

Preface

In this History of Tolland an attempt has been made to bring up to date all of the information contained in the former Histories of Tolland, as written by Loren P. Waldo, J. R. Cole and many others. It therefore seems both fitting and proper that we use the words of Loren P. Waldo as a preface to this History of Tolland. These are his words:

> I have some hope that this history will, at least, be the means of rescuing some incidents from oblivion that might otherwise have been forever lost; and if it shall awaken any interest in the subject of local history, I shall be fully compensated for the labor I have expended.
>
> The leading idea which seemed to control the acts of the first settlers of Tolland, was the establishment and support of institutions for public worship. Next to this, they regarded the maintenance of the government under which they lived, as a conscientious duty. They were also an united people, remarkable for their stability of character and freedom from schism and discontent. This is evidenced by the tenure by which all offices, civil military, and ecclesiastical, were held. These offices were regarded as having been instituted for the benefit of society rather than as rewards for partisan services. They were also essentially a moral as well as a religious people. To do right, was the great object of their lives.
>
> In the light of this thought, how important is the question, is our work done, and well done? Is there nothing more we can do to make life more desirable, and the world better and happier? Are we prepared to put off the armor and leave the field? But if anything remains to be done, let us improve the present moment to accomplish it; nor let our efforts cease until the great work of life is ended.

In these days of unrest, we might do well to ask ourselves the same questions that Loren P. Waldo has asked. This is where the study of History can play a very important part in the development of our youth today. History can teach us about those elements of good government that can make a nation great and also the pitfalls of corruption that can undermine a great nation and cause its downfall; as many nations have failed in the past. We do hope that the youth of Tolland will study this History of Tolland and through it develop a pride in being a citizen of Tolland and a desire to make our community and our nation a better place in which to live.

Tolland, Connecticut, Sept. 1, 1971
HAROLD WEIGOLD

The Tolland Historical Society, Inc.

Due to the enthusiasm generated during the week long celebration of Tolland's 250th anniversary, in May 1965 the newly formed Junior Women's club decided, as their first project, to create an Historical Society for the benefit of the entire community. Its purpose was to preserve the artifacts and traditions of Tolland's past.

The Society was formed in 1966. The first officers were: President - Mrs. Harold W. Garrity; Vice President - Mr. Jean Auperin; Treasurer - Mr. Emory Clough; Secretary - Mrs. Dennis Hart. Over the years, the Friends of Tolland had collected numerous local memorabilia. These antiques were turned over to the Society, which arranged them very attractively in the old Post Office owned by Bertha Place and became the first museum. It was dedicated and opened to the public on May 30, 1967.

The organization has flourished during the few years of its existence and has now two Major projects. The Benton home, which was donated Dec. 13, 1969 by Mr. William Shocket and Mr. Charles Goodstein and is now open to the public two days a week during the summer.

A new Museum has been established in the former Tolland County Jail, which was given to the town in 1968. The new Museum has grown rapidly and is well equipped with the old equipment and artifacts of early Tolland life. It is open to the public on Sunday afternoons.

As a third project the Historical Society is sponsoring this new History of Tolland to preserve and bring up to date all of the interesting historical facts concerning the town of Tolland. It believes that the people of Tolland will take more pride in the heritage of their town, if they have this information readily available.

Up to this time our main sources of information concerning the History of Tolland is contained in *The History of Tolland*, written by Loren P. Waldo in 1861, and *The History of Tolland County*, written by J. R. Cole in 1888. Also *The Commemorative Biographical Record of Tolland and Windham Counties*. The object of this book is to compile all of the historical information from all sources into one book and to bring it up to date. To accomplish this, many of the people of Tolland have contributed information and photographs to make this book possible. The late Mrs. Charles Daniels contributed much in her History of the Congregational Church and Mrs. John H. Steele about the Methodist Church in her personal notes concerning Tolland. The *Two Hundred and Fiftieth Anniversary Book* also contributed many articles written by Tolland people.

The compiling and editing of this information was done for the Historical Society by Mr. Harold Weigold, who is a native born resident of Tolland.

The Title of this Book

The title of this book refers to the old post roads that passed through Tolland. In the early days, the mail was called "Post" and from 1796 to 1807 was carried on horseback or sulkey. After 1807 until 1851, regular stage coach routes were established between New York and Boston and Norwich and Springfield, passing through Tolland. Some of these post roads had toll gates of which there were several in Tolland. It is known that one was in Skungamaug and one on the Old Stafford Road. Leonard Loomis kept a toll gate for the Turnpike Company from 1837 to 1847 near the old Loomis home on route 195. With the coming of the railroads, the carrying of mail was gradually transferred to the railroads from the stage routes and eventually the railroads eliminated the stage routes.

Our Sponsors

The Tolland Historical Society is especially grateful to our contributing sponsors for their generous contributions, which have made the publication of this book possible.

Mr. William A. Shocket
Senator William Benton
The Crandall Family

HISTORICAL SOCIETY SPONSORS

Mr. & Mrs. Jean G. Auperin
Mr. & Mrs. John Burokas
Mr. & Mrs. F. S. Carpenter
Grace and Emery Clough
Alice and Ira Creelman
Arlyne and Harold Garrity
H. David Garrity
Miss Bernice A. Hall
Eleanor Meacham Jenks
Robert F. Jenks
Helen E. Lees
Miss Mary R. Leonard
Mr. & Mrs. Duane A. Mathews
Mrs. Helen L. Needham
Mr. & Mrs. E. C. Patapas
Miss Bertha M. Place
Mr. & Mrs. Harold Weigold

Introduction

A certain tract of land of about thirty six square miles in what is now the State of Connecticut was named TOLLAND in the year 1715. Perhaps, for our practical purposes, the History of Tolland should commence at that time, but this tract of land had existed as such for many millions of years. Surely, during all of those years, there must have been many factors that eventually shaped the destiny of Tolland, as we know it now.

Until recently, Connecticut was part of a vast wilderness and was inhabited only by wild animals until the coming of the Indians, several thousand years ago. The Indians hunted and fished in Connecticut but had no effect upon changing it from a wilderness.

In 1492, Christopher Columbus, discovered America and opened it up for exploration by all the other European countries. The news of the discoveries of Columbus spread swiftly over all of Europe and soon many nations were making plans to share in this great discovery.

Spain was very active in exploring and establishing colonies in America, but limited its activities to Florida, Mexico and South America. The French started exploring Canada in 1534 and claimed all of the land bounding the St. Laurence River, the Great Lakes and the Mississippi Valley. This left the eastern shores of the present United States open for colonization by the English and Dutch. The Dutch first settled around New York and claimed Connecticut as part of the Dutch Settlement. They held this land from 1609 until 1674 when all Dutch settlements in America came under English control. The English first established colonies in Virginia in 1584 and at Plymouth in 1620. By 1640, more than 20,000 Englishmen had come over to New England. Five separate states or colonies were established.

Some of the Indians living on the Connecticut River and afraid of the Pequot Indians, went to the Governors of Plymouth and Bay State Colonies and invited them to settle on their river. The Governor of Plymouth colony, after investigation, sent in 1633, William Holmes with the frame of a house and whatever was necessary to finish it, by boat. Sixty more families moved from Dorchester to Windsor in the summer of 1635.

Windsor grew and thrived and in time she needed more expansion; so after moving somewhat to the northward and the westward and southward to meet Hartford — she expanded across the river into what is now East Windsor. This was a gradual expansion, as each generation had to have new lands for the younger sons. The original homesteads were usually taken over by the oldest sons. In order to take care of this expansion, the town of Windsor had purchased from the Indians all of the lands due east of Windsor as far as the Willimantic River.

Meeting House Hill
The First Settlement in Tolland

By 1713 the town of Windsor had gradually expanded eastward across the Connecticut river into East Windsor. It would seem logical that this expansion would continue from East Windsor to Ellington and Vernon to Tolland. However, in 1713 the town of Windsor decided to establish a settlement in Tolland. There must have been some very good underlying reason to pass over Ellington and Vernon to settle Tolland. They, no doubt, were concerned by the fact that the southern part of Tolland, which they had bought from the Indians was also sold by Joshua Uncas, Sachem of the Mohegans to another group of men from Hartford. Another reason may have been that the towns of Mansfield and Coventry were already being settled and the encroachment of settlers from these towns upon lands which rightfully belonged to the town of Windsor.

They evidently decided that the best way to establish their rights to this land, was to settle it with men from Windsor, because they reasoned that actual possession and settlement of the land would give them priority over the claims of others. This reasoning may have helped to establish the boundary between Tolland and Coventry, however, the proprietors of Coventry did sue the proprietors of Tolland and in 1724 the General Court decided that the proprietors of Tolland had to pay three shillings per acre for all the lands in question.

On April 18, 1713, the town of Windsor appointed a committee comprised of Colonel Matthew Allyn, Roger Wolcott, Timothy Thrall and John Ellsworth, to lay out a town and establish a settlement in Tolland. It was at this time that Roger Wolcott proposed the name of TOLLAND for the new township in honor of Tolland Parish in England, from which town he had emigrated. The name of Tolland appeared in the resolution of the Assembly of May,

1715, which granted the new township to the petitioners of Windsor. These men from Windsor most likely followed the old Connecticut trail, which ran from Hartford to Boston through Bolton and then on to Mansfield, Putnam and Boston. They evidently travelled to Bolton and then north and east until they arrived in the vicinity of Grant's Hill.

In 1861, Loren P. Waldo wrote *The Early History of Tolland* and much of our information about early life in Tolland will be obtained from this book. So at this point it is perhaps fitting and proper to quote some of his opening passages about the early history of Tolland as follows:

> The territory now called Tolland, prior to the year 1700, formed a part of the vast wilderness that covered the western continent before the treck of civilization ever visited these shores, and was inhabited only by wild beasts or wilder men. In looking back through the long vista of years since this town was first known, we can discover no incident of thrilling interest connected with its history. We can point to no spot where the white and red men have met in mortal combat; nor where hostile armies have sought for vengeance in the bloody encounter. We do not know that the barbarian war-fire has ever shone upon these hills; or that the savage war-whoop was ever heard in these valleys. We have no legend of the Indian's stealthy tread — or his merciless attack upon the innocent and defenseless; or of our soil ever reeking with human blood. Nor can we find the footsteps of any distinguished personage upon its territory who has attracted the gaze of the world by his deeds of daring or acts of self-devotion. The history of Tolland, in short, is not calculated to interest the marvelous, nor produce wonder and astonishment in the reflecting; but like a gentle current, bears upon its quiet bosom facts worthy of our notice, and which may afford us both instruction and amusement.

Mr. Loren P. Waldo describes the first settlement in Tolland as follows:

> The earliest of these records I have been able to find is under date of April 18, 1713, at which time a committee was appointed "to lay out a settlement upon the east side of Windsor upon lands formerly purchased of the Indians." This committee performed the duties assigned them and made a report of their doings commencing in these words:
> "A chronicle of the acts of the committee empowered by the town of Windsor to lay out a plantation from the east side of Windsor upon lands formerly purchased of the Indians, April 18, 1713. The committee went upon the land to be laid out, and laid out and bounded highways and several lots as followeth. A highway of twenty rods in breadth, and running due north upon the hill called THE MEETING HOUSE HILL, between the first furlong of lots on the said hill on the east side of the

highway and the second furlong of lots on the west side of the highway; and is marked out by several marked trees, and stakes and heaps of stones, and goes the same breadth and point of compass until it pass the brook that runs up out of Cedar Swamp."

Then follows a record of seventeen lots of land containing forty acres each, laid out on each side of this highway, — eight of them being on the east side of the highway, bounding west upon it, and nine lots being on the west side of the same, bounding east upon it. These lots were each forty rods in width and one hundred and sixty rods in length, being forty rods upon the highway and extending one hundred and sixty rods in rear from the same. One of the lots on the east side of the highway is bounded north on the brook, which is no doubt the stream that runs up out of Cedar Swamp. The lots on the east side were numbered from one to eight inclusive, and were granted by the committee to Samuel Pinney, Jr., Hezekiah Porter, Sergt. Henry Wolcott, Joseph Porter, Nathan Gillett, and Samuel Forward. Those on the west side were numbered from one to nine inclusive and were granted to Enoch Loomis, Cornelius Birge, Simon Wolcott, Jr., Joshua Loomis, Sergt. Henry Wolcott, Noah Grant, Joseph Rockwell, Jr., Thomas Grant, and Josiah Rockwell. The first and sixth lots on the east side of the highway do not appear to have been assigned to any one.

It has been a matter of some inquiry where this first highway was located, for it is evident that its location was intended to establish the center of the new town. From the record we learn that it was "twenty rods in breadth," and ran "due north upon the hill called Meeting-house Hill, between the first furlong of lots on the said hill on the east side of the highway, and the second furlong of lots on the west side of the highway," and that it goes the same breadth and point of "compass until it pass the brook that runs up out of Cedar Swamp." Here we have the point of compass — "due north," — the width of the road — "twenty rods," — the name of the hill where located — "Meeting-house Hill," — and its northern terminus — "the brook that runs up out of Cedar Swamp." Now is there any locality that will answer this description?

Some persons have supposed that the village of Tolland is located on this highway. The street, they say, runs nearly north and south, sufficiently to answer the description "due north;" that it is, or was before trespassed upon and shorn of its primeval capaciousness, nearly of the requisite width; that it is the only eminence in town that can be justly called meeting-house hill, for no other hill was ever honored with an edifice of this character, and the stream of water north of the village known as "Spencer Brook" is the brook that was described as running up out of Cedar Swamp. But a little attention will satisfy the casual observer that the present village could not have been the locality described in this record. For the course of the street is not "due north" but several degrees to the west of north, and before we come to Spencer Brook it is north-east. Nor was the street ever twenty rods wide, during its whole length, nor is there any evidence that it was ever called "Meeting-house Hill." It must be borne in mind that this record was made April 18, 1713, more than two years before the charter of the town was granted, and before its locality or extent could be known. The town of Coventry was incorporated in 1711, but its northern boundary was not then established, as we shall hereafter have occasion to see; and hence the proper place for the center of the contemplated new township must of necessity then have been a matter of speculation. It is true, our ancestors in locating a township first sought for an eligible location for a meeting-house, and an indispensable requisite for such location was high land. True to these instincts, the committee that located the first road in Tolland, and laid off the first lots to settlers, commenced upon the highest ground that then was supposed to be nearest the center of the contemplated town. As I have already said, the north line of the town of Coventry was then unknown, but was then and for many years thereafter claimed by the Windsor men to be one mile further south than it was finally found to be. There can therefore be no doubt that the first location of highways and lots in Tolland was made upon Grant's Hill, and not upon the hill where the village is now located. This locality answers the description in the record, the course of the road now on Grant's Hill is generally north and south, and it crosses the brook that runs up out of Cedar Swamp, and the only such brook in Tolland. The name "Meeting House Hill" was doubtless given to it because it was intended for the center of the new town, which could not even be regarded as a town without containing a meeting-house. But we are able to make this thing certain by the following facts which are conclusive upon this point. The record before spoken of shows that several lots of forty acres each were, by the committee who laid out this road, located on each side of it, and were granted to particular individuals. The survey of one of these lots is in these words, copied from the record afore said: —

> The seventh lot is by the committee bounded east by the "highway", south on the sixth lot; west on undivided lands; north on the eighth lot; and containing forty acres, being in breadth forty rods north and south, and runs from the street one hundred and sixty rods west. This lot is by the committee granted to Joseph Rockwell, Jr.

The sixth lot described in this record was by this committee granted to Noah Grant, and the eighth to Thomas Grant.

On the first book of records of lands of the town of Tolland, at page seventy nine, I find a record of a deed of land from Joseph Rockwell of Windsor, in the county of Hartford, to John Abbott, of Andover, Mass., a blacksmith; dated March 14, 1719-20, which land in said deed is described as follows:

> My dwelling house and house lot in the township of Tolland, said lot containing forty acres, being forty rods in breadth, and one hundred and threescore rods in length, be it more or less, butting and bounding west upon my own land lately set out to me by the committee of the town of Tolland in our first division of lands appertaining to or belonging to said home-lot, of forty acres, bounding easterly on the town highway, and south on the home-lot of Noah Grant, and north by lands firstly belonging to Thomas Grant, Jr., of Windsor, but now in possession of Nathaniel Wallis.

This is the same place once owned by Alfred Young and later by James A. Brown, situated on Grant's Hill.

These are the conclusions that Mr. Loren P. Waldo arrived at from studying the facts that he had at hand and he evidently arrived at the correct conclusion. The following study of the Grant's Hill area not only upholds his conclusions but adds certain revealing facts that eliminate any doubt about the location of the first settlement in the town of Tolland.

Now a study of Grant's Hill does not readily reveal the true facts. It is hard to conceive of a highway that was 20 rods wide or 330 feet wide, especially on Grant's Hill. The present road is quite crooked and certainly bears no resemblance to a road 20 rods wide. However, one strange thing is noticeable about this road and that is that some of the houses were set way back from the road. This seemed unusual, since on most roads, the houses are all set quite close to the road. In looking over the National Geological Survey maps of this region, one is impressed with the fact that when they stated that the road was laid out "due north", that they referred to the fact that boundaries at that time were laid out by compass and of course they used the magnetic north. The south boundary of Tolland was laid out on magnetic east and west and thus slopes up about 13° to the true-north in running from west to east.

Now, one is readily impressed by the fact, that the Grant's Hill road does lie fairly close in the direction of the magnetic north. Now by drawing parallel lines on each side of the road that are just 20 rods apart, and drawn exactly "due north", these lines will be perpendicular to the Tolland — Coventry line also. We then find that these two lines will hold the Grant's Hill road within their boundaries for over a mile of length and immediately, the old houses that seemed scattered helter-skelter over the landscape, fell into perfect alignment along the outer edge of the 20 rod wide highway. We also find that the stone wall beside the New Road is exactly perpendicular to this 20 rod highway and runs due east and west for the first half mile. Now, if we take this as a base line and use it as the dividing line between Lot #5 and Lot #6, we can lay out 8 lots on the east side of the highway and nine lots on the west side. If the lots on the west side are numbered from 1 to 9, we find that the names of the lot owners fall at the right place. Lot #7 is the same as the records say, was allotted to Joseph Rockwell and who later sold it to John Abbott. Noah Grant becomes the owner of Lot #6 and Thomas Grant becomes the owner of lot #8, as stated in Mr. Waldo's History of Tolland. On the east side you will note that Lot #1 and Lot #6 were left vacant. It seems reasonable to assume that Lot #6 was left vacant, in order to have space for the meeting house, which would be centrally located. Perhaps also for a school and town hall. The #1 lot was evidently not claimed at that time.

It is surprising how many of the present stone walls run due east and west and many fall at the lot line boundaries. There is even a pile of stones as a marker for the north-west end of the highway, near the brook.

The layout of "Meeting House Hill" was made in 1713 and these men thought they were near the center of Tolland, but when the final Coventry — Tolland line was established in 1720, they found that they were on the extreme south end of the town. When the first meeting house was to be built in 1722, the other settlers in

Tolland insisted that it be built in the center of Tolland; so it was built in what is now called Tolland Street. The plan for "Meeting House Hill" was then abandoned. However, several of the old houses still remain on the edge of the original 20 rod highway. After the plan was abandoned the owners of the lots on Grant's Hill got permission from the town to move their boundaries from the 20 rod highway out to the edge of the present highway. The map of the original "Meeting House Hill" layout does not leave much doubt that Grant's Hill was the first settlement in Tolland.

A record of some of the owners of three of the lots in the original plan is as follows:

OWNERS OF LOT #7 — GRANT'S HILL — WEST SIDE

1713　Land grant to Joseph Rockwell of Windsor.

1720　Land deeded by Joseph Rockwell to John Abbott of Andover. Sometime during this period, land sold to Alfred Young.

1853　Alfred Young sold land to Mr. Kimball and Mr. James A. Brown, who was Mr. Kimball's son in law.

1857　The original house was torn down and a new one was built.

1868　The land and house was sold to Charles Underwood. Mr. Underwood rented the property to Jaynes Babcock.

1871　Mr. Underwood resold the property to Mr. Kimball. On Oct. 22, 1873, Mr. Gilbert P. Babcock, the son of Mr. Jaynes Babcock, married Inez Brown, the granddaughter of Mr. Kimball and the daughter of James A. Brown.

1884　Mr. Kimball deeded the property to his granddaughter, Mrs. Inez Brown Babcock.

1912　The house burned down and was rebuilt.

1927　Mrs. Babcock sold property to Mr. Steero of New Britain.

1932　The house burnt down and was again rebuilt.

OWNERS OF LOT #8 — GRANT'S HILL — WEST SIDE

1713　Land grant to Thomas Grant of Windsor.

1719　Thomas Grant deeded property to Nathaniel Wallis.

1816　Deed by David Dart to Harry Coggswell. 3-12-1816.

1863　Deed by Sarah and Gilbert Preston to Reuben and Albert Whitman. 3-3-1863.

1864　Quit claim deed by Albert Whitman to Reuben Whitman.

1888　Deed by Reuben Whitman to William D. Round. 11-8-1888.

1919　Deed by Probate Court to Alvah and Enoch Rounds.

1935   Deed by Jennie A. Sands, former wife of Enoch Rounds, to Hazel Forryan. 8-9-1935.

1946   Deed by Hazel M. Forryan to Chadbourne Knowlton.

1947   Deed by Chadbourne and Wilma Knowlton to Robert Mc-Hutchison, on Dec. 1, 1947.

OWNERS OF LOT #7 — GRANT'S HILL — EAST SIDE

1713   Land grant to Nathan Gillett of Windsor.

1716   Land deeded by Nathan Gillett to George Bradley.

1724   Land deeded by George Bradley to Noah Grant. Noah Grant was the original proprietor of Lot 6 on the west side of the highway. He was Noah Grant, the great, great grandfather of President Ulysses Grant. He most likely lived in a log cabin on Lot #6 on the west side of the highway, until he bought Lot #7 on the east side, in 1724. He lived there until he died in 1727.

1805   Ebenezer Grant to Oliver Grant — Probate Court 10-3-1805.

1853   Oliver Grant left property to his wife and children and all deeded to George M. Grant, on Aug. 22, 1853.

1854   George M. Grant deeded the property to Edwin L. Grant.

1855   Edwin L. Grant deeded the property to James J. Andrews. James J. Andrews sold the property to Smith H. Brown.

1889   Smith H. Brown sold the property to his son David Brown.

1895   David A. Brown sold the property to Michael and Opolene Reiske, on April 15, 1895.

SETTLER'S ROCK, *on Gehring Road, Tolland's first settlers were believed to have used this rock for shelter on the night of their arrival to lay out a town on Grant's Hill.*

FIRST SETTLEMENT IN TOLLAND - APRIL 18, 1713.

Meeting House Hill - now Grant's Hill.

SETTLER'S ROCK GEHRING ROAD. GRANT HILL ROAD

Marker School

9. Josiah Rockwell

8. Thomas Grant.

Rounds

Samuel Forward # 8.

7. Joseph Rockwell Jr.

Nathan Gillett # 7.

Steero

Reiske

6. Noah Grant.

Vacant # 6.

New Road.

5. Henry Wolcott.

Joseph Porter # 5.

4. Joshua Loomis.

Henry Wolcott # 4.

3. Simon Wolcott Jr.

Silhavy

Hezekiah Porter # 3.

2. Cornelius Birge.

Samuel Pinney Jr. # 2.

Hannon

1. Enoch Loomis.

Vacant # 1.

Tolland - Coventry Line.

Dimensions of lots = 1/8 mile x 1/2 mile.
           = 40 rods x 160 rods.
           = 660 feet x 2640 feet.

Width of proposed highway = 20 rods or 330 feet.

MAGNETIC NORTH
TRUE NORTH

*The research and layout of the village on Meeting
House Hill was done by Mr. Harold Weigold.*

The prize red oxen that belonged to the late Edwin J. Crandall. He often exhibited them and entered them in contests at the Rockville Fair. About this time in 1902 he served as first selectman.

Scraping roads with oxen in 1904. In this picture the lead oxen were driven by John Weigold.

Oxen headed for the Stafford Fair in 1916.

The village blacksmith shop. The village blacksmith shop was located opposite the Jewett home in Tolland Street. It was operated by a Mr. Price for many years.

The J. P. Root Store, which later was operated by L. Ernest Hall, has now been operated by the Clough family for a long time.

The Crandall Cider Mill on Cider Mill Road produced cider for the town for many years. The pond which produced the water power for the mill is now owned by the town and is used as a bathing facility.

The Establishment of Tolland Township

The record of the early formative years of Tolland Township are taken directly from Mr. Loren P. Waldo's *History of Tolland,* and is as follows:

The first movement towards an act of incorporation for the town was made in the year 1713. The earliest record is under date of May 9, 1713, and is in the words and figures following, viz.:

To the Honorable the General Assembly in Hartford, May 14, 1713:

"The petition of us the subscribers humbly showeth: That whereas your petitioners being inhabitants of this colony, and the descendants of those that have for a long time contributed to the support of the same, being through the numerous increase of our families much straitened for want of land whereon to make improvement and get out livelihood: and being encouraged by your honors' wonted goodness to encourage the settling of plantations in the waste lands within the colony, and having viewed a township of land on the east side of the great river, ordered by the town of Windsor and the heirs of Mr. Thomas Burnham, deceased, to be settled into a plantation bounded as in their agreement doth fully appear; — many of us having already been out with the committee and taken up lots in the same, and shall with those that are desirous to settle with us, speedily settle a fair town there if the government discourage us not; we therefore humbly pray your honors would grant that a township may be made of said land, and that they may be patented to and holden by such inhabitants as shall be admitted by the committee appointed by the town of Windsor, and heirs of Mr. Thomas Burnham, deceased, and your petitioners shall ever pray". Dated, May 9, 1713.

This petition is signed by the following persons, viz.:

Baker, Joseph	Grant, Samuel	Porter, Nathaniel
Barber, Benjamin	Grant, Noah	Porter, Joseph
Birge, Cornelius	Grant, Nathaniel	Rockwell, Joseph
Bissell, Josiah	Gridley, John	Rockwell, Samuel
Chapman, Henry	Hoskins, Anthony	Stiles, Thomas
Chapman, Simon	Holcomb, Benaiah	Stiles, Henry, Jr.
Cook, Nathaniel	Huntington, John	Skinner, Joseph
Cook, Ebenezer	Loomer, H.	Stoughton, Israel

Cook, Daniel	Loomis, Stephen	Smith, Philip
Drake, Nathaniel	Loomis, Ichabod	Watson, Nathaniel
Eno, John	Loomis, David	Wolcott, Roger
Ellsworth, Samuel	Loomis, Joshua	Wolcott, Charles
Edgar, Thomas	Marshall, Samuel	Wolcott, Henry
Eggleston, Thomas	Mills, Jedidiah	Willes, Joshua
Farnsworth, Joseph	Phelps, Joseph	Willes, John
Gillett, Cornelius	Phelps, William	Willes, Joshua, Jr.
Gaylord, Jonas	Pinney, Humphrey	Willes, Samuel
Griswold, Daniel	Pinney, Jonathan	Warren, Robert
Griswold, Thomas	Pinney, Nathaniel	Loomis, Daniel
Gillett, Nathaniel	Porter, Daniel	59 in all.

The next movement was at the General Assembly in May, 1715, when the following petition was presented:

"To the Honorable the General Assembly sitting at Hartford, May 12, 1715; The petition of the town of Windsor humbly showeth: — That your petitioners did in the year 1636, purchase of the Indians certain lands on the east side of Windsor; and since the town has immeasurably increased and many inhabitants forced to seek after new settlements, and the town did in conjunction with the heirs of Mr. Thomas Burnham release their claims to said lands unto such sober inhabitants as should orderly settle on the same, paying only the prime cost; and therefore several sober and religious persons viewing the same are very desirous to settle the same, and several families are already there, giving a fair prospect of a likely town — if this Honorable Assembly would graciously grant a town there, and the land to be holden by such as shall orderly settle on the same: which we pray this Honorable Assembly would graciously do; and we beg leave further to move them thereto by the following considerations:

1. The Assembly hath hitherto done the like on like occasions, and it hath been found the best way to settle the country quietly.

2. Our purchase was improved before his Majesty for obtaining the colony patent, and he by it moved thereby to grant the lands to the colony: — Therefore we pressing the same arguments to the Assembly, hope to find the same favor.

3. It is most reasonable the ancient inhabitants who have supported the colony should by the government be allowed to settle the lands before strangers and without paying excessive prices to all pretenders, which hath led us into all imaginable confusion already.

And your petitioners shall ever pray."

At a town meeting in Windsor, March 21, 1714-15, it was voted; that the above petition should be preferred to the General Assembly in May with their desire it may be granted.

Test, John Moore, Register.

This petition is now on file in the archives of the state at Hartford, and at the Assembly in May, 1715, the following resolution was passed.

And it is further resolved by this Assembly upon the petition of Windsor men that they shall, after the regulation of Coventry according to the foregoing act of this Assembly, have a town-ship of six miles square laid out to them which shall be called Tolland, bounded on the south with Coventry, and east with the Willimantic river; and in case the claimers mentioned in the preceding act shall pay in proportion to what is in the said act settled with respect to Coventry, and also by their inhabitants therein seated by Windsor committee as in the aforesaid act is provided for the like quantity of land, the said inhabitants settled by Windsor committee to pay all the charges of laying out and settling the said land, — that a quitclaim of this governments claims shall also be in like manner executed by the Governor and Secretary and delivered to the claimers, for the claim of this government for so much of the said township as shall fall within the bounds of the said claimers. And it is further resolved that a quit claim of this governments right shall also be executed in like manner by the Governor and Secretary to Col. Matthew Allyn, and Roger Wolcott Esqr., Timothy Thrall and John Willsworth all of Windsor, in trust for themselves and such others as shall by them be admitted to settle in said township, for all that part of said township that lieth without the bounds of said proprietors claims as aforesaid. Provided the said Allyn and others do pay to the public treasury of this colony for the said land in proportion to what is in this act before stated in respect of Coventry; and it is further provided that none of the claims in the foregoing act shall be construed to oblige any of the aforesaid inhabitants seated on any of the said lands, who have procured the claims of the said proprietors and have instruments under their hands to show for the same, and it is also to be understood and it is hereby resolved that the said proprietors if need be, shall give further and better assurance to the said inhabitants to whom the said proprietors have sold their claims and received the money for the same. Provided also, that the above mentioned claimers do or shall well and truly pay or cause to be paid into the colony treasury the aforesaid sum or sums on or before the 15th day of May next, or else they shall not claim the benefit of this act, any thing herein contained to the contrary notwithstanding.

By this resolution, the Windsor men became entitled to a township six miles square, to be bounded south on Coventry and east on the Willimantic river, and to be called Tolland. The fee of this territory was to be vested in Matthew Allyn, Roger Wolcott, Timothy Thrall and John Ellsworth in trust for themselves, and for such others as should by them be admitted to settle in the township. These gentlemen, it will be perceived, were the committee who located the first highway, and made the first allotments in Tolland, April 18, 1713. These trustees, on the 11th day of May, 1719, conveyed by deed of that date, the north part of Tolland to fifty-one persons named in said deed; the portion of land conveyed in said deed was described as follows:

Bounded south on a line east and west at the south end of Shenups pond, east on Willimantic river, and is to be in length from Willimantic river west six miles, and in breadth is from said line drawn east and west at the south end of Shenups pond so far north as to make the six miles from Coventry north bounds.

The following are the names of the grantees in this deed:

Baker	Eaton, Daniel	Paulk, Samuel
Benton, Samuel, Sr.	Ellsworth, Jonathan	Porter, Hezekiah
Benton, Samuel, Jr.	Ellsworth, John	Porter, Daniel
Benton, Joseph, Sr.	Forward, Samuel	Rockwell, Samuel
Benton, Joseph, Jr.	Gillett, Nathan	Royce, Joseph
Bellell, Ephraim	Grant, Noah	Rockwell, Joseph
Birge, Cornelius	Grant, Nathaniel	Stearns, Shubael
Birge, Joseph	Hatch, Joseph	Stoughton, Thomas
Brace, Stephen	Hinsdale, Barnabas	Taylor, Nathaniel
Cook, Daniel	Huntington, Chris.	Tucker, Ephraim
Coy, Samuel	Huntington, John.	Utley, Samuel
Chapman, Simon	Loomis, Enoch	Wolcott, Henry
Caswell, Matthew	Loomis, Moses	Wolcott, Simon
Drake, Joseph	Loomis, Joshua	Wallis, Nathaniel
Ellis, Thomas	Nye, Ebenezer	West, Samuel
Eaton, William	Pinney, Samuel	Willis, Joshua
Emmons, Peter	Peck, Joseph	Whipple, Thomas

I cannot find any record of the original title of the southern part of the town before the year 1717, of which I shall by and by speak. There can be no doubt it was, by some conveyance, vested in the committee who commenced making the allotments in April, 1713. The petition of the town of Windsor contains an allegation that the town did "in the year 1636 purchase of the Indians certain lands on the east side of Windsor," and "did in conjunction with the heirs of Mr. Thomas Burnham, release their claims to said lands unto such sober inhabitants as should orderly settle the same," which clearly evinces the fact that some portion of the territory contained in the proposed township had already been the subject of a conveyance. And the resolution of the General Assembly which authorized the conveyance to Matthew Allyn and his associates only so much of the land that was within the six miles square "that lieth without the bounds of said proprietors claims as aforesaid." It is therefore obvious that the title to the south part of Tolland was originally derived from the Indians, and it was the source of bitter controversies during the early settlement of the town. From what tribe of Indians this title was obtained, does not appear. Before the settlement at Windsor in 1633, the territory now embraced in the

State of Connecticut was inhabited and probably owned by several small Indian tribes. But the boundaries between these tribes were never very well defined, and indeed, in some instances, different tribes claimed the same land, and the early settlers not unfrequently received deeds of the same land from different sachems or Indian chiefs. That portion of Connecticut situated east of the Connecticut river was inhabited and owned by the following Indian tribes, to wit: The Pequots, who were located between the Niantic and Paucatuc rivers, and extending from the shore back into the country. The Mohegans, supposed to be a branch of the Pequots, whose principal town was between New London and Norwich, but whose territory extended north into the southern part of Tolland county. The Nehantics of Lyme, and the Podunks of East Windsor and East Hartford. The Nipmucs of Massachusetts had a few sparse settlements in the northern portion of Tolland and Windham counties. The town of Windsor, on the west side of the river, was subject to the Tunxis, a tribe that inhabited the valley of Farmington river. As I have said, it nowhere appears from which of these tribes the settlers at Windsor purchased lands on the east side of Windsor in 1636, for it is probable that the Mohegans, The Podunks, and the Nipmucs might have each claimed the territory. Whatever may have been the claims of others, it is certain the Mohegans regarded a portion of the territory now included within the boundaries of Tolland as their own, and hence we find that one of their sachems named Joshua, as early as the year 1675, undertook to dispose of it by will — as by the following extract from the record of it will appear.

> Item. I give and bequeath all that tract of land lying from the mountain in sight of Hartford northward to a pond called Shenups, east to Willimantic river, south by said river west by Hartford bounds, except three hundred acres already sold to Major John Talcott, and two hundred acres to Capt. Thomas Bull, and according to a draught or map drawn and subscribed with my own hand, bearing date with there presents.) viz.: to Mr. James Richards, Mr. Samuel Wyllys, Capt. Thomas Bull, Mr. Joseph Haynes, Mr. Richard Lord, Major John Talcott, Mr. John Allyn, Mr. Ebenezer Way, Bartholomew Barrett, Nicholas Olmsted, Henry Hayward, Mr. Joseph Fitch, Thomas Burnham, and William Pitkin, to be equally divided amongst them, into so many parts as there are persons, and also Nathaniel Willett to have an equal proportion amongst them. Dated at Pettupaug 29 Feb. 1675. Compared Feb. 8, 1686. John Allyn, Secry.

This will describes that portion of the town of Tolland not included in the deed of Matthew Allyn and others, and is that part of town where the first surveys were made by the proprietors' committee. I have no evidence that this tract of land was ever divided among the legatees according to the provisions of the will, and probably it never was. The Thomas Burnham named in this will, was doubtless the Thomas Burnham whose heirs united with the town of Windsor in releasing their claims to the territory of Tolland "unto such sober inhabitants as should orderly settle the same," and hence the first settlers had whatever right was vested in Windsor by virtue of their purchase of the Indians in 1636, and also the right Thomas Burnham acquired under the will of Joshua. But the legatees of Joshua were dissatisfied with the action of the first settlers, and prosecuted them for trespassing upon their rights. The settlers resisted this claim of the legatees, and made it on common cause, defraying all necessary expenses from the common treasury of the proprietors of the township. The first suit was commenced in April, 1724, by one Joseph Baker against one Shubael Stearns. In September, 1724, the proprietors, at a meeting held for that purpose, appointed Francis West, Daniel Eaton, and Shubael Stearns a committee to agree with the claimants, "With power to go to the General Court at New Haven." It appears that this committee attended the General Court at New Haven, where a committee was appointed "to treat with the proprietors of Tolland." This controversy was of great importance to the proprietors, and no doubt very seriously affected the early settlement of the town. It extended to a very large portion of the land included in their charter and went to the validity of their title. After various conferences between the committee above named, the matter was finally compromised, and the General Assembly, at its session in October, 1724, passed an act that the proprietors of Tolland should pay to the legatees of Joshua at the rate of six pounds per allotment, or three shillings per acre for the land, and that the legatees should release all their title to said lands. This action of the General Court was not acceptable to the legatees and they seemed unwilling thus to give up their claims; — and as late as October, 1728, or four years after the decision of the General Court above-mentioned, other suits were commenced upon the same claims. The proprietors held a meeting, October 28, 1728, and chose a committee consisting of Deacon Francis West, Capt. Hope Lathrop,

Lieutenant John Huntington, Sergeant Samuel Benton, and Sergeant Samuel Chapman, "to go to the legatees of Joshua and in the name and behalf of the proprietors to take a quitclaim deed of all their claims to the lands in Tolland." They also solemnly obligated themselves "to pay all such sums as said Committee should be compelled to pay in the business of their office." This committee promptly attended to the business assigned them, and in a few months obtained proper conveyances from the legatees of Joshua which put an end to this expensive and important controversy.

It is a matter of some doubt at what precise time the first settlement was made in Tolland. The opinion generally prevails that the first permanent settlement was in 1715, but I am satisfied it was at an earlier date. It is certain that roads were laid out, and allotments of lands made to individuals in April, 1713. Tradition informs us that the persons who executed this work provided themselves with a temporary home, under a large shelving rock, now situated on the west side of the highway, leading to Bolton, near the north bank of the brook that runs across the road this side of the present residence of Alden B. Crandall. The walls of the dwelling, as well as the roof, being of stone, it received the name of Stoney house; and this gave name to the brook that runs by it, which is in the early records of the town called Stoney House brook. While it is probable that the residence of persons at this place was temporary, yet there are several facts tending to show that permanent settlements were commenced in about 1713. "The petition to the General Assembly for an act of incorporation, dated May 9, 1713, alleges that many of the petitioners have been out with the committee and have taken up lots in the same; and shall with those that are desirous to settle with us now settle a fair town there," etc. The petition of the town of Windsor for the same object, alleges "that several families are already there, giving a fair prospect of a likely town," etc. This petition is dated March 21, 1714-15. The resolution of the General Assembly under date of May, 1715 speaks of the inhabitants thereon seated by the Windsor committee; — from all of which it is evident there must have been settlements in Tolland before May, 1715. And further, in the records of the marriages, births and deaths in the town, we find the records of several births in Tolland, prior to May, 1715. The earliest of them is that of Amy Hatch, a daughter of Joseph Hatch, who was born October 10, 1713. Margaret Pack, a daughter of Joseph Pack, was born January 7, 1715; Joseph Hatch, son of Joseph Hatch before mentioned, and as tradition says the first male child born in Tolland, was born Sept. 12, 1715. Joseph Pack had land assigned him in the early allotments, and his name and that of Joseph Hatch are among the earliest upon the records. From these facts I am confident the first settlement in Tolland must have been made in the year 1713.

As I have already intimated, there was early a difficulty about the true location of the north line of the town of Coventry. The Windsor proprietors, under date of May 1, 1716, petitioned for a "final settlement with the legatees of Joshua; for setting of bounds with the town of Coventry, concerning which there is much difficulty;" also, "that we may have privilege to choose a town clerk and other officers as the law directs." This petition purports to be the petition "of us the subscribers, inhabitants of Tolland," and was negatived by the Assembly. The following are the names of the petitioners to wit:

Baker, Joseph	Ellis, Thomas	Stearns, Shubael
Benton, Joseph	Grant, Nathaniel	Willes, Joshua
Birge, Cornelius	Loomis, Joshua	Wolcott, Henry
Benton, Samuel	Mather, Joseph	Taylor, Nathaniel
Bradley, George	Porter, Hezekiah	16 in all.
Bissell, Ephraim	Porter, Joseph	

In May, 1718, a petition was presented to the General Assembly, as follows, to wit: "A petition of us the subscribers, inhabitants of Tolland, relative to Coventry lands."

Signed by the following persons:

Baker, Joseph	Loomis, Joshua	Slafter, Joseph
Benton, Joseph	Loomis, Enoch	Slafter, Antony
Benton, Daniel	Nye, Ebenezer	Stimpson, James
Birge, Cornelius	Pack, Joseph	Stoughton, Thomas
Cook, Daniel	Porter, Hezekiah	Taylor, Nathaniel
Drake, Joseph	Porter, Joseph	Willes, Joshua
Eaton, William	Rice, Joseph	Wolcott, Simon
Grant, Noah	Rockwell, Joseph	25 in all.
Hatch, Joseph	Stearns, Shubael	

I am unable to ascertain at what time the line between Tolland and Coventry was finally settled, but I have no doubt it was done before 1720, in which year a committee appointed by the General Assembly, located the town of Tolland and defined its boundaries. The following is a copy of their report:

> This may certify whom it may concern, that we, James Wadsworth and John Hall, on this day of October, A. D. 1720, being properly assisted by Thomas Kimberly, surveyor and in company with sundry men of the town of Tolland, did pursuant to an act of the General Assembly of this colony, held at Hartford May 12, 1720, survey and lay out the north and west bounds of the town of Tolland; and for that end we went to the north-east corner of the town of Coventry; and from thence due north (by the needle of the instrument,) six miles, at the end whereof to wit, in an east line by the needle, at or on the west bank of Willimantic river, we erected a heap of stones for the north-east corner of the township of Tolland, and marked a red oak tree on the south side with the letter T; and from thence ran upon a point west (by the needle,) six miles seventeen rods and thirteen links to a white oak tree marked and a heap of stones about it, standing on the southerly side of a hill, which tree is the north-west corner boundary of said Tolland; and from the said tree to run south, five degrees west to Coventry north-west corner; (this 5 degree variation was most likely made so as to divide the shores of Shenipset Lake equally between Ellington and Tolland). The land contained within the said town lines, and the said river which is the east bounds of said town is of the contents of six miles square. The chainmen were under oath as the law directed.
>
> A true copy of record. (Signed,) JAMES WADSWORTH,
> Examined by Hez. Wyllys, Sec'y. JOHN HALL.

From this certificate it is very evident that the north line of Coventry was substantially settled before October, 1720, and became the basis of the action of the above-named committee in locating the north and west lines of the town of Tolland. But there were subsequent negotiations between these towns upon this subject. The towns of Coventry and Tolland appointed a committee of three from each town to agree about the dividing line, and they were empowered to make a final issue and determination of the lines between the towns. This committee consisted of Samuel Parker, Joseph Strong and Thomas Root, of Coventry; and Joseph Hatch, Daniel Eaton and Noah Grant, of Tolland, and met on the 6th day of February, 1722, and agreed that the dividing line between the two towns should be the line run by Capt. John Hall, and Mr. Kimberly, and that the same should thereafter be perambulated according to law. They further agreed, "that Francis West and Joseph Benton, being in Coventry, might pay their public dues in Tolland, with three acres of land a-piece about their houses, and counted inhabitants of Tolland, as if Tolland had took them in; they and their heirs and assigns living on the three acres of land where their houses now stand." Francis West found it impracticable to reside in one town exercise town privileges in another, and he very soon removed his house from Coventry to Tolland. This house is the one lately occupied by Billaky Snow, now deceased.

It would seem that the settlement with the legatees of Joshua, and the establishment of the line between the towns of Coventry and Tolland, might sufficiently quiet all conflicting claims and remove all doubts respecting the corporate powers of the town of Tolland and the title of its inhabitants to the territory within the limits of its charter. But lest there might be some defect in the previous proceedings, or some omission which might cause further difficulties, the town procured from the General Assembly, at its session in New Haven, October, 1728, the passage of a resolution confirming and establishing every thing that had been previously done. This resolution, after reciting the resolution of May 12, 1715, recognizes the survey made by Messrs. Wadsworth and Hall in 1720, and also the deed to the proprietors of Tolland, dated May 11, 1719, and then declares that the proprietors "held the lands of the said township as one entire propriety; and that all the said proprietors shall have equal interest and benefit by force of the patent by the said assembly granted to be executed to the said proprietors in usual form."

In pursuance with this resolution a patent was issued by the Governor, countersigned by the Secretary of State, dated the 2nd day of Nov., 1728, in and by which all the powers, privileges and franchises before granted to the Windsor men, were ratified and confirmed, and the title to the land within the boundaries of the town as described by the survey of Messrs. Wadsworth and Hall, was fully, clearly, absolutely given, granted, ratified confirmed unto Henry Wolcott, Stephen Steel, Francis West, together with the rest of the proprietors of the town; and to their heirs and assigns, and such as should thereafter legally succeed to, and represent them forever in such proportion as they the said proprietors, partners and settlers, or any of them respectively had right in, or were lawfully possessed of the same. Also authorizing and empowering said proprietors and inhabitants of said town, from time to time, and at all times forever thereafter, to exercise and enjoy all such rights, powers, privileges and franchises in and among themselves, as were given, granted, allowed and exercised and enjoyed by and amongst the proprietors of other towns of the colony, according to the common approval custom and legal observance and guaranteeing to said grantees, their heirs and assigns legally representing them, "a good, pure, perfect, absolute and indefeasible estate of inheritance, in fee simple, in the lands described, to be holden of his majesty his heirs and successors, as of his majesty's manor of East Greenwich in the county of Kent in the Kingdom of England, in free and common socage, and not in capite nor by knight service, yielding therefor and paying unto our sovereign Lord King George, his heirs and successors forever, one fifth part of all ore of gold and silver, which from time to time and at all times forever thereafter, shall be there gotten, had or obtained in lieu of all services, dutys and demands whatsoever."

There is no positive evidence that the territory within the limits of Tolland was ever occupied by the Indians, other than for hunting and fishing. Formerly our ponds and streams were stored with excellent fish, and our forests were filled with a great variety of wild game, which during certain portions of the year invited the attention of the savage inhabitants occupying the land near the sea-shore. I have myself heard some of the aged people say, they had seen shad and salmon caught in large quantities in Willimantic river, between Tolland and Willington, and so plentifully were salmon caught, that fishermen had a standing rule that they would not sell a certain number shad to one person unless he would take a certain quantity of salmon. The Indians in their summer visits to this town, found it necessary or convenient to erect wigwams of Indian huts, — traces of which in the western part of the town, on lands lately owned by Mr. Ephraim West and Mr. Timothy Benton, were visible within the recollection of some of our oldest inhabitants. A few families may have occupied these huts, but they left the town before its first settlement and none of the red men have ever dwelt here since. We have but few objects to which any Indian name was ever known to be attached. The Indians gave the name of Wangombog to a large portion of country in the southern part of Tolland county, adjacent to the large pond known by this name, situated in the town of Coventry. A portion of the town of Tolland was within the territory called Wangombog, and several of the early deeds recorded in Tolland, describe the land conveyed as situated in Wangombog. The same name is given to the locality of the land conveyed in the will of Joshua, before mentioned. The pond on the west side of Tolland, was by the Indians called Shenipset, which by an easy corruption is now pronounced Snipsic. This word is variously spelled in the old records — sometimes Shenipset, Shenaps, and Shenips.

The small stream running east of the village was by the Indians called Skunkermug — sometimes in the old records written Scungamuck. These Indian names, though less euphonious than some of our more modern ones, I hope will be perpetuated. Indeed I entertain some doubt whether they will sound any more harsh in the ears of our posterity than Bald Hill, Sugar Hill, Buff Cap, Goose Lane, or Cedar Swamp — all of which are the recognized modern names of well-known localities.

Colonial Life of the Early Settlers: 1715 — 1780

The first problem of these original settlers was of course to build their shelter homes. In fact, some of the first settlers, while laying out the first highway and lots on "Meeting House Hill" lived under a large shelving rock which can still be seen on the north side of the road leading to Bolton.

The first homes of the settlers were crude shelters, to prepare boards they had to be sawed by hand or split out with an ax. The first roofs were thatched with grass. Soon they learned to saw cedar logs into short lengths and split them into shingles. These shingles were found to be very durable, some lasted nearly a hundred years. The first chimneys were made of wood covered with clay, but were soon replaced with stone, as the wooden ones caught fire too often.

The cabins were heated by a large fire-place, since stoves did not come into common use until after 1750. Most of the large fire-places contained a stone oven for baking. All food was usually prepared by boiling in a large iron kettle hung over the fire.

The first windows were usually made of oiled paper and were protected by heavy wooden shutters, to be closed during the night. The lighting in the daytime was dim at its best and at night they used pine knots, which were burned in a corner of the fireplace. In some places fish oil with a wick was used for lighting and later on the tallow candle was developed. These were replaced with whale oil lamps, which gave the equivalent light of three tallow candles.

To light a fire in the fire-place in colonial days was a real task, as a spark had to be made with flint and steel, which had to ignite tinder, usually old linen cloth. To get a fire going good, usually took one half hour, if the person was skilled at making fires. Matches of course were not used until about 1850. After the fire was started it was carefully kept from going out, and when this did happen it was usually easier to go to the nearest neighbor's house for some live coals.

The kitchen was the only room that received any heat and was therefore the living room for the family. The children usually sat at both ends of the fire-place to keep warm. On real cold nights, they had to crowd within a few feet of the fire to keep warm. The other rooms were always cold and cheerless. Only the use of thick feather beds kept the children warm while they slept.

Furniture in colonial homes was simple and crude. Tables, chairs, and beds were made from rough hand sawed boards. Even many of the dishes, plates and spoons were carved out of wood. As time went on these were replaced with pewter and iron and eventually by china and silver.

Food by the first settlers was mainly obtained from the abundant game and fish of the land and streams. Venison meat was most common, also wild turkeys, ducks, partridge and quail. Various fish were caught in the streams and lakes. Later on, after the fields were cleared, they raised corn, pumpkins, beans, peas, turnips, parsnips and carrots. Sugar was obtained by boiling down maple sap and also some use was made of wild honey.

Clearing of the land around the homestead was a tremendous job. First, the trees had to be cut and the stumps burned out. Many of the fields were covered with stones of various sizes and these had to be removed. Since there was no wire to build fences, they used these stones to make stone walls to serve as fences, which were very permanent and also served as excellent permanent boundary lines.

A good water supply was also one of the first necessities of the new homestead. Each farm house therefore had a well. A well was usually ten to thirty feet deep and walled up with field stones. The first wells used a well sweep and bucket. This consisted of a pole about fifty feet long and about five inches in diameter, supported in the middle, so that it could swing up and down, on another pole at a height of fifteen feet. One end of the top pole was weighted down with a stone to keep that end on the ground. The other end was directly over the well and to it a thin pole about two inches in diameter and twenty feet long was fastened. This reached to the top of the well and a wooden bucket was fastened to it. By pulling this pole and bucket down into the well, the bucket filled with water and was hauled up again by the thin pole, while its weight was partially balanced by the stone on the back end of the sweep. The quality of the water obtained from wells in Tolland was generally very good. Water was the only drink that the colonists could obtain; as tea and coffee were unknown.

Apple trees were soon planted and when they began to bear, the apples were ground and pressed for cider and later on in the winter this turned into vinegar. Cows were soon obtained from England and milk, butter and cheese came into general use.

Sheep were raised to produce both food and clothing. Clothing for the colonists was hand made by the housewives. They spun the hemp and wool and then wove it into cloth, from which their clothes were made by hand. This usually kept all hands busy during the long winter evenings, for the making of their clothing was a long and tedious process.

Very little travel was done in these early days and that mostly on foot or by canoe on the water. Later when horses could be obtained, travel was mostly on horseback and it was a long time before wagons were used. At first there were no roads, only paths made by the Indians. These paths gradually developed into roads and are the cause of so many of our roads being so very crooked.

The education of the early settlers left much to be desired. Most of the people had very little education, many could not write at all. Some that came from England were well educated and they helped to establish schools; so that the children could read the Bible and take part in forming the laws of the colony and its government. The first schools were for boys only; so that many mothers taught their own children to read and write at home. In many cases they allowed the neighboring children to come in. Sometimes they received a small fee for this. Much of their teaching was with the Bible as their text book. The first school houses were single room houses that would accommodate from twenty to fifty children.

The early settlers were very religious and the meeting house or church was the center of each community. The early churches were crude buildings and were unheated. There were rough benches for the people to sit on, but there were no cushions or carpets and usually no musical instrument. The services were several hours long and every member of the parish was expected to attend. These early settlers considered attending church a very serious matter and they would not allow any unnecessary work to be done on the Sabbath day.

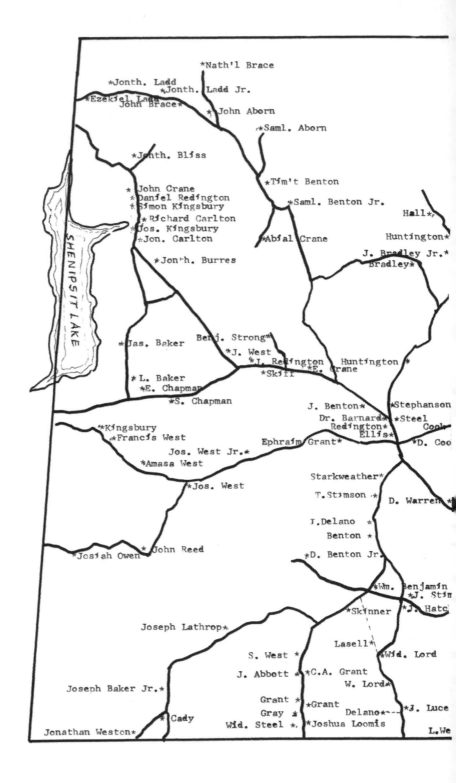

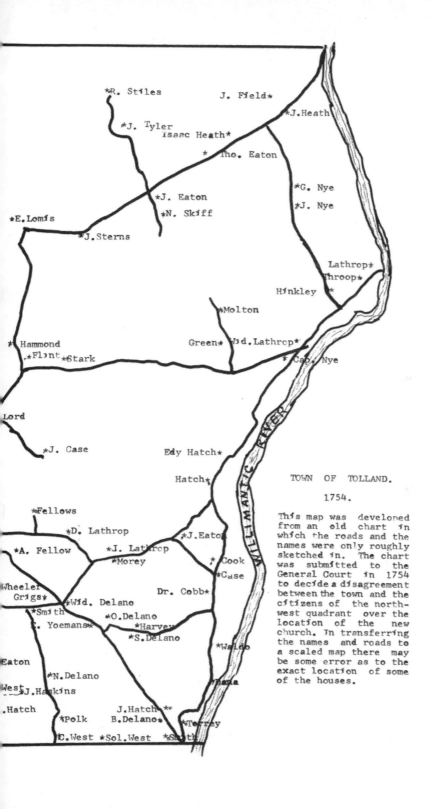

R. Stiles   J. Field

*J. Tyler   *J.Heath
  Isaac Heath*

          *   Tho. Eaton

                    *G. Nye

*J. Eaton   *J. Nye
*N. Skiff

*E.Lomis

  *J.Sterns

                         Lathrop*
                         Throop*
                    Hinkley
                       *
           *Molton

Hammond   Green Wid.Lathrop*
 *Flint *Stark   * Cap. Nye

Lord

  *J. Case
           Edy Hatch*

           Hatch*   TOWN OF TOLLAND.

                                1754.

*Fellows   This map was developed
                             from an old chart in
  *D. Lathrop   which the roads and the
                             names were only roughly
*A. Fellow   *J. Lathrop   sketched in. The chart
           *Morey   *J.Eaton was submitted to the
                             General Court in 1754
                     *Cook   to decide a disagreement
                    *Case   between the town and the
Wheeler   Dr. Cobb*   citizens of the north-
Grigs*   west quadrant over the
  *Wid. Delano   location of the new
*Smith   church. In transferring
  Yoemans   the names and roads to
     *O.Delano   a scaled map there may
         *Harvey   be some error as to the
      *S.Delano   exact location of some
                    *Waldo   of the houses.

Eaton

West
   *J.Haskins   *Hala

Hatch   J.Hatch
     Polk   B.Delano
  *C.West *Sol.West *Smith *Terrey

The early settlers had to work from early morning to late at night. Their only sport was to hunt and fish and even this might be considered as work in those days; as it was necessary to hunt and fish to obtain enough food to feed the family. One of their more pleasurable tasks was collecting chestnuts, hickory nuts and butternuts and also wild grapes and cranberries in the fall of the year. The forests of Tolland were of great worth to the early settlers. The great trees of the forest were sources of shelter and fuel. They used the pine, the hemlock, the oak and the chestnut to build their log cabins. From other trees such as hickory, elm, birch, ash, sycamore, maple, butternut, willow, poplar, beech and cherry they made farm tools, fences, posts, bridges, household utensils, furniture, water wheels, clocks, wagons and sleds. In those days the trees were free from disease and pests. There was no chestnut blight, no elm tree disease, no gypsy moths, no apple borers, no pine blister rust and many other diseases that affect our trees now. Our trees have also paid the price of civilization. This resulted from bringing trees and plants in from Europe and Asia to the United States.

We owe a lot to the first settlers for the form of democratic government that we now have. The founders of Hartford, Windsor and Wethersfield, while following the teachings of the Rev. Thomas Hooker drew up what they called the Fundamental Orders as a basis of good government. These Orders contained the principles of government that Hooker had summarized in his sermons. Five of the most important ones were as follows;

1. All the authority of government comes directly from the people.
2. The number of men that the towns shall choose to help make their laws shall be in proportion to the population of the town.
4. All freemen who take an oath to be faithful to the State shall have the right to vote.
5. New towns may join the three original towns and live under the same government.

On October 10, 1639, the General Court of Connecticut made laws under the Fundamental Orders for the towns of Windsor, Wethersfield, and Hartford. These laws were also to apply to all other towns that later joined the Connecticut government. These laws authorized to establish a town government. This town government was to consist of not less than three men elected by the people. These men were to have control of town affairs and were called "Select Men."

The towns were also authorized to establish town courts and these courts were to have power to determine all matters of trespass or debt not exceeding fifty dollars in value.

The General Court further ordered in 1639 that each town keep permanent records of all lands bought or sold, of all deeds, mortgages, probate affairs, and of all other important town matters.

Such was the beginning of town government in Connecticut over three hundred years ago. Tolland still has a town meeting form of government, where the legislative branch is the town meeting, and the administrative branch consists of the selectmen and other elected or appointed town officials.

TOLLAND VILLAGE IN 1888

There is no record of just how Tolland Village was originally laid out. Evidently the village was created, when the settlers decided to build the first meeting house in Tolland Street, rather than on Grant's Hill. The meeting house was built in what is now the center of the green and the towns people laid out a road on either side of the meeting house, which later was extended to the north to form the double road and green of the present village.

In his *History of Tolland County,* J. R. Cole described the village of Tolland in 1888 as follows:

Of the many villages scattered throughout New England, few boast of such elevated location, beautiful and well kept streets, romantic beauty and absence of disfiguring dwellings as Tolland. Situated on elevated ground, it possesses natural drainage facilities, consequently the sanitary conditions are excellent, and the longevity of its inhabitants is proverbial.

The street proper is one of extraordinary width and beauty, flanked on either side, and extending its entire length, with residences of modern architecture, beautiful in design and appearance. Beautiful shade trees adorn either side of the street, affording shelter from the sun in the summer, and adding not a little to the picturesqueness of the village. Between the two driveways is a plot of well kept ground, which affords ample place for the innocent amusements which engage the attention of the people in summer, such as croquet, lawn tennis and kindred amusements. Concrete or stone walks extend the length of the street, which is about one-fourth of a mile. Water is obtained from a brook having its source in hills north of the street, is very clear and healthful. With all these natural facilities and healthful sanitary conditions, it is not a matter of wonderment that Tolland was noted as a summer resort for city people. For many years it was the seat of considerable manufacturing, notably hats, spoons, clocks, carriages and leather, but like many other villages settled in New England under similar circumstances, its manufacturing interests gradually diminished until nothing is left except one manufacturing establishment, which discontinued operations in the early 1920's.

Being the county seat, Tolland was, in earlier times, the abiding place of men eminent in law, medicine and theology, and the descendents of some of the settlers are not unknown to fame at the present time.

In 1888, the village is described as follows:

At the lower end of the village is a little one story house near the forks of the road, where Jeremiah Parish lived. Doctor Gurden Thompson, a prominent physician, lived on the Holbrook property, later owned by W. R. Ladd. He practiced medicine in the village for many years. Judge Elisha Stearns lived in the house later owned by Frank T. Newcomb, as a residence and post office. The post office was kept by Judge Stearns in his old law office. The State Bank was kept there one year, while the new bank building was building. The house now owned by Doctor W. H. Clark was built forty years ago by W. Wescott. The next house north was the residence of Jonathan Barnes. It was gambrel roofed. Sheriff Gilbert's house came next. It had two stories and an ell.

At that time a peach orchard extended from where a hotel was formerly kept by a Mr. Shepherd, on that corner to the County House. The store just north was built by Danforth Richmond as early as 1815. The County House was then similar to the Stearns house, with a long ell, with wood house back of it. The jail was built back of the house. The next house north was the store of Everett Chapman. It was a two-story house with an ell in the south part. It is now owned by Albert Hawkins and has not been used as a store for thirty years. The property of Mrs. Benjamin Lathrop was then owned by Captain Barber, and where William Sumner's house stands, Captain Barber kept an old, rickety blacksmith shop. Just north of this shop stood the old gambrel roofed school house. This was the old academy building. It was moved away twenty-five years ago. The school was kept in an upper room. Judge William Strong, late associate Judge of the supreme court of the United States, taught for three or four years. He was the son of the Reverend William Strong, of Somers. After leaving here he studied law in Harrisburg, Pa. Professor Hubbard succeeded as teacher, but the school never prospered after Mr. Strong left. This school was chartered in 1828, but only flourished a very few years.

Gurdon Isham owned a hat shop next door north of the school house. It has since been much altered and is now owned by Lull & Sumner. The two-story parsonage house next north of that was moved a few years ago. It is now owned by R. H. Agard. It was the residence of Ansel Nash. Reverend Abram Marsh also lived there. He was pastor of the Congregational church for a period of thirty-eight years. The house now owned by Charles A. Hawkins was built by Lyman Kibbee. Reverend Mr. Williams lived in the next house, now torn down, and the barn just above was a blacksmith shop. The barn is now the property of Charles Underwood.

Beginning at the north end of the village and coming south on the west side of the street the first house we come to was the property of Doctor Abijah Ladd. The dwelling house of F. P. Mock was then a store. The house now occupied by E. O. Dimock was the property of William Eldridge, father-in-law of Judge Waldo. The latter was married in this house. The property now owned and occupied by A. M. Hawkins was owned and occupied as a residence by Luther Eaton, the father of Senator W. W. Eaton. Below this was a tailor shop, on the site of the Baptist Church, and owned by Mr. Eaton Taylor, postmaster and tailor. Mr. Taylor had but one leg. The fine residence of Mr. Charles Underwood stands on the site formerly occupied by a barn. Doctor G. H. Preston lives where Joseph Pitkin did. The house now owned by Lucius S. Fuller is the old Benjamin Ashley house. Colonel Elijah Smith kept a hotel in what is now called the Tolland House for many years. He was succeeded by Benjamin Fuller, and his successors were Ansel Barber, George H. Olmstead and Stephen Ives, of Meriden, the present owner. Mr. Ives has turned the hotel into a summer boarding house. The proprietors of the County House have been as follows: Abiel Ladd, Joseph Burnham, Samuel Kent, Lucius S. Fuller and Mr. A. L. Kurau, the present jailer, who is now in charge of the hotel.

The store now kept by A. J. Morton was built fifty years ago by Elijah and Eli Smith, twin brothers. The old court house, built sixty-five years ago, then stood in the middle of the street. It was a gambrel roof house. The present court house stands on the site of Mr. Williams' old tavern.

The bank was built in 1829. It stands on land owned by Calvin Willey, and sold by him to the bank company. The presidents of the Tolland County Bank have been: Elisha Stearnes, John H. Brockway, Alvin P. Hyde, Charles Underwood and Lucius S. Fuller. On the 6th of June, 1865, it was changed into the national bank. The charter expired June 6th, 1885. Mr. Fuller has been president for many years. The cashiers have been: Elijah Chapman, Jonathan R. Flynt, George B. Hastings, Charles A. Hawkins, Arthur J. Hawkins and Mr. Frank T. Newcomb, who became cashier in 1882.

The Tolland County Insurance Company was organized in 1828. The presiding officers have been; John Fitch, Ariah Ladd, Clark Holt, Solyman Taylor and Lucius S. Fuller, who has been president for the past fifteen years. The secretaries have been: Jeremiah Parish, Jeremiah S. Parish, Clarke Holt, John B. Fuller and Edward E. Fuller, the present incumbent. The gross assets of this company in June, 1887, were about $90,000.

The residence now owned by Noah Moulton was Calvin Willey's old stand. Mr. Willey was postmaster as early as 1815. The house now owned by John D. Fuller as a place of residence was built and occupied by Calvin Willey as a store. The site now occupied by James E. Underwood was occupied by a gambrel roofed house. It was bought by Judge Waldo and torn down. The house of F. H. Underwood stands on the old Brooks site. Next south was the old Ashbel Steel place, which was used for a school house. Mr. Lucius S. Fuller taught both before and after the building was moved. Doctor Potwine lived in this house. Joshua Griggs now owns it.

Joseph B. Pitkin owned a store at the south end of the village, years before either Stafford Springs or Rockville had a beginning, and did a large business. It was on the west side of the street. Mr. Pitkin was succeeded by Obed Waldo, who kept store here for twenty-two years. Judge Waldo then bought the property, and Cooley and Waldo traded there for a while. Sheriff Rider bought it finally.

In 1970 the following people lived in Tolland Street, starting from the north end and going clockwise around the green: C. Preston Meacham, Jonathan Potter, Frank Merrill, Parsonage — Rev. Donald Miller, Mrs. Eleanor Meacham Jenks, Frederick Carpenter, Harold Garrity, Tolland County Mutual Aid System, County House and Jail, Clough's Store, Miss Elizabeth Hicks, Howard Tourtellot, Dominick Riley, Furlonge Flynn, Town Hall, John Tweet, Mrs. G. Roy Brown, Charles Loetscher, George Meacham, Southernmost Point — Charles MacArthur, — West side starting north — Hilton Pierce, Walter Palmer, Jr., Glenn Pfistner, Hicks Memorial School, Kenneth Kaynor, David Serluco, Maurice Meacham, Harvey Clough, Congregational Church and House, Savings Bank of Tolland, Tolland Public Library, Miss Bertha Place, Joseph Krawczyk, Paul Meyer, William Anderson, Donald Duncan, St. Matthew Rectory, Mrs. John Aborn, Malcolm Matthews, Grange Hall, St. Mathew Church. On the Rockville Road — Left side, Walter Anderson, Mrs. Aaron P. Pratt, Post Office. Right side — Arthur Carney, William Bradshaw and Duane Matthews.

Tolland Green — Tolland Connecticut.

Tolland Street in the Horse and Buggy Days.

Tolland Green — showing Court House and Church.

*Tolland Street after the hurricane of 1938, showing the Steele House
and Library.*

The Daniel Benton Homestead on Metcalf Road was built around 1720. The former home of the Bentons, four of whom served in the American Revolution, it has an intriguing history including the quartering of Hessian mercenaries in its cellar. This home still contains the original panelling, floors, five stone fireplaces, small hand-made window panes, and has candlestick fixtures throughout. It is now owned by the Tolland Historical Society.

This colonial house on the green in Tolland was once the home of O. P. Waldo, who was the postmaster and had the postoffice in his home.

Jeremiah Parish house built in the triangle on the southern most point of the green. It is one of Tolland's Cape Cod type houses.

The Sumner Home in Tolland represents the true beauty of some of the homes on Tolland Street. It is now owned by Mr. Harold Garrity.

Noah Grant, the great, great grandfather of the President Ulysses S. Grant lived in a house where the present Reiske house stands. He bought the property in 1724, but died in 1727. The property remained in the Grant family until 1855.

The Danforth Home of Mile Hill is one of the real old houses in Tolland. Sgt. John Cady is believed to be the builder. Unique features such as crossed "summers," all stone bake ovens and a lone bake oven, believed to be the only one of its kind in Connecticut, make this home a prize exhibit for Tolland. It has three fire places on the first floor as well as a tap room. The second floor has a ball room with a fireplace. It was the home of the Gideon Brown family for many years.

This house was the Weigold homestead from 1888 until 1964. Most of the land bounding on the Coventry line and on both sides of the Skungamaug River, in the south part of Tolland was granted to Francis West, the father of Zebulon West, who was a very prominent citizen of Tolland. He sold part of his lands to Joseph Luce, who lived in the ell part of the house in 1754. The front part of the house was built at a much later date.

This picture shows the original fire place in the above house together with the bake ovens. The fireplaces have been restored to their original state as they appeared when they were first built. This work has been done by Mr. Donald Barrows, the present owner. He is at present, remodeling it in its original colonial style.

Mrs. John Aborn's House is outstanding with history significant to the religious life in town. Jesse Lee stopped here and preached in 1790. The first annual conference of the Methodist Church was held here. Bishop Asbury also preached here. In 1886, the house was purchased by the Methodist Church as a home for its ministers. Many people of the parish enjoyed in the Parsonage.

Aerial View of Tolland Center facing Southwest

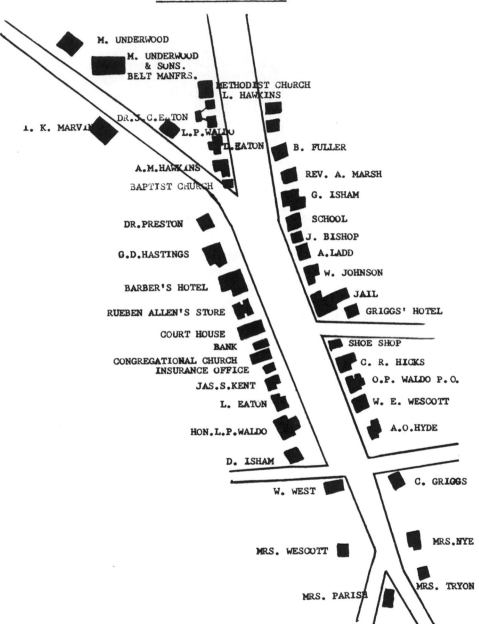

TOLLAND STREET IN 1857.

Churches in Tolland

The Congregational society was organized in 1722 or 1723. The first settlers of Tolland exhibited a very strong attachment to religious institutions. Being lineal descendants of that band of pilgrims that left their native land to seek across the trackless waters an asylum where they could worship the God of their fathers unmolested, according to the dictates of their own consciences, it is not strange that they should regard the social organization as entirely imperfect without a spiritual leader to break to them the bread of life. A minister and a house for public worship were not only regarded by them as essential to their happiness, but as indispensable to their wordly prosperity; and thence all sacrifices necessary to the attainment of these objects were most cheerfully made. The early records of the town furnish conclusive evidence of their intense zeal upon this subject and their great liberality in a cause so near their hearts. They were authorized by the general assembly to choose town officers in the year 1717, and the first town clerk and select men were chosen in that year. In the year 1719, when probably there were not over twenty-five families in town, a vote was passed appropriating eighty acres of land for a minister's lot, and offering salary of seventy-five pounds, or two hundred and fifty dollars a year, making an average of ten dollars annually to each family.

On the 19th day of November, 1719, the proprietors of the town voted to build a meeting house thirty feet square, and appointed Noah Grant, William Eaton and Joseph Benton a committee "to order the affairs of the meeting house." There was, as usual some difficulty in locating this house; and the records show that several meetings were held on the subject, which served to delay the building of the house for several months. The spot where it was finally erected was agreed upon February 5th, 1721-22, which was on the hill a little east of the present residence of Mr. William West. At a previous meeting held on the 31st of January, 1720-1721, the town had voted to build a meeting house thirty feet long and twenty-eight feet wide, with eighteen feet posts. They also voted that the frame of the building should be raised by the last day of the month of June next following, and that the sides should be covered and the floors laid and windows put in by the last of the following November. It is not probable that any very serious efforts were made to comply with these votes, for we find the record of a town meeting held on the first of May of the same year, at which it was voted that the building should be forty-five feet long, thirty-five feet wide and twenty feet between joints. As this is the last vote on the subject of dimensions, it is fair to presume that the house was finally built as last prescribed and was probably raised in the spring of 1722.

It does not appear when this house was dedicated to the worship of God, yet there can be no doubt public worship was held in it early in the year 1723. October 4th, 1725, a tax of four pence on the pound was laid to defray the expenses of furnishing the meeting house. February 28th, 1726, it was voted to build pews upon that part of the floor that was raised above the rest.

In December, 1728, it was voted to build a house about twenty feet by fourteen near the meeting house to accommodate the inhabitants living remote from the meeting house with a place to spend the intermission between services without troubling others. December 9th, 1730, the town voted that the select men should procure at the town's cost what was necessary for the pulpit. December 8th, 1730, it was voted to do something toward repairing and finishing the galleries. From 1744 to 1749 liberty was given various persons to erect pews in the galleries at their own expense and for their own accommodation.

It would seem that this house did not answer the purpose for which it was designed, for we find that before it had stood thirty years, to wit, on the 28th of January, 1751, the town, by a vote of nearly two to one, voted that it was necessary to build a new meeting house. This time must have been one of unusual interest, for at this meeting we find that no less than twenty-eight persons were admitted inhabitants of the town, and one hundred and ten votes were given upon the question, viz., seventy in the affirmative and forty in the negative. Three unsuccessful attempts were made to rescind this vote, but the town adhered with increased majorities each time to its first decision. The location of this house was a matter of more than usual interest. The inhabitants of the western and northwestern portions of the town insisted on a site at the north end of the street, while those of the southern and eastern portions were equally strenuous for its location at the south end of the street. The matter was at first submitted to the town, and a majority of votes decided in favor of the southern location.

There was then no road leading into the street from the eastern part of the town, except the one leading from near where the old meeting house stood, and of course all persons attending meetings from that part of the town would have to come into the street at the south end; this doubtless had its influence in determining the location of the house. Tradition says that the influence of the Honorable Zebulon West, whose residence was in the southern part of the town, had great weight in the final settlement of this question. The minority did not readily submit to the decision of the majority as they appealed to the General Court and obtained a committee to review the proceedings of the town, but after several public hearings the location fixed by vote of the town was finally confirmed.

On the 24th day of December, 1753, the town voted to build a new meeting house fifty-six feet long and forty feet wide. This house was raised in the month of May, 1754, and was so far finished as to be used for public worship in the spring of 1750. It was erected without a steeple and not until the year 1792 did the town come to the conclusion not to dispense with this appendage any longer. At a town meeting held on the 12th day of January, 1792, they voted, "That the town will build a steeple to the meeting house, provided, that a bell can be procured and given to the town without burdening the town with any expense for said bell." The bell was to be procured by voluntary subscription, and such progress was made in this direction, that the town, at an adjourned meeting on the second day of February, 1792, voted "to raise a tax on the last August list two pence and one farthing on the pound to build a steeple on the meeting house in Tolland."

It is a traditional fact that the inhabitants of the north western portions of the town were very much opposed to the project of building the steeple, and it is said that General Chapman and his uncle, Simon Chapman, were the only persons from that quarter of the town who voted in the affirmative on this question. It is also said that the old feud growing out of the location of the meeting house was revived and had its effect upon those who voted in the negative. It seems the people were hardly satisfied with the action of the town on this subject and another town meeting was called, as will appear by the following vote copied from the town records under date of April 25th, 1792.

> Voted at said meeting that the town consider the first article in the warning for a town meeting at this time first (viz.) whether they will reconsider the vote passed at a former town meeting to build a steeple to the meeting house. Voted, to take that up first. The question was then put whether the town would reconsider their vote passed at a former meeting to build a steeple to the meeting house. Negatived by the whole.

The following vote furnishes some evidence that the old difficulty about the location of the house was not entirely forgotten. It is under date of May 4th, 1792, and is as follows:

> Voted to choose an agent to send to Hartford to attend the General Assembly at the present session to oppose the memorial of a number of inhabitants of the town of Tolland, referred to said assembly praying for liberty to move the meeting house in said Tolland to some other place near the center of said town."

It is probable the steeple was built and the bell procured and in use before December 3rd, 1792, for on that day a town meeting was held at which the following votes were passed: "Voted that a tax of one penny three farthings on the pound be laid and collected on the last August grand list to pay up the committee the residue of their bills for building the steeple to the meeting house; and the overplus, if any, to remain to defray other town expenses. At the same meeting voted, that the selectmen of said town procure Mr. Hanks to run over the bell, if he will do it on reasonable terms and to hang it again in the steeple."

Mr. Hope Lathrop, an influential citizen, was very active in procuring subscriptions for the bell. It is said he went into the western part of the town to obtain funds for this purpose, and being universally refused, he became a little excited, and declared that those who would not give anything for the bell should not "hear it ring."

The collection of the tax for building the steeple was resisted by the people in the western part of the town, and the collector, under the direction of the selectmen, distrained an ox, the property of Nathaniel Kingsbury, Jr., to pay his tax. This Nathaniel Kingsbury was an elder brother of Deacon Jabez Kingsbury, whose grandchildren still own and live on the farm owned by him during his life time. Mr. Nathaniel Kingsbury brought an action against Daniel Edgerton and others, then selectmen of Tolland, to test the legality of this tax. The writ was dated January 28th, 1793. The facts were agreed to by the parties, and the cause was carried to the supreme court of errors. Two questions were made in the case: 1. — That the town had no right to tax its inhabitants to build a steeple and 2. — If it had this right, it could only be exercised by a vote of two-thirds of the voters at a legal meeting; and inasmuch as the tax in question was laid by a majority vote only it was not legally laid. But the court ruled both questions in favor of the town, and the plaintiff had to pay the costs.

Tradition informs us that the first public use to which the bell was put was tolling for the death of Captain Hope Lathrop, who was so active in procuring it and that it was cracked on that occasion. He died November 8th, 1792, and the meeting to have Mr. Hanks recast the bell was held December 3rd, 1792; a fact that corroborates the traditional evidence.

Although this meeting house was so far finished as to be used for public worship in 1755, it was not entirely completed until several years afterward, for there is record of a vote passed on the 3rd of March, 1760, raising a tax for finishing the meeting house, which was made payable the first day of November then next following. The interior of this house was fitted up with square pews, having seats usually on three sides, so that a large portion of the audience had to sit with their sides or backs to the minister. These pews furnished very indifferent accommodations for worshippers who indulged in the somniferous habits of some of the present generation. This meeting house was taken down in the summer of 1838, being eighty-four years after its erection. The present meeting house was erected and dedicated on the 25th day of October, 1838.

The present building has changed but little in its exterior appearance in these 131 years. The steeple is said to be copied from the original in Tolland, England, and its peculiar notched construction is very different from other New England churches. The windows at that time were of plain glass; the doorway has been altered.

In 1893, extensive alterations were made in the interior. Mr. Ratcliffe Hicks, Mr. William Sumner and Mr. William Holman were the committee in charge. The old interior had contained boxed pews, brass lamps, wood stoves and galleries. Music was provided by cello and melodeon.

The church parlors were renovated in 1949. Church members volunteered to remodel the entire basement. A heating system, new kitchen and Sunday school rooms were provided. About $12,000 was raised by convass, the Congregational Building Society loaned $7,500; securities were sold, and a mortgage given.

The war between the states and the opening of the west triggered a long decline in New England towns. Tolland was no exception and the population decline was felt within the church. Young men discovered that better farms were to be found to the west and industry moved to the cities. The intensive type of farming that had been in favor could no longer be made economical. An exodus was one that lasted for one hundred years. By 1919, the Congregational and Methodist Churches had grown quite small, hardly more than 25 members in either church.

In 1920, after much discussion, planning and prayerful thought, the Lee Methodist Episcopal and the First Congregational Church of Tolland constituted themselves as the Federated Church of Tolland. Both congregations maintained an identity and affiliation with sectional and national groups. New members could choose to join the Congregational, Methodist or Federated Church. Ministers were to be drawn alternately from Congregational or Methodist headquarters. It was decided to use the Congregational Church as the building for worship. The Rev. William C. Darby from the Methodist Church of Moosup was chosen as the first pastor.

The Federated Church was governed by a Federated Board, which met regularly and whose members were appointed by the respective congregations. Each church had retained financial independence, with envelopes printed in different colors. Each treasurer paid into the Federated fund. It was a noble attempt in 1920 to foster unity in the community regarding religious work, thought and service. When the Federation was discontinued in June, 1958, the Methodists were given a chance to automatically become Congregationalists. Several Methodists did not so choose and joined either the Rockville Methodist Church or some other Methodist Church.

THE CHURCH BELL

In 1792, a steeple was built on the church in Tolland and a bell was purchased by subscription to be cast by a Mr. Hanks of Mansfield. The bell became cracked, when it was first tolled for the death of Mr. Hope Lathrop, who had been very active in procuring it. It was returned to Mr. Hanks for recasting.

Fancy loves to regard the old bell as a faithful companion to generations of men, women and children of this town during the one hundred and seventy eight years of its life up to the present day. In early years it seems to have suffered many ills. Quaint records tell us of frequent repairs on its tongue, the hook, the yoke, the "giting" and the "wheel". In 1807, Hymen Smith received $3.69 for ringing the bell at the death of Phillice and for helping Capt. Ezra Chapman mend the bell and for one quart of brandy used at that time and for mending the sealing hammer. In five years a new "roap" became necessary. Could it be that frequent ringings and tollings wore it thin within the horny-handed grasp of the ringer? Or did a bit of mischief spring from that disgruntled west part of the town?

Despite these variations of health the bell has persisted to a lusty old age and still sounds forth its call to worship in pleasant tone though it is heard less often than of yore when the daily noon hour was struck and also the curfew at nine. Climb to the present belfry, its second home, and you may read upon the sides of the bell bits of its life history as follows:-

South side:

"1010 lbs. Clinton H. Mcneely Company, Troy, New York."

North side:

Congregational Ecclesiastical Society of Tolland, Conn."

"This bell was originally cast in the year 1792, Recast same year — again 1826 — refounded in its present form in the year 1880. "Let Him That Heareth, Come."

The bell ringer was an important personage in those old days. His task was no light one in the way of physical exercise and called for carefulness and dexterity. Seth Eaton is named as an early ringer, from November 6, 1802, and for a year's service, including also "sweeping meeting house," he was paid twenty dollars. The salary for this work was gradually increased until we find a contract in 1816 between the selectmen and Hymen Smith that he should "Ring the bell and toll for all deaths and funerals within the town and on all other occasions where it is necessary for the bell to be rung and to sweep the meeting house when necessary for the sum of $85.00 per year."

The bell foundry is one of the most useful industries, which has its origin in this town of Mansfield. Col. Benjamin Hanks, one of the pioneers in the silk manufacture business at Hanks Mill in Mansfield, also established there a bell foundry. It was in this place, a short distance south of the Hanks Bros. Silk Mill, that the first church bell was cast in America.

Col. Hanks first established himself in the watch and clock business at Litchfield, Conn. in 1778. He built and put up the first tower clock in the city of New York on the old Dutch church on the corner of Nashua and Liberty streets. It was a unique affair, being wound by the aid of a windmill attachment. In 1785, he returned to Mansfield and established the bell and bronze cannon foundry business, the latter being also the first cast in our country. He employed many men and among cannon cast, were two Bronze four pounders belonging to what was then the first Conn. Artillery. They bore his name and were carried by more modern weapons of warfare and these ancient relics are now preserved at the Hartford Arsenal as mementos of the past.

Col. Hanks died in West Troy, N. Y., aged 65 years. Twelve years prior to his death he established his third son, Julius Hanks in the foundry business at Troy, which he has successfully operated. The latter was thoroughly instructed in the business, as well as in the manufacture of mathematical and surveying instruments. One of the graduates of his works was Andrew Mcneeley, who married Philena, eldest daughter of Rodney Hanks, a brother of Col. Benjamin Hanks. Mr. Mcneeley succeeded Julius Hanks in 1826, making church bells a speciality. During his business career of a quarter century upwards of seven thousand bells were cast. In 1851, Mr. Mcneeley died, leaving a good name and valued reputation to his two sons, Edwin A. and George R. Mcneeley, who continued the business under the name of Andrew Mcneeley's Sons until 1863 when the firm was changed to E. A. and G. R. Mcneeley.

MINISTERS OF THE CONGREGATIONAL CHURCH

The Reverend Stephen Steel was the first minister of the town and was officiating in the months of January and February, 1719-20. He was graduated from Yale College in 1718. The town voted to give the minister sixty pounds a year and not to build him a house, but they finally gave him seventy-five pounds and agreed to build him a house. On June 19th, 1723, is this record: "Voted, that the church hath liberty to ordain Mr. Stephen Steel pastor of a church in Tolland. Voted, that the charge of Mr. Steel's ordination is done at the expense of the town. Voted, that Noah Grant shall be one to see that provision be made for the ordination of Mr. Steel. Voted, that Daniel Cook shall be one to take care that provision be made for the ordination of Mr. Steel."

From documents and records it is apparent that the church of the Congregational Society in Tolland was organized between the month of May, 1722, and the month of June, 1723, but at what precise date, or who were its first officers or members cannot now be accurately ascertained. The Reverend Stephen Steel was ordained as pastor of the church and society in Tolland in 1723, but the precise date is not known. He continued to be the pastor of the church until the 21st day of December, 1758, when the connection between him and the church and society was amicably dissolved by the parties, on account of his ill health. He died in Tolland on the 4th day of December, 1759, in the sixty-third year of his age. Mr. Steel was a native of Hartford, where his father was a farmer. Mr. Steel married Ruth, daughter of Colonel Hezekiah Porter, of Hadley, Mass. Their children were; Ruth, Stephen, Eleazer, Elisha, Sarah, Mehitable, James, John and Aaron.

It is not possible to give any very distinct idea of the person or character of the Rev. Stephen Steel. Unfortunately, he left no publication, nor does any manuscript exist from which his intellectual and literary attainments can be estimated. He once preached the annual election sermon at Hartford, but omitted to furnish a copy for publication. The fact that he was selected for this service, is evidence that he was a man of more than ordinary ability, for in his day none but clergymen of very respectable attainments were honored with this distinction. His correspondence with the town, and the satisfactory arrangement made with its agents, when his health became so much impaired as to disable him from performing the duties of his ministerial office, give unmistakable evidence of his concilatory spirit, his disinterestedness and his unaffected piety. He had then been the sole minister of the town for nearly forty years, had commenced with it in its infancy, when it was nearly an unbroken wilderness, containing less than twenty-five families; had seen the population increase to near one thousand, and had the satisfaction of knowing there was not, at the time of his resignation a single dissenting worshipper in the whole number, nor the least want of unanimity on ecclesiastical affairs in the whole town.

The Rev. Mr. Nathan Williams succeeded the Rev. Stephen Steel and received a unanimous call from the town to settle in the work of the ministry in Tolland, on the 26th day of November, 1759 — they offering to pay him two hundred pounds (Six hundred sixty-six dollars and sixty-six cents) as a settlement, and eighty pounds (two hundred sixty-six dollars, and sixty-six cents) as a yearly salary. This proposition was accepted, and the Reverend Nathan Williams was ordained April 30th, 1760. He continued the sole pastor of the church and society until January, 1813, a period of nearly fifty-three years, when the Reverend Ansel Nash was settled as his colleague. Doctor Williams continued to reside in Tolland until his decease, on the 15th of April, 1829, at the age of ninety-four years. He was born at Longmeadow, Mass., November 8th, 1735, was a son of Reverend John Williams, the celebrated minister of Deerfield. The Rev. Nathan Williams of Tolland and Mary Hall, of Wallingford, were married October 20, 1760. They had the following children: Nathan, Eliakim, William, Mary, Ruth, Abigail, and Isaac.

The Rev. Doctor Williams holds a prominent place in the history of Tolland. He has done more than any other person to form the character of its inhabitants. He was their only minister for more than fifty years, and occupied a prominent and influential position for nearly seventy years of his life. In person he was about five feet nine inches in height; rather stout, with a body symmetrical and well proportioned. He was easy and graceful in his manners, social in his habits and interesting and instructive in his conversation. He was punctilious in etiquette, careful in his personal appearance, precise and select in his language, and in every way a model gentleman of the old school. As a preacher he adhered to the tenets of the old divines, was strictly orthodox as the term was then understood, but was quite liberal for the age in which he lived. He was a good scholar, well educated, with a fair intellect, and good common-sense. His public performances were very creditable, and quite acceptable to parishioners. Several of his sermons and other religious compositions were printed, and will compare favorably with similar productions of his associates. Several copies of them are now deposited in the library of the Connecticut Historical Society at Hartford.

Mrs. Mary Williams was a perfect model for a minister's wife. Intelligent without vanity; complacent without sycophancy; devotedly pious without any forbidding pretensions, she exercised a salutary influence without any apparent effort. She taught by example as well as by precept; she attended to the duties of her own household, and cared for the wants of her dependants, feeling that her happiness was best promoted when she was contributing to the enjoyment of those around her. She was an economist, not for the purpose of acquiring wealth, but on account of the example to others. Doctor Williams possessed more of this world's goods, comparatively, than now ordinarily falls to the lot of country ministers, but it was never ostentatiously used. His house always exhibited comforts without extravagance, and great order and neatness without luxurious elegance.

The Reverend Ansel Nash was settled as the colleague of Reverend Doctor Williams in the month of January, 1813, and continued to be the active pastor of the church and society until the month of May, 1831, a period of a little more than eighteen years, when he resigned upon his own request, with the consent of a majority of the church and society. Mr. Nash was born in Williamsburg, Hampshire county, Mass., on the 16th of January, 1788. He graduated at Williams College in the year 1807, at the age of nineteen years. He pursued his theological studies at Andover, Mass., and was licensed to preach in the year 1810. He came to Tolland in the latter part of the summer of 1812, received a call, and in January, 1813, was ordained as the colleague of Doctor Williams. His salary was six hundred dollars a year; one hundred of which, a few years later, he generously relinquished annually, in consideration of the pecuniary circumstances of the society. He was married to Eunice Jennings, of Windham, Conn. on the 24th of May, 1813, with whom he lived until his death. He left no children. He departed this life August 11, 1851 aged sixty-three years.

Mr. Nash was a man of marked ability. To a mind naturally

quick and active, was added the polish of a finished education; and aided by a memory that garnered the choicest treasures of both ancient and modern literature, he was prepared to acquit himself creditably on the theatre of life. His sermons were characterized rather for their logic than their rhetoric, and contained more of argument than imagination; still they were both attractive and instructive. He could not be said to be eloquent in their delivery, but was earnest, forcible and serious, and particularly successful in securing the attention of his hearers. In extemporary prayer he possessed peculiar gifts. He seemed to apprehend the secret desires of the most obscure worshiper present, and would present them at the mercy seat in language that raised the mind from earth to heaven, and imbued it with that fervency which makes prayer importunate and effectual.

In social life, Mr. Nash was open, frank, and sometimes a little abrupt. He carefully noticed passing events, and was free to make them topics of general remark; and it was sometimes supposed these occupied too much of his time as a religious teacher. And yet he was never light nor trifling, and was always ready to defend the religion he professed, whenever and however assailed. He was forward in all efforts for public improvement in the town in which he lived — particularly those which had for their object the education of the masses. He took especial interest in the establishment of an academy in Tolland; and was for a long time chairman of the board of trustees. It may not be invidious to remark, that the academy ceased to exist about the time of Mr. Nash's leaving the town, and there has been no special effort since to revive it. He was a valuable member of society; an intelligent and interesting preacher; a worthy and revered pastor; and a most constant and sincere friend.

After the resignation of Mr. Nash, the Rev. Abram Marsh became the pastor of the Congregational Church and society in Tolland, which position he held for a period of thirty-eight years. He was installed on the 30th day of November, 1831. Mr. Marsh was born in Hartford, Vermont, June 15th, 1802. He was educated at Dartmouth College, where he was graduated in 1825, pursued his theological studies at Andover, Mass., and was licensed to preach in 1828. He supplied a church in Redding, Vermont, about two years, a portion of which time he was the principal of an academy at Thetford. He married Miss Rhoda Short, of Vermont, January 25th, 1829. She died in Tolland, August 17th, 1840, leaving two sons.

Mr. Marsh married Miss Mary H. Cooley, of Norwich, Conn., Apr. 6, 1842.

Mr. Marsh was a man of strong convictions and yet kindly in his attitude towards individual offenders and when it became necessary to speak for his principles, he attacked the sins and spared the sinners. In this connection it is told of him that, being strongly opposed to the sale of intoxicants in our town, he preached a vigorous sermon upon the subject with plain reference to a certain distillery, but without allusion to the men running it.

It is evident from all records that this long pastorage was a fruitful one and gained for Mr. Marsh genuine confidence and respect from the entire community. When he began there were one hundred and sixty-six members of the church, a decrease from the high water mark of Mr. Nash's day. Perhaps the exit from country village to town had already begun. It certainly became a marked feature of those years, 1831 to 1869. Although two hundred and fifty-five were added to the church from time to time, at the close of Mr. Marsh's ministry there were but one hundred and four members, of whom twenty were absentees. The young men in particular left, as was true in many rural communities. More than three times as many male members were dismissed by letter as were received.

A depleted church therefore meant no reflection upon the affection between people and pastor nor upon the sermons of these thirty-seven years. Possibly there came to be a sameness and heaviness about the sermons for a record reads that when in the thirty-eighth year a committee visited Mr. Marsh and suggested his resignation, they informed him that "the people had come to the judgment that his sermons would be more useful to a people unaccustomed to him and his sermons, than here."

It is a tribute to the spirit of this pastor, that he quietly agreed with his people and withdrew, to take up work elsewhere for a few years.

A Rev. H. M. Holliday followed Mr. Marsh and immediately demanded a raise in salary from $600 to $1,200 which the society reluctantly agreed to, but Mr. Holliday intimated increasing strength his ministry might bring to the church, would be ample to meet the emergency. However, no such strength came but debt instead. Mr. Holliday was obliged to take his ambition elsewhere in one year.

About four years were filled with supplies until in 1874 the fifteen year pastorate of Rev. Charles N. Seymour began. Mr. Seymour's family occupied a parsonage which the church had acquired by the bequest of one of its members, Miss Ruth Hatch, 1874, situated just below the southern end of the street.

Unlike the four previous pastors, Mr. Seymour was well advanced in years and in pastoral experience elsewhere when he came to Tolland. An active worker he was tramping the country roads east and west, north and south, to visit his families.

His pulpit work is remembered not so much for its direct and stirring appeal as for thoughtful topic elaboration with perhaps undue reflection upon the present day. Mr. Seymour sounded as if "the old times were better" but acted as if these were pretty good times after all! Ill health was the cause of Mr. Seymour's resignation in 1889.

The Rev. Aurelian H. Post was engaged in 1892, "to serve for a year, more if acceptable," as proved to be the case, so that he was with the church ten years.

A choice man was Mr. Post, scholarly, kindly genuine, although so modest and quiet that the pure gold of his character was not immediately discovered. He could hardly be called, in modern parlance, a "good mixer", indeed social amenities appeared to burden his retiring nature. Yet in pastoral attentions he was faithful and sympathetic.

In the spring of 1904, after two years of "supplies", The Rev. H. T. Barnard of West Stafford, Conn., was engaged "to act as pastor of this church for the year ending March 13, 1905, and to so continue until further action is taken". No further action was desired or necessary for three years, during which Mr. Barnard endeared himself to the church and community by his loving spirit, his kindly and genial social ministries and his helpful words from the pulpit. Both Mr. and Mrs. Barnard brought a valuable asset to the town in the way of music. A village church seldom received such an uplift in its singing power as came by these two voices, Mrs. Barnard's in the choir, the pastor's ringing from his place in the pulpit.

During the interim between the close of Mr. Barnard's pastorate, December 1907 and June 1st, 1908 the pulpit was supplied by Rev. Mr. Berg, a student at the Hartford Theological Seminary. The Rev. Robert M. French of Hadlyme was then engaged for five years. He grew into the esteem and love of the people, to be followed by the Rev. Burt F. Case who also made for himself a warm place in the hearts of the community. These two, friends of each other and of a wide circle in Tolland, complete the list of pastors who built up and sustained the church in its separate denominational life.

An important step taken during the pastorate of Mr. French was the revising of the original creed of the church and the printing of a manual, completed July 1, 1913. The names of fifty-three persons are given as members in this manual. At one communion service in 1909, Mr. French received into membership fifteen young people.

Mr. Case will be remembered as the War pastor among other counts, and an indefatigable, persistent loyal patriot he showed himself to be, leading the community in "drives" and assisting in other war work.

The Rev. William C. Darby, first pastor of the Federated Church, was a young man, well liked by all, but most particularly by the young folks. Mr. Darby was instrumental in organizing and provided leadership for the use of the Methodist Church as a Community House. The teen-age boys' and girls' basketball teams were very active and the former first selectman, Carmelo Zanghi was the girls' coach. Rev. Darby left in 1930, after getting the Federation off to a good start. He went to California to live.

Rev. James A. Davidson and Mrs. Davidson (of the Congregational denomination) were a delightful couple, who brought a serenity and dignity to the parish life. In their quiet, efficient way, they carried on the work of a real community church.

Rev. Valentine S. Alison and his wife Sylvia with their children, brought young life back to the parsonage. Both minister and his wife were active, hard working people. Mrs. Alison was beloved by all who knew her. She is buried in the North Cemetery of Tolland. The family had, before her death, moved to a Presbyterian parish in northern New York state; as Rev. Alison wished to return to his own denomination.

Rev. Ernest O'Neal, Jr., ordained Methodist minister, and Mrs. O'Neal were a devout, dedicated young couple. Their sojourn in Tolland was short. After leaving Tolland they went to Latin American countries as missionaries — a field for which they were studying while in Tolland.

Rev. Hollis French and Mrs. French were also devout Christians. He was a graduate of Wesleyan University and the Northern New York Conference School of Technology. He was well read and interested in nature. Mr. French had a brilliant mind and was a real scholar. He has done a great deal of writing. He served as pastor from July 23, 1944 until May 1946.

The Rev. and Mrs. Philip King were an ideal couple. He was very devoted and kind and gave some wonderful sermons. He knew how to manage the affairs of the church. They were active in promoting the church and brought deep spiritual feeling to their associates.

The Reverend William C. H. Moe, D.D. was born in 1876. His early childhood was spent in the Madison County Home, New York. After a full career of service in the ministry, Dr. Moe came to Tolland in 1948. National attention was focused on him in the Saturday "Evening Post" for his work as Chaplain of the Tolland County Jail, which was of more than passing interest.

In 1955, Mr. Moe preached his sermon "Story of the Ecclesiastical Society." arguing that the church rightfully belonged to all its members. As an outcome, the Society deeded its property to the Church. Later Dr. Moe impressed upon the Church its duty to provide a parsonage, which would not only provide a comfortable home but would reflect in a measure the regard of the Church for its ministers. In 1958 the congregation voted to accept plans for a new parsonage.

On June 12, 1955, an Honorary Doctorate of Divinity was conferred on William Collins Hainsworth Moe, by Dartmouth College . "Your life has been immense in all the directions that count: courage, conscience, competence, kindness and generosity — you came to Dartmouth as a pastor of the Congregational Church in Norwich, worked through its college to graduate Summa Cum Laude with the class of 1910."

In 1957, Dr. Moe tendered his resignation, but his work has continued. He still visited the jail, hospitals, children and the aged, bringing a gentle faith, his life a daily sermon of the brotherhood of man and the fatherhood of God. He died June 27, 1971.

The Rev. Frank C. VanCleef came to the church in February, 1959, and was its pastor until Oct. 13, 1963. He was soft spoken and very deliberate in his preaching and his sermons were well prepared with topical subjects and with sincere Christian devotion. He was always pleasant in his visits to members of the congregation.

The Rev. Donald Miller, the present pastor of the Congregational Church, came on April 12, 1964. He has been well accepted by the congregation and is a very active worker for the church. He is especially liked by the young people.

LIST OF CONGREGATIONAL MINISTERS

Rev. Stephen Steel	1723 - 1758
Rev. Nathan Williams	1760 - 1813
Rev. Ansel Nash	1813 - 1831
Rev. Abram Marsh	1831 - 1869
Rev. H. M. Holliday	1869 - 1870
Rev. Charles N. Seymour	1892 - 1902
Rev. Henry T. Barnard	1904 - 1907
Rev. Robert M. French	1908 - 1913
Rev. Burt F. Case	1914 - 1920

THE FEDERATED CHURCH

Rev. W. C. Darby	1920 - 1930
Rev. J. A. Davidson	1931 - 1933
Rev. Valentine S. Alison	1934 - 1941
Rev. Ernest E. O'Neal, Jr.	1941 - 1943
Rev. Hollis French	1944 - 1946
Rev. Philip King	1946 - 1948
Rev. William Moe	1948 - 1957

THE UNITED CONGREGATIONAL CHURCH

Rev. Frank C. VanCleef	1959 - 1963
Rev. Donald G. Miller	1964 -

During this period there were many supply or substitute ministers that occupied the church pulpit during those times when there was no regular minister assigned. These supplys deserve much credit for keeping up the church spirit, during those times when the parishioners had no regular minister to advise and to console them. Some of these supply ministers were as follows: Rev. George E. Sanborn, Rev. I. W. Fitch, Rev. G. W. Morrell, Rev. W. B. Ronald, Rev. W. V. Berg, Rev. Abby, and the Rev. Allison R. Heaps.

THE METHODIST CHURCH

In May, 1789, at the Conference held in New York, Jesse Lee was appointed as the preacher for New England. On the 11th of June he arrived in the State of Connecticut and six days later preached his first sermon in New England at Norwalk. Five years before, at the invitation of Bishop Asbury, Lee adjusted his affairs, procured a horse, saddle bags, a Bible and a hymn book, the necessary equipments for a Methodist minister in those early days and started out on a career which has made his name immortal. In 1790, the Hartford circuit included Wilbraham, Mass., Tolland, Hartford, Windsor, Suffield, Granby, Enfield, Waterbury, Middletown and other nearby towns. Jesse Lee preached the first Methodist sermon ever heard in Tolland, April 2, 1790. Many were converted, and a class was formed.

Monday, August 11, 1793, the first Methodist Annual Conference ever held in Connecticut and the second in New England was held here. Ten of twelve ministers were then present. The sessions of the Conference were held in the northeast corner room of the house now occupied as a parsonage. The preaching service was held in the partially finished chapel. Bishop Asbury was present and preached on II, Timothy II:24-26, "The servant of the Lord must not strive," etc. The text was peculiarly apt for the people and the time, for Rev. Williams of the Congregational Church had recently bitterly attacked the Methodist Church usages and doctrines. Dr. Williams afterwards acknowledged his mistake, and invited Methodists to hold prayer meetings at his home.

On Monday, October 4, 1790, Jesse Lee arrived at the Conference then in session in New York. He asked for additional workers for New England. The appointments for this section were as follows: Presiding Elder, Jesse Lee; Fairfield Circuit, John Bloodgood; New Haven Circuit, John Lee; Hartford Circuit, Nathaniel B. Mills; Boston Circuit, Jesse Lee and Daniel Smith. As Tolland was included in the Hartford Circuit, we find that Nathaniel B. Mills was the first preacher appointed to Tolland, although Jesse Lee preached the first Methodist sermon there.

At the Conference at New York in 1791, Lemuel Smith and Menzies Rainor were the preachers appointed to Hartford Circuit.

During the year an "extensive reformation prevailed on this circuit." At Tolland and the neighboring villages the interest was especially profound. Asbury estimates that 150 souls were converted here. In 1792, Hope Hull, George Roberts and F. Aldridge were appointed to Hartford Circuit. The revival spirit which had begun here the year before extended like fire under the labors of Hull and his colleagues. It left in Tolland such distinct traces that a small society was formed and a chapel erected. With this society the Conference met in 1793. This Conference was the first ever held in Connecticut and the second in New England.

The first Methodist meeting house or chapel in Tolland was erected in 1793. It stood on the same site of our present Lee church. In 1807, a lease for the land on which the chapel was built was given to the trustees of the Methodist society. A copy of the lease now in possession of J. P. Root, chairman of the present board of trustees, reads as follows: "Know all men by these presents: That we, Thomas Howard and Harvey Howard both of Tolland, in Tolland County, for the consideration of the love, goodwill, and affection, which we have and bear towards the Methodist religion, do lease unto Elijah Haskell, John Norris, John Stanley, Samuel Norris and Moses Barnard, all of Tolland, Trustees, — for and during the term of nine hundred and ninety-nine years — ."

The sessions of the Conference were held in the house now used as a parsonage, while the preaching service was held in the unfinished chapel, Bishop Asbury preaching from II, Timothy II:24-26.

In 1794 Tolland Circuit appears for the first time in the Conference returns. The first Methodist meeting-house was erected on land owned by a Mr. Howard. In 1807 a lease for the land on which the chapel was built was given to the Trustees of the society. Among the large number of useful men converted at about this time, 1816, were Erastus Benton, Sanford Benton, Seth Crowell and Eleazor Steele. All natives of Tolland, and grand and powerful Methodist preachers.

In August, 1794, Bishop Asbury is again in Tolland. He writes in his journals as follows: "Thursday, the 7th, a day of rest and affliction of body. Came to Tolland very sick. I find my soul stayed upon God in perfect love, and wait His holy will in all things."

On Thursday, September 11, 1794, Jesse Lee, as presiding elder, rode into Tolland, only to find the little band of Methodists wreaked by persecution. He preached on the text Acts XVII: 6.

In 1800 Rev. John Broadhead, presiding elder, and Rev. S. Bostwick, at Tolland, jointly sent a letter. In it they say: "There has been a great work in Tolland, in the old town; but it afterwards broke out in another part of the town, and about 65 members were added."

Asa Kent was pastor part of the year 1802. He afterwards wrote of that year thus: "D. Ostrander, the presiding elder, took me to Tolland circuit, to take the place of E. Batchelor, who was sick. I stayed there till November 8, and received $12.83: poor encouragement, so far as money was concerned. My clothes were threadbare — entirely out — after more than a year's travel, and I had been obliged to borrow money to get along, besides giving my note for my horse; but faith in God gained the victory."

The oldest records of the Methodist Episcopal Church in Tolland date back to 1839, and only one preacher was appointed that year, indicating that Tolland had become a separate station.

In 1832 Rev. R. E. Allen began his ministry at Tolland. In 1880, he wrote: "Tolland! What associations it awakens! Tolland circuit was my first in the itinerant life, and can I forget it? Never, never! Oh, how I would like to go back to that old battlefield and see and experience what I then saw and experienced. The Sabbath appointments for the circuit were Tolland, Stafford Springs, West Stafford, Square Pond, and Willington."

In 1860, George A. Morse was stationed at Tolland. He preached two years, teaching school in winter. He was very successful in teaching some of the most wicked men in town. But this was not all, for he found here a certain young lady, Miss Sarah A. Chapman, who afterward became his wife.

In 1873, Nelson Goodrich was appointed to this charge, and began to hold meetings in the east part of the town, at what was then known as Tolland Depot. Under his labors and those of his successor, Rev. L. S. Godell, there was a general awakening. So in 1874 a new society was formed, consisting of thirteen members, and Nathan Pierson appointed leader. In 1876 a meeting-house was built. This church was Wesley Chapel.

On Wednesday, May 5, 1880, the present Lee Church was

dedicated, Rev. Samuel McBurney preaching the dedicatory sermon. For some time the need of a parsonage had been felt. Finally in the fall of 1886 an opportunity presented itself. A house near the church was secured for $800. The sum of $435 was immediately spent in putting the building in good condition.

The second Lee Methodist Church, which was built in 1880 was used by the Methodists until 1920, when they were joined to the Federated Church. The Methodists deeded the church to the Federated Church, who in turn sold it to the Grange in 1959. It is interesting to note that this church was built on property which did not belong to the Methodist Church. Erected in 1794, the property was deeded to the trustees of the Methodist Society in 1807. Deeded by Thomas and Harvey Howard whom we must credit as just men, the instrument covers a leased period of 999 years and is valued in town goodwill and affection to the Church.

Many of the older residents who remember the last days that the Methodists used this as a separate church, recall the Gospel Hymns sung out on a summer night. There was an intensity of feeling that would not be "sophisticated" today. The Methodist parsonage for many years was in the house that presently is the home of Mrs. John Aborn.

The early history of the Methodist Church was taken from the Souvenir History of the New England Southern Conference by Rev. Rennetts C. Miller in 1897.

METHODIST PASTORS

	Jesse Lee		
1790	Nathaniel B. Mills	1839	Benj. C. Phelps
1791	Lemuel Smith	1849	Winsor Ward
	Menzies Rainor	1841-42	L. Leffingwell
1792	Hope Hull	1843	C. Turner
	George Roberts	1844	Abram Holway
	F. Aldridge	1845	William Leonard
1793	Joseph Lovell	1846	H. Torbush
1794	Lemuel Smith	1847	L. Dow Bentley
	George Pickering		William Dixon
1795	Christopher Spry		Rev. Mr. Stoddard
	Nicholas Snethen		Josiah Benton
1796	Evan Rogers	1848	William W. Hurd
	Thomas Cooper	1855	H. W. Smith
1797	Sawrence McCoombs	1856	Jabez Pack
1799	Daniel Ostrander	1858	Caleb D. Rogers

1800	Abner Wood	1860	T. W. Douglas
1801	Augustus Jocelyn		George A. Morse
	Henry Eames	1861-62	George A. Morse
1802	Elijah Batchelor	1863	L. A. Dunham
	Alexander McLean	1864-66	Benj. M. Walker
1803	Augustus Jocelyn	1867-68	H. H. Arnold
	Elijah Batchelor	1869	F. A. Metcalf
1804	John Gove	1871	E. L. Latham
1805-6	Noble W. Thomas		W. Dixon
	Benj. Hill	1872	E. L. Latham
1807	Hollis Sampson	1873	Nelson Goodrich
	G. R. Norris	1874	L. S. Goodell
1808	Benj. F. Lombard	1875	S. G. Ashley
1809	Benj. P. Hill	1876-77	J. Cooper
	William P. Hinman	1878	J. O. Dodge
1816	Solomon Winchester	1880-82	William Turkington
	Nathan Paine	1883	F. A. Crafts
1817-39	Benj. Sabine	1884-85	J. H. Sherman
	Ebenezer Blake	1886-88	J. B. Ackley
	Daniel Dorchester	1890-93	John Thompson
	M. Fifield	1894-96	J. B. Ackley
	William Ramsdell	1897-99	J. Q. Adams
	---Hascall	1900-04	W. T. Johnson
	---Otis	1904-06	J. H. Allen
	John W. Case	1907-10	J. A. Wood
	---Wolcott	1911-19	J. N. Geisler
	E. Withey	1920	W. H. Barber
	A. Hale		
	---Haywood		
	R. W. Allen (1832)		
	and others		

THE NEW LIGHTERS

Between the years 1740 and 1751, the people of New England were electrified by the eloquence of the celebrated Whitefield, whose preaching was mainly instrumental in forwarding the great revival of religion that then spread through the land. The followers of Mr. Whitefield were called New-lights, and were not very favorably regarded by the more staid religious community. Their success, however, was so great, that many of the clergy who were then supposed to have permanent livings, were opposed to the revival, fearing that they might be deserted by their hearers, and be compelled to preach to empty seats. Many of them carried their opposition so far as to re-fuse the revival preachers the use of their pulpits, and actually procured the enactment of a law that under certain limitations confined all preachers to their own parishes, — an opposition as useless as unwise, and only encouraged the very thing it was intended to prevent. The minds of people, having become excited by the fervor of the new teachings, could not relish the dry, formal services of the settled clergy, which they supposed were conducted by a set of graceless mercenaries, without any of that unction which characterized the performances of the New-lights. The town of Tolland shared the advantages, or disadvantages, of these movements; but the innovators were treated with more favor by the then settled minister, Rev. Stephen Steel, than their associates received from the clergy generally; and the wisdom of the course pursued by Mr. Steel, growing out of his forbearance, catholicity, and kindness, is evidenced by the fact, that in a very few years this sect entirely disappeared from the town, and left him in charge of a respectable congregation without any open dissension.

Among the persons in Tolland who adopted the New-light ideas, no one became so much distinguished as Shubael Stearns, Jr. He united with them about the year 1745, became a preacher, and continued with them about five or six more years. In the year 1750 or 1751, he also became acquainted with the Baptist denomination; renounced the usual tenet of infant baptism, and was himself rebaptized by Rev. Wait Palmer, in Tolland, in the year 1751. On the 20th day of May, in the same year, he was ordained to the work of the ministry by Mr. Palmer and Rev. Joshua Morse. Several persons in Tolland attached themselves to Rev. Mr. Stearns, among whom were one or two by the name of Paulk. Mr. Stearns and his companions left Tolland in the year 1754 and finally settled in North Carolina at Sandy Creek. He organized the Sandy Creek Baptist Church. This church is recognized as the mother church of the Southern Baptist Convention, the largest Protestant denomination in America.

THE OLD BAPTIST CHURCH

In 1807, the bustling community had need for a third church. The Baptist church was organized in June, 1807. Their first minister was the Reverend Augustus Bolles, who was ordained pastor in the year 1814. The services at his ordination were held in the Congregational meeting house. He continued their minister three years. The next settled minister in this society was Reverend Levi Walker, Jr., who was ordained in June, 1833, and was succeeded by Reverend Sylvester Barrows in the year 1836, who continued their minister until the year 1841. Since the departure of Mr. Barrows the following have supplied the Baptist church and society; Reverend John Hunt, one year; Reverend Thomas Holman, one year; Reverend Percival Matthewson, one year; Reverend Homer Sears, three years; Rev. Thomas Dowling, four years; Reverend Joseph A. Tillinghast, a little more than a year, until his death, August 7th, 1859. Reverend C. L. Baker and others have occasionally supplied the pulpit to this time. Reverend B. J. Savage is the last pastor.

The house belonging to the Baptist Society was built by subscription in 1832, and has been thoroughly repaired. Before the building of this house the congregation had held meetings in the old school house of the Center district. Baptisms were performed in Phillips Pond, which is located at the foot of Jail Hill.

After the Baptist church and society was discontinued in 1887 the building was used as a private school in the 1890's. It also served as a hat shop, a meat market and a general store. It was removed in 1908 and was rebuilt into a house on Torry Road.

THE NEW FIRST BAPTIST CHURCH OF TOLLAND

The new First Baptist Church of Tolland is temporarily holding its services in the gym of the Hicks Memorial School located in the center of Tolland. Sunday school is at 9:00 A.M. and the Morning Worship service is at 10:00 A.M. On Sunday evening there is a Training Institute at 6:30 P.M., followed by the Evangelistic service at 7:30 P.M. Due to the lack of a building the Wednesday prayer service is held in the parsonage and in various homes of the members and friends. There are now about 60 members.

The Southern Baptist Convention is assisting the Baptist Church in Tolland in its start. It had its beginning as a Fellowship meeting in Stafford Springs under the leadership of its founder, David Calderwood. As the work grew Arthur Field became the mission's director and preacher, and in July of 1968 moved to Tolland. In January of 1969 the mission was constituted a church and called its first pastor, Rev. Herbert P. Clough. A new church is being planned.

ST. MATTHEW CHURCH

St. Matthew Catholic parish was established in June, 1964 in accordance with the changing needs of the community. Land had been purchased in the northern portion of the center of the town, between Rockville, Stafford and Dunn Hill roads.

The Rev. J. Clifford Curtin, the first pastor of St. Matthew Church was born in Hartford, Conn. and graduated from Hartford Public High in 1940. He attended St. Thomas in Bloomfield, Conn. until 1944 when he entered the Grand Seminary of St. Bernard, Rochester, New York, to study philosophy. At Christ The King Seminary of St. Bonaventure's University in Alleghany, New York, Father Curtin studied theology. He was ordained on May 3, 1951, at old St. Joseph's Cathedral, Hartford.

Father Curtin's first assignment was at St. Mary's Parish, Coventry, and he served there until 1956 when he was transferred to St. Bernard Parish, Rockville. In 1958, Father Curtin went to St. Michael's Parish in Pawcatuck, Conn., until June of 1964 when he was named by Bishop Hines as first pastor of the newly-established parish of St. Matthew in Tolland, Conn. Father Curtin took residence in the classic 175 year old rectory building on Aug. 18, 1964. The white wooden frame building, dominated by enormous twin maples, has long been a landmark in Tolland. It had been known as the Old Squirrel Inn, and more recently at the turn of the century as the Tolland Inn. Its centuries-old panel wood of pumpkin hue, its wide plank flooring, its several utilitarian fireplaces, and all structural foundations have been excellently maintained throughout the years. New furnishings in keeping with the colonial theme help to preserve the pristine neatness of earlier Pilgrims who may have lodged there. This fine old home has served many Tolland citizens including members of the Eaton family and ministers of the Baptist church.

Services were first held in the Grange Hall and then in the Hick's Memorial School gym. Construction of the new church began in April 1965.

The esthetic appearance of St. Matthew Church is modified colonial in a style that blends with the surrounding countryside of this typical New England town of Tolland. The exterior is Belden Colony, a rose-blended brick. The aluminum-covered spire crowned by a gold leafed cross which soars to a height of 80 feet above the village green. The total seating capacity of the church is 750 parishioners.

Dedication Day of St. Matthew Church was on May 30, 1966. Organizations of the Church are St. Matthew Holy Name Society (men); St. Matthew Ladies Guild; C.Y.O. for High School young people; and a Men's Choir organized in March, by Mrs. Harold Garrity, the church organist.

THE ROCKVILLE-TOLLAND SEVENTH-DAY ADVENTIST CHURCH

The Rockville-Tolland Seventh-day Adventist Church was organized on Dec. 8, 1956 with twenty-one charter members. The first official meeting of the group, which was composed mostly of members of the Prospect Avenue Hartford Church, was held on Nov. 3, 1956, at the Masonic Temple in Rockville, which place was to remain its meeting place until October of 1964 when the group began to meet in the Full Gospel Church. The congregation was to make another move in the fall of 1965, to the Willington Congregational Church before finally moving to its own house of worship on Route 30 in Tolland in Jan. 1967.

John Haywood was the minister of the local church when it was organized, followed by H. Ward Hill in 1960 and O. J. Mills in mid-1962. Since the middle of 1964 an assistant pastor has worked with the local congregation to further the work in the area; the present assistant pastor is Wayne Willey whose predecessors were Mark Findley, Alexander Fuleki, David Johnston, and Russell Burrill.

The nucleus of the building fund came from the sale of the Woodward property in Vernon, which had been given to the local church. Volunteers of many faiths, from local and distant places, helped the church to be ready for occupancy within ten months of ground breaking in March 1966. The pews were donated by the Suffield First Baptist Church and the altar chairs by the Collinsville Congregational Church. The pulpit was hand crafted by Ernest Anderson, and the building was designed by Edmund Van Dyke Cox with a sanctuary to seat one hundred fifty.

At the time of the church's consecration in 1967 there were twenty-seven members; presently the membership is forty-one. The increase in membership resulted largely from an evangelistic effort in March 1967, conducted by Pastor James Gilley and David Peterson.

Young men of the church are non-combatants, serving in the medical corps of the armed services but not bearing arms, and therefore, are classified as conscientious cooperators. The church is known for its observance of the Sabbath as set forth by Biblical decree, its welfare work, its health reform, and its Five Day No Smoking seminars.

About seventy years ago a Seventh-day Adventist group was known to have met here in town, though the date and place are not now known. Some believers went on foot or by buggy to worship in the home of Dr. Marsh in Mansfield, and later they went to Willimantic for services.

The Rockville-Tolland Seventh-day Adventist Church was built in 1966 near Leonard's Corners.

The present Congregational church was built in 1838. It has been remodeled and improved several times since then. The original church was built in 1722.

The first Lee Methodist church and parsonage. The church was erected in 1793.

The Baptist Church was built in 1832 and was used as a Baptist Church until 1887. It was finally removed in 1908 and was rebuilt into a house on Tory Road.

The second Lee Methodist church was built in 1880. It was used by the Methodists until 1920.

St. Matthew Church. The construction of St. Matthew Church was started in April 1965. It was designed to blend in with the surrounding countryside of this typical New England town of Tolland.

Schools in Tolland

As early as 1650, the Connecticut colony ordered every township of fifty families to maintain a school to teach reading and writing. Tolland must have had its first school within a few years after its founding in 1713. Until 1780 only boys went to school. It was not thought to be necessary to educate girls, as most of them would marry and become housewives.

Before the Revolutionary War about the only books used in the schools were the Bible, The New England Primer, and the Psalter or psalm book.

The first attempt at education was in the housewives' houses before schools were built. There they would teach a few neighbor children reading and a few simple facts. Later in colonial times nearly all teachers in the schools were men, as only the men had higher education. Still later nearly all the teachers in the primary grades was then thought to be suitable only for women. Today the number of men and women teachers is about evenly divided.

The first schools in Tolland were small one room buildings constructed of wood. As one entered the school, he crossed a large flat rock at the threshold and was in a partitioned cloakroom, about four feet deep, extending across the front of the building. The walls of the cloakroom contained pegs for hanging coats; lunches brought from home were to be left here.

Passing through the cloakroom, one entered the single class room which was finished with a varnished wainscot, chair rail and plastered walls and ceiling. The floors of the room sloped toward the center where the teacher sat. The children sat in tiers around the teacher. When it was time to recite, the teacher would call, "first class", and the whole class would turn in unison, swinging their legs over the plank benches. Books, pencils, paper and slates were furnished by the student's parents. There were no wells on the school properties and water was brought in a pail from the nearest house, and was drunk from a common dipper.

In later years these schools were modernized by replacing the plank benches with regular student desks, which varied in size, so that the older students sat in the larger desks in the back of the room. All of the students faced the teacher who usually sat on a raised platform in the front of the room. Often the seats were made for two pupils to sit together, sharing the same desk.

At first there were no blackboards, and pupils wrote their lessons on slates which were placed on the teacher's desk to be corrected. Then they were washed with a damp cloth. Sometimes a child would carry a slate with very good work home to show his parents. Later parents bought books. Paper was used only for special work. Writing books were made of large sheets of paper stitched together. Students copied directly from the teacher's note book. At first pens were made from pigeon quills, and ink was commonly made from soot and vinegar. Later wooden pens with steel points were provided, and each desk had an ink well.

Lessons were usually recited in unison. Early lessons in arithmetic included such a sample as "twelve sacks equals one load," and "ten cowhides equals one dicker." Reading, arithmetic, geography, spelling and grammar came to be taught, and daily periods were spent in penmanship.

The school hours were usually from nine A.M. to four P.M. with an hour or a half hour for noon lunch. Recesses were for fifteen minutes in the morning and afternoon. Most children carried their lunches in small tin pails, as very few lived close enough to go home. The lunches were lined up on a shelf in the cloak room, and in the winter they often froze.

A pail of water stood on a bench in front of the room with a tin cup or dipper hanging above it. Everyone used the same cup, sometimes during winter colds, carefully rinsing it out before using it. Water was often carried from a spring or brook or sometimes from a well of a house near the school. It was a special privilege to go after the water each morning. Two boys would bring the water back with a stick carrying the pail between them. It was a daring game to swing the pail on the stick over their heads as fast as possible to see if they could make it without spilling the water. If they were quick or lucky they made it. If not, they had to return for another pailful and run the risk of a scolding from the teacher for being late. This was especially true if they spilled it just before arriving at school after a half mile walk with the water.

School opened with a prayer or a Bible reading. A poem might be recited together, and on special days the teacher told what the day was about. Often on Friday afternoons there were special exercises, such as spelling bees, reading matches and songs, poems and story telling. In later years there were spelling bees between schools. Reading aloud had to be done with the voice pausing for a comma, colon or semi-colon, and a longer pause for a period. The voice had to be raised properly for a question and dropped just right for a period or exclamation. Students gathered flowers and made charts in the spring, and a prize was given to the pupil who could identify the most flowers.

The district or the town furnished the furniture, the water pail and dipper, and the broom and dustpan. The stoves burned wood, and a typical winter's supply was an order for four cords of white oak or walnut and four cords of birch or chestnut. The lowest bidder got the contract.

The stove sat in the middle of the classroom with a long pipe going up through the ceiling, or reaching across the room and out through the wall into a chimney. The children who sat farthest away from the stove might shiver in their seats in the coldest weather. At other times the stove might get red hot and everyone would roast or get very sweaty in his long woolen underwear. Often the stove insisted on smoking in spite of open dampers, and everyone would start to cough and produce tears. Lessons would be stopped while the doors and windows were opened to air the classroom. It didn't help matters if the teacher discovered the damper in the stovepipe closed tightly with a stick so that smoke could not escape. Placing a flat stone on top of the chimney gave the same effect. Of course every boy was innocent, but it usually meant a longer lesson with extra work to do. Discipline often was handed out by the teacher in the form of standing students in the corner, or with a crack over the knuckles with a ruler. Sometimes a birch switch was used for really bad boys.

The teacher cleaned her own classroom and made the fires in the winter. She often had to shovel a path from the road to the door. Before schools had electric lights, most of them could not be used after dark. If the school was used for an evening meeting, oil lamps had to be used, as they were in the homes. Dark days in school found pupils squinting with their books or papers close in front of them. A special privilege was to be allowed to dust, clap erasers, or bring in the wood for the fire in winter, and carry the water pail.

The children all looked forward to recess, when many games were played. Some of these were Jump Rope, Tag, I Spy, Follow the Leader, Hide and Seek, Run Sheep Run, Bean Bag (before balls were common), Fox and Geese, and Haili Over. This last game was played by tossing a ball over the roof of the school. If it was caught, the boy shouted, "Haili Over!" and they changed sides of the building, each side choosing one boy from the other side.

In winter there was sliding, and sometimes skating as well as snowball fights with snow forts. Often a number of snowmen were made, some of them quite large. At Christmas the teacher furnished each child with a bag of hard candy, and the children brought a gift of a fancy handkerchief or cup and saucer or vase for the teacher. Special exercises with everyone speaking a piece were held.

On May Day, children tried to hang a May basket filled with flowers and candy on the teacher's doorknob without getting caught. Usually they were, and the teacher shared the contents of the basket. Finally, the last day of school brought the long awaited picnic, when sandwiches, cakes and cookies were brought and as a special treat ice cream was served.

The first school societies were formed in 1798 in each section or "district" of town with fifty or more families. Eventually Tolland had a total of thirteen school districts, with a one room school in each. Only the men were voters, and they gathered in each district once a year for the school meeting. Each family was taxed according to the number of children who went to school. The Committeemen were elected, and they hired the teacher and attended to repairs. The teacher was paid a small amount each week or month, and was boarded by each family according to the number of pupils in each.

The school year was usually broken into two terms, a winter and a summer one. Records for the Grant Hill District for 1852 tell that the winter term was to begin on the first Monday after Thanksgiving and run for three and a half months. The summer term was to begin on the first Monday of May and run for sixteen weeks, right through the summer. This was necessary because the winter term often was much shorter than planned because of bad weather and the difficulty of getting there.

Here, without frills or spoiling, children received a basic education that served them in good stead all the rest of their lives. No time was wasted on unnecessary subjects to the detriment of the three "R's". All our school problems today have their roots, if not their counterparts in the past.

The public school of early nineteenth-century New England was the product of a century and a half of educational development before it and the forerunner of our town and state systems today. The tiny, one-room district schoolhouse crowded onto a triangle of land at a crossroad or placed on some valueless acreage without shade, play space, or access to water, had yet in 1800 and 1820 come a long way from the schooling provided in the seventeenth century.

Connecticut in the year 1700 became the first colony to require adequate teaching for the body of its children. It provided that every town having seventy or more families must employ a full-time instructor to teach the children to read and write; towns with fewer families must employ a teacher for six months of the year.

The thirteen districts, each with its one room school and what happened to them follows:

District #1. The "Street" school, originally stood on the north end of the green. In 1863 it was moved to the site of the present Hicks School on the south end of the green. The original building was destroyed before the move, but the newer one was of two stories, with the first four grades downstairs and the last four grades upstairs. These last four grades, called Tolland Academy, was chartered in 1818.

In 1908 this building was moved to the green in front of the Town Hall and was on stilts while the Hicks building was being built. In the summer of 1908, it was dismantled and moved to Rhodes Road to be reassembled into a packing shed for small fruits. Only the old bell was moved into the new school, which is a much larger brick building, donated to the town through the generosity of the Hicks family.

District #2. Grant Hill Road. The first building was a small white one which had as many as thirty pupils in its small room in all eight grades. When it burned in 1918, it was over 125 years old. It was replaced by another one, which is now a private dwelling, on the corner of Gehring and Grant Hill Road.

District # 3. Cedar Swamp School. This was a small school on Mile Hill Road, above Wagner Road, facing east, it burned in 1910, was rebuilt in 1911, and sold at auction a year or two later for a private dwelling.

District #4. The school originally was on an old highway leading from Buff Cap Road to North River Road. Later it was moved to North River Road and was remodeled in 1850 and again in the early 1900's. It was finally sold at auction and has been remodeled as a dwelling.

District #5. The White School, which got its name because it was the first school in town to be painted white. Earlier schools were either unpainted or were often painted red. It was built at the intersection of Routes 74 and 30 on the Leonard property and was moved across the road to its present location. In 1917 it was completely rebuilt, and is now Tolland's main fire station.

District #6. This school was located on South River road, near Walbridge Road. It was near the Willimantic River, and fell into ruin many years ago.

District #7. This school was on Rhodes Road, at the top of the hill, and was moved once. It was made into a private home, but burned many years ago and was not rebuilt.

District #8. The Snipsic School, was on Snipsic Lake Road, near the lake. It was moved to its present location and remodeled in the early 1900's. It is now a private home.

District #9. This school was on Anderson Road, near the corner of Baxter Street. This district was combined with district #7 and was then known as the District 7 & 9 school. The building was repaired in 1915, and is now a private home.

District #10. The Skungamaug School, was on Tory Road, at the corner of Charter Road. It was built in 1864 and is now a private home.

District #11. The school was called the Lord School House after a family who lived nearby. It was on old Crystal Lake Road, and burned in 1906 and was never rebuilt.

District #12. The Sugar Hill School, was on Cook Road. It had old style benches on three sides of the room and the children sat facing the walls with the teacher behind them. When the pupils were called on to recite, they had to stand up, turn around and step over the benches before they were ready. The old equipment in this school was removed about 1900, and the building lasted only a short time afterward.

District #13. The Buff Cap School, was on Buff Cap Road and was built in 1857, burned in 1868 and was rebuilt in 1869.

In 1899 the thirteen districts were placed under town management. Tolland did not have its own high school until 1967, and many years ago only a few pupils went on to Rockville High School. By horse and buggy it took over an hour to reach Rockville High School. In winter travel was by sleigh over the snow drifts. Students had to buy their own books and stationery.

As the population fell away, some districts were abandoned. Later when transportation became practical the district schools were closed in accord with changing methods of teaching. The last district school to remain in operation was Grant's Hill, which was finally closed in 1946.

By 1800, Tolland was very prominent in politics and law, and the primary school education was insufficient. The Tolland Academy was chartered in 1818. The Reverend Ansel Nash, graduate of Williams College and Andover Theological Seminary, was hired as assistant to Dr. Williams in the Congregational Church. There could be no doubt of his ability; not only did he lead two revivals within the Church but he became principal of the Academy. The Academy was on the second floor of the old "Street" School. At that time this school was located on the east side of the Green about midway from the jail to the present parsonage. When the building was sold in 1908, it was moved to the farm of John Rhodes, and was used as a berry house.

The declining population during the last half of the nineteenth century was, no doubt, a factor in the demise of the Academy. The importance of education was still clear, however, and about 1890 a private school was organized in the village. Robert Tongue was the teacher and about twelve or fifteen students were enrolled. This private school was held in the Baptist Church at the north end of the Green.

About 1907, there was a private kindergarten in the village, conducted in the wing of the Waldo House, now the property of Howard Tourtellot. Miss Bertha Place of Tolland was a teacher in this school. The Tolland Cooperative Kindergarten was established in 1953. In 1965, 44 children attended in two sessions. This kindergarten was held in rooms of the Congregational Church.

The first modern school built in Tolland was the Ratcliffe Hicks Memorial School, built in 1908. It was the legacy of Mr. Ratcliffe Hicks to the town of Tolland. The quality of this building was unsurpassed and it was for many years considered one of Connecticut's finest schools.

During the building of the Hick's Memorial School in 1907-1908, the old school stood on wooden ties in the middle of the green in front of the Town Hall. In the fall of 1908 before Oct. 17, 1908 dedication of the new school, classes were held in the old school and in the Town Hall.

The district schools had scarcely closed their doors, when the Hicks building began to become over-populated. The auditorium was partitioned, and later the gymnasium. The building was added to twice, and in 1962-1963 school year the Meadowbrook School of twenty rooms was built on the Minnie Helen Hicks' Memorial property. Considerable controversy existed over size and location of the building. The final building of 31,000 square feet and with a pupil capacity of 630 pupils was built at a cost of $440,968.

In 1940 there were two teachers in the Hicks building. Twenty-five years later there are forty-three teachers and three administrators in the two buildings. About eighty children have increased to 1036 during this time.

For many years Tolland's students attended Rockville High School. Later they were schooled in the new Ellington High School. In September of 1964 we were again in attendance at Rockville, and will remain there until September 1967. That year Tolland began operation of its all-electric High School in Connecticut. Comprehensive in scope, it will have an area of 120,000 square feet and will house 1,500 children in its ultimate capacity. It was built at a total cost of $1,710,000.

In 1968, Phase II of the Tolland High School was completed for use on March 1, 1968. Phase II, the Arts and Science Center, includes 14 specialized classrooms and a lecture hall with a total of 37,000 square feet. It was built at a total cost of $865,000. Phase III, though still in the future, will make available more classrooms, an auditorium and other educational advantages when needed.

In 1969 a new addition to the Meadowbrook School of ten rooms has been built at an additional cost of about $280,000. This has been necessary by the rapid increase in the population of Tolland and by the fact that a state law was passed requiring that all towns must provide a kindergarten school for all pre-school children.

In the fall of 1969 another new grade school is in the process of being built. It is known as the Middle School and will provide an additional 32 rooms. The amount of $2,260,000 has been appropriated by the town to build this school. It will be built next to the Meadowbrook School.

SCHOOL REPORT OF 1877

Under the old system of having a school in each district, we find that there were 12 separate schools in the 13 districts. The 7 and 9 districts were combined into one school.

In the report of the Board of Education of the Town of Tolland for the year ending August 31st 1877, we have the following summary of the school activities:

DISTRICT	TOTAL EXPENSE	TEACHERS' WAGES	FUEL AND INCIDENTALS
1	$ 288.45	$ 262.00	$ 26.45
2	90.00	84.50	14.50
3	214.55	198.00	16.55
4	190.00	182.00	8.00
5	196.50	181.00	15.50
6	100.00	87.50	12.50
7 & 9	190.00	174.00	16.00
8	194.35	180.00	14.35
10	98.62	84.00	14.62
11	160.00	148.00	12.00
12	160.00	148.12	11.88
13	160.00	145.50	14.50
Total	$2042.47	$1874.62	$176.85

DISTRICT	MONTHLY TEACHERS' WAGE	AVERAGE ATTENDANCE
1	$36.00	37.16
2	28.16	10.81
3	32.00	25.80
4	24.00	20.50
5	28.36	23.30
6	25.00	12.95
7 & 9	26.00	19.83
8	24.00	12.60
10	28.00	7.75
11	27.00	14.77
12	26.00	11.25
13	24.00	17.44

There was both a winter and summer term in all schools except 2, 6, and 10, which only had a winter term.

The above shows the cost of education in 1877 and in comparison the cost of education in 1970 is as follows:

The Board of Education and Education Association have approved an agreement reached by their contract negotiating committees.

Under terms of the agreement, to be effective from July 1, 1970 through June 30, 1971, there will be 12 steps on all salary schedules, ranging from $7,300 to $11,100 for a B.A. degree with $600 additional for a M.A. degree and $600 over the M.A. for the sixth year certificate.

The rate for substitute teachers has been increased to $25 per day, and pay for homebound instruction at $7.50 per hour.

The first modern school built in Tolland was the Ratcliffe Hicks Memorial School. It gradually replaced all of the district schools after several expansion programs. The quality of this building was unsurpassed and it was for many years considered one of Connecticut's finest schools.

The Center District School was the first to be replaced by the Hicks Memorial School. Many of Tolland's prominent citizens received their education in this school.

The Grant Hill School was the last district school to be closed in 1946. The original school burned in 1918 and was replaced by another building that is now a private dwelling. One of its popular schoolteachers was Miss Mary Leonard.

The River District #4 school was originally on an old road leading from Buff Cap Road to River Road. It was moved to River Road and remodeled in 1850 and again in the early 1900's. It was finally sold at auction and has been remodeled as a dwelling.

The White School
The #5 District School was built on the Leonard property and later moved to its present position across the road. It was completely rebuilt in 1917 and after the district schools were closed it became Tolland's main Fire House.

The 7 and 9 School.
The districts 7 and 9 school on the corner of Baxter and
Anderson roads, was originally the #9 school, but was later
combined with district #7 on Rhodes Road. Perkins L. Lathrop
taught here in 1874 when only 16 years olds.

The Buff Cap School
The district #13 school, known as the Buff Cap
school, was on Buff Cap Road and was built in 1857,
burned in 1868 and was rebuilt in 1869. It was
remodeled in the early 1900's and is now a private dwelling.

TOLLAND SCHOOL DISTRICTS.

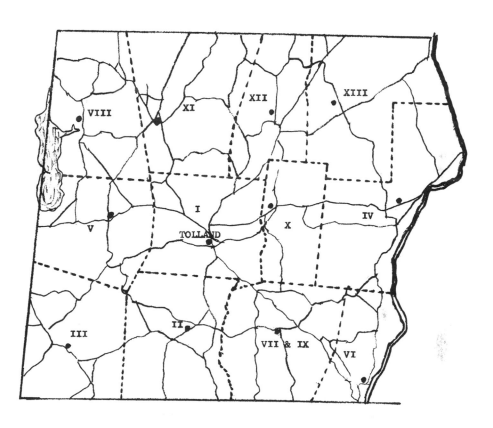

I	Street School	VII & IX	Seven and Nine
II	Grant's Hill	VIII	Snipsic School
III	Cedar Swamp	X	Skungamaug
IV	River District	XI	Lord's school
V	White School	XII	Sugar Hill
VI	Peck's Bridge	XIII	Buff Cap.

Military History of Tolland

The first record of any military organization in Tolland is under the date of October, 1722. The General Assembly then approved of Joseph Hatch as Lieutenant, and John Huntington as Ensign of the train-band in Tolland. The number in the "train-band" was probably then too small to make a captain necessary. The following record, copied from the archives of the train-band in this town:

> Major Wolcott, Esq. Pursuant to that order from yourself to the drawing of the first company in Tolland, to a choice for their commissioned officers for said company in Tolland; said company accordingly met on the 20th day of April and orderly chose Lieutenant Joseph Hatch, captain; Ensign John Huntington, Lieutenant, and Joseph Pack, Ensign.
> EBENEZER NYE, Military clerk

Samuel Chapman was chosen in 1735, to succeed Joseph Hatch as captain of this company. By a return bearing date September 13, 1737, it appears that the roll of this company contained the names of eighty-seven rank and file. The militia were afterwards divided into two companies called the North and South companies; the division of the companies was a line nearly east and west through the town, passing across the south end of the Street; and west of the Street was represented by the road running west from the present residence of Mr. William West to Vernon line. The extent of the participation of Tolland in the wars previous to that which commenced in 1755, cannot now be ascertained. All that is known with certainty is, that Captain Samuel Chapman Sen., commanded a Company in the expedition to Louisburgh in 1745, where he died the following January; and that Samuel Baker, son of Joseph Baker, in that, or a former war, died in captivity among the French and Indians.

In the year 1756, the colonies raised an army of seven thousand men for the purpose of aiding the mother country in an expedition against Crown Point, and placed them under the command of Major-General Winslow. Azariah Wills, of Tolland, enlisted under Captain John Slap, in the service of the Colonies, on the second day of April, 1756, and served until the 25th day of June following, when he was unfortunately taken prisoner, with others, by the French and Indians, between Albany and Hoosick, and carried to Canada. He remained a captive and endured great hardships until November, 1758, when he attempted to return with Col. Schuyler and Major Putnam, but while on his journey home he was taken sick and died on the eighteenth of November, 1758. How many others from Tolland were in this expedition it is impossible to say.

In August, 1757, there was an alarm that a powerful force of French and Indians was on the way to attack Fort William Henry. Volunteers were called for, and Connecticut instantly poured forth several thousand. On the roll of Capt. Samuel Stoughton's company are found the names of the following men of Tolland:

Ens. Samuel Chapman	John Eaton	Samuel Aborn
Serg. Solomen Wills	Ichabod Hinckley	Jonathan Ladd., Jr.
Daniel Baker	George Nye	Simon Chapman
Elihu Johnson	Timothy Delano	Francis West
John Abbott, Jr.	William Benton	Rufus West
Abner West	Solomon Loomis	Joseph Davis
Jacob Fellows	Samuel Huntington	John Stearns
Thacher Lathrop	Jabez Bradley	Amos Ward
Nathan Harvey	Samuel Barnard	28 in all.
David Hatch	Samuel Benton, Jr.	

The French general, Montcalm, had prosecuted the siege with his usual vigor; and the Fort was compelled to surrender before any of the volunteers could arrive. Those from Tolland went no further than Kinderhook, in the State of New York; and returned home, receiving pay for only fifteen days' service. Pay was allowed for four horses from Tolland to Kinderhook, L2, 3s., 9d.; for nineteen from Tolland to Litchfield, L4, 18s., 11d.; and for two to bring them back from Litchfield, 14s., 5d.

For the campaign of 1758, Connecticut agreed to furnish five thousand men; and a company was formed in Tolland and its vicinity, of which Samuel Chapman, of Tolland, was Captain. Twenty-one of the men are recognized as belonging in Tolland, and probably there were others. Most of the remainder would be recognized by their names as having gone from the towns of Somers, Mansfield, Willington, Bolton, Coventry and East Windsor.

In the year 1762, the King of England made a requisition upon the colonies for troops to join in the expedition against the island of Cuba; and a company was raised in the eastern part of the State, of which Col. Israel Putnam was, by one of the then formalities of the service, nominally captain, but really under the command of its first lieutenant, Solomon Wills of Tolland. This company went to the island of Cuba, and was present at the siege and capture of Havana, but was not in any serious engagement. One of the men on the roll related afterward, that the principal fort had been undermined and blown up, so that a column of British regulars carried it by assault, this company had the sad duty to perform of clearing the fort and burying the dead. The destruction of life was very great; the dead were represented as lying in windrows. The pools of blood were so deep in some places in the fort that, as the informant said, he was compelled to step over his shoes in human gore while removing the dead. Although this company was not under fire during the whole of this campaign, the mortality of its members was unparalleled. Of the ninety-eight persons of which the company was composed and who actually reached the Island, only twenty-two ever returned to their native land. Of the twenty-seven enlisted from Tolland and its vicinity, only four escaped the arrow of the fell destroyer. The names of two of these four persons were Solomon Wills and Edward Hatch. John Barnard, John Burrows, Constant Crandall, William Eaton, Aaron Eaton, Leonard Grover, Judah Hatch, Noah Stimson, Ezra Waldo and Oliver Yeomans of Tolland, are known to have died on the Island of Cuba. There were no deaths in the company before the month of August. As returned on the roll, the deaths were in August, fifteen; in September, eighteen; in October, eighteen; in November, eighteen; and in December, seven. Total, seventy-six. The survivors were paid off December 11, 1762. The average term of service was about thirty-five weeks.

The war of the Revolution commenced in 1775, and was most vigorously supported by the people of Tolland County, particularly by the town of Tolland. Their experience in the war of 1755, known as the French war, had made them acquainted with the trials and hardships of military life, and prepared them for the duties of the camp in the approaching struggle with the mother country. Not only did the town furnish its full quota of men and officers for the field, but it was also forward in contributing to the relief of those who suffered for advocating the principles that led to our national independence. The first town meeting touching the difficulties between the colonies and England was held on the fifth day of September, 1774. Ichabod Griggs was chosen moderator. The following is a copy of the record of that meeting:

Voted, That Messrs. Samuel Cobb, Solomon Wills and Eleazar Steel be the delegates to attend the county meeting at Hartford on the 15th instant.

Voted, That Messrs. Stephen Day, James Chamberlin, Hope Lathrop, Joseph West and Simon Chapman, be a committee to receive and transmit to the town of Boston and Charlestown, such charitable donations as be subscribed for the use of the poor and necessitious inhabitants of those towns.

Voted, That the selectmen empowered and directed by the town to procure powder and other ammunition fully to supply the town stock, in proportion as the law directs at the expense of the town.

The appointment of the committee to receive charitable donations for the use of the poor and necessitous of the towns of Boston and Charlestown, was not an unmeaning formality, but was prompted by that generous sincerity with which the people of that age were actuated. The following copy of a letter dated Boston, October 24, 1774, about six weeks after this appointment, will show the object the town had in view, and the efficiency with which the committee discharged its duties.

Gentlemen: This is to acknowledge the receipt of your kind and generous donation of ninety-five sheep by the hand of our worthy friend Mr. Hope Lathrop which shall be applied to the relief of our poor sufferers by means of the cruel and oppressive port bill, — according to the intentions of the generous donors. We are still struggling under the heavy load of tyranny. Our troubles are exceedingly great, but the kindness and benevolence of our friends in Tolland, as well as other places, greatly refreshes and raises our spirits. You may depend upon it, that by divine help and blessing, Boston will suffer everything with patience and firmness that a cruel and arbitrary administration can inflict upon us, even to the loss of fortune and life, rather than submit in any one instance to the power of tyranny. We trust we have a righteous cause, and that the Supreme Ruler of the Universe will in his own time and way, arise and scatter the dark clouds that at present hang over us. We submit to him and ask your prayers at the throne of grace for us. The sincere thanks of this committee in behalf of this greatly distressed and injured town are hereby presented to our worthy friends in Tolland, for their kind assistance in this our day of trial. We are with great esteem, gentlemen, your friends and fellow countrymen.

HENRY HILL, per order of the Committee of Donations

All these proceedings were preliminary to the commencement of hostilities, which event occured at Lexington, Mass., April 19, 1775. When the news of this transaction reached Tolland, a company of men was immediately formed from this and several neighboring towns, which, under the command of Capt. Solomon Wills, served in Col. Spencer's regiment at Roxbury, near Boston, from May 1, to December 1, 1775, a period of eight months.

The number on the roll are — officers and musicians, eighteen; privates, eighty. Total, ninety-eight. The names indicate that the men were from Tolland, Somers, Stafford, Willington and Coventry. Arrangements for enlisting were made in Tolland and men engaged on the day the news of the battle of Lexington reached the place. It is known that other persons from Tolland were at Roxbury, but were either temporary substitutes, or in other companies; among them were Joshua Griggs and Solomon Eaton. Thirty four are known as belonging in Tolland, which town was ascertained the previous year to contain twelve hundred and forty seven white, and fifteen black inhabitants. The last survivor of the Tolland men on the roll was Capt. Ammi Paulk, who died in 1843.

The war had now continued about five years, and the issue was still doubtful. The credit of the government had depreciated, and the circulating medium of the country had become nearly worthless. The army began to complain as well for the non-payment of its wages as the worthlessness of the currency in which it was paid. It was impossible to find men willing to leave their families for the continental service, without further guarantees that their services should be fairly compensated. The town of Tolland was required to furnish sixteen men for the continental army for the year 1780, besides its quota of cavalry. In order to obtain this number by voluntary enlistment, the town, on the 26th day of June, 1780 voted that the wages of forty shillings per month should be kept good, and made up to each effective man belonging to the town who should enlist to serve until the last day of the then next December in the Connecticut line of the continental army; in wheat at four shillings per bushel; rye at three shillings per bushel, and Indian corn at two shillings per bushel. And as a further encouragement the town voted to pay each man that should so enlist, the sum of thirty shillings, lawful money, on the first day of January then next. By the same vote they extended the benefit of the same allowance to such effective men as should enlist into the cavalry to serve in the continental army the same time. These several obligations made it necessary for the town to provide means to discharge them, and many expedients were resorted to, to sustain the plighted faith of the town. Taxes payable in provisions as well as money, were laid; and such taxes as would frighten the tax payers of modern times.

It is impossible to estimate with accuracy the number of men belonging in Tolland who served in the army of the revolution. The quota usually assigned to it was from sixteen to twenty one. I understand this did not include those who served in the cavalry. There can be no doubt that the town constantly had no less than twenty-five men in the field, besides those who served in what were called the short levies, and when the entire military force of the town went on some alarm or emergency. Nearly twenty can be enumerated as having gone from the present limits of the fifth school district; and probably more than one hundred and fifty persons, residents of Tolland, comprising nearly every man of suitable age and strength, participated in that struggle by marching against the enemy. Several persons were in the field during almost the entire war, among whom Capt. (afterwards Gen.) Elijah Chapman, Jonathan Luce, Isaac Fellows, Solomon Eaton, and Elihu Johnson are remembered. Several times almost the entire active male population was absent in the army, and ordinary work upon the farms was done by female hands.

Although Tolland furnished its full proportion of men in the revolutionary contest, and although so many of them perished in the service, yet it has not been ascertained either by record or traditionary evidence, that any were slain in battle except Amos Cobb and John Lathrop, before referred to. The record of John Lathrop's death, in the Town clerk's office, is as follows; "John, the son of John Lathrop, and Lucy his wife, departed this life December the 10th day, 1780, by the sword of the enemy at Horseneck." He was under eighteen years of age, and was struck dead by a blow on the head with a sabre, by a dragoon. Col. Solomon Wills, to whose wife Mr. Lathrop was nephew, assisted in wrapping him in his blanket and laying him in the grave of the soldier.

Nor is there now any evidence that any Tolland soldier received any dangerous wound, or so severe as to occasion his dismissal from the service.

In concluding the general subject of the revolution, it should be remarked that there were no Tories in Tolland. With the exception of two or three odd, crusty, eccentric men, who generally opposed what others approved, and who being in the main respectable persons, whose whimsical opposition was generally amusing, there was entire unanimity in tyranny of England until the final establishment of American Independence.

THE WAR OF 1812

This conflict between the United States and Great Britain took place between 1812-1814. In attempting to crush Napoleon, Great Britain tried to regulate American shipping between the West Indies and Europe. America objected to the searching of her vessels by British cruisers and to impressing of her seamen into British service.

Feeling against Britain rose to a high pitch, due to the eloquence of Clay and Calhoun, and resulted in a declaration of war on June 18, 1812.

The United States immediately started operations against the Canadian border with no success, until Commander Perry defeated the British fleet on Lake Erie and captured the entire fleet. William Henry Harrison then was able to invade Canada with troops and defeated the British and burned Toronto.

Britain then enlarged her Atlantic fleet and made several landings, resulting in the burning of Washington, but they were repulsed at Baltimore. Britain then made an attack on New Orleans, but the genius and valor of Andrew Jackson repelled the British, who lost 2036 men, on Jan. 8, 1815. However, a treaty of peace had already been signed on Dec. 14, 1814 and when the news arrived, all hostilities ended.

The following is a record of veterans of the war of 1812, who are buried in Tolland cemeteries:

Ashbel Chapman, Chelsey Chapman, Aaron Bernard, Joel Eno, John Kimball, Dimock Willis, Eli Baker, Harry Coggswell, Levi Edgerton, Russell Fitch, John Lathrop, Martin Phillips, John Warren, Nathan Williams, Calvin Fuller and Elijah Smith.

THE CIVIL WAR

The great Civil War between the states, commenced actual hostilities in the attack on Fort Sumter at 4:20 on the morning of April 12, 1861. The news flashed over the country and aroused an intense and universal excitement in all the north. Many refused to credit the tidings and the surrender of the fort so speedily announced. All doubt, however, was soon dispelled by the publication of the president's proclamation on the 15th, calling for 75,000 volunteers in order to suppress the rebellion and cause the laws to be duly executed. This proclamation was received by the free states with enthusiastic approval and they vied with each other in their proffers of men.

As the War Between the States proceeded we find a record of Company K from Tolland. The following is condensed from the History of the Twenty-second Regiment, Connecticut Volunteer infantry, written by Capt. John K. Williams, Company H.

This regiment, with the exception of Company K, was recruited from Hartford County and was the first to respond for the call of the President for "three hundred thousand militia to serve for nine months," dated August 4, 1862. Its personnel was of superior intelligence, for the term of service attracted many occupying responsible positions, from which they could not absent themselves for a longer period.

The officers elected George S. Burnham as their Colonel. Under his skillful instruction the regiment acquired a degree of military efficiency and discipline rarely obtained by any command in so short a time.

The regiment went into winter quarters at Miner's Hill, near Falls Church, Virginia, about eight miles from Washington. This regiment here entered that part of the Army of the Potomac which was assigned to the defense of Washington. While encamped under shelter tents at Miner's Hill, the regiment felled trees and built for itself log cabins which it occupied from November 25, 1862 til February 12, 1863.

On June 9th the regiment formed a part of the advance column in the "advance on Richmond," and moved by way of Williamsbury and Chickahominy River to Diascund Bridge and Chickahominy Church. This force moved by way of the York River, the whole expedition being known in history as the "Blackberry Raid." Returning to Yorktown, the 22nd embarked by steamer for home on June 26th and was mustered out July 7, 1863.

Fortune favored this regiment in that none of its members were killed in action, but the frequent commendations of brigade commanders for its promptness and efficiency in circumstances of danger are proofs that it was "not lacking in bravery." Forty-three members of Company K, twenty-second regiment Infantry were listed as of Tolland.

Of the one hundred seven Tolland men in the Civil War not all fared as well as those of the Twenty-second Regiment. Twelve died, eight were captured, others were wounded and ten deserted. These ten were members of the Litchfield County Regiment of Heavy Artillery. One hundred twenty-nine died and one hundred ninety-four were wounded. One wonders whether these men were not fighting under some of the most severe conditions of the war, which persuaded them "to go home." Three men from Tolland were members of the Twenty-ninth Regiment Infantry (colored).

THE SPANISH AMERICAN WAR

During the presidency of Wm. McKinley, our Country became involved in another war, which fortunately proved to be of short duration. This time it was a conflict with Spain growing out of an insurrection in Cuba, which called forth the sympathy of Americans, because of the terrible suffering of the Cubans, involved in financial interest in the U.S. and led to the sending of the U.S. battleship Maine to Havana, where she was destroyed by an explosion, which may have been accidental, but which was generally believed to have been caused by some one in sympathy with the Spanish in their attempt to subdue the Cubans.

On April 11, 1898, Pres. McKinley asked Congress for authority to use the military and naval forces of the U.S. to bring an end to hostilities between Spain and Cuba and to secure the establishment of a stable government for Cuba. This meant war. Military preparations and action were hurried. The war was fought in Cuba, Puerto Rico, and the Philippines and everywhere the United States was successful. By fall the war was over. So brief and one sided a war, did not call for large enlistments and there were only a few men from Tolland that were serving in the regular armed forces. Among these are listed the following men:

Martin Laubisher, John F. Haun, George N. Aborn and John J. O'Neal.

WORLD WAR I

World War I was fought between 1914 and 1918. It started as a local conflict between Austria-Hungary and Serbia on July 28, 1914. By Aug. 1, 1914, Germany declared war on Russia and eventually it became a global war, with Germany, Austria-Hungary, Turkey and Bulgaria as the central powers against the Allies, mainly Great Britain, France, Russia, Italy and the United States.

The United States entered the war in April, 1917, after Germany had declared a policy of unrestricted warfare against all shipping in and out of Great Britain. Germany made an all out effort to advance on the western front and at first succeeded, but was gradually driven back. This defeat resulted in the abdication of Kaiser William II in early November with the formation of a German Republic on Nov. 11, 1918.

For the war the United States had mobilized 4,355,000 men of which 126,000 were killed and 234,000 were wounded.

Tolland contributed its share of men to this great conflict and the Roll of Honor for Tolland in World War I holds the following names:

Harris Lamphear Andrews
Orris Joseph Ayers
John Timothy Bowler
Gordon Newton Christopher
Louis Richard Czegledy
Steve Dezso, Jr.
Christopher John Duell
Theodore Roosevelt Gardiner
Cornell Augustus Green
Joseph Mathias Gritsch
Ralph Henry Haun
Gottlieb Mathew Held

George Elliot Metcalf
Leslie Raymond Metcalf
Arthur Morgansen
Frank Joseph Nedwied, Jr.
Joseph Nestowitz
Carlton William Newman
Clifton Charles Newman
Michael Reiske
Louis Alva Rounds
William Sumner Simpson
James Lynd Taylor
John Joseph Wagner

Ichabod Tilden Jewett
Lewis Kenneth Laubscher
Hugh Lewis
Mildred Anna Metcalf, Nurse

Roy Waldo
Clifford White
Howard Alva White
William Rudolph Wochomurka

Tolland Gold Star List

Mildred A. Metcalf   Clifton Newman   James Lynd Taylor

WORLD WAR II

World War II began on Sept. 1, 1939 with the invasion of Poland by Germany. France and the United Kingdom immediately declared war on Germany. Italy entered the war with Germany in 1940 and Germany invaded Russia, June 22, 1941.

With the attack of Japan on Pearl Harbor on Dec. 7, 1941, Germany then declared war on the United States and the conflict became a global one. Before the war ended with the unconditional surrender of Germany on May 9, 1945, and of Japan on Sept. 2, 1945, a total of 70 nations were involved. It was a conflict between the Axis Powers, consisting of Germany, Italy, Japan and their satellites. Germany was under the leadership of Adolph Hitler, who had risen to become the Nazi dictator of Germany. The Allies consisted of the United States, the United Kingdom, the Union of Soviet Socialist Republics, China and their allies.

The casualties of the United States totaled 1,151,588 men. Of this total 294,578 were killed and 707,324 were wounded with 28,002 reported missing. The cost of the war to the United States was about $825,000,000,000.

Tolland, as usual, contributed its share of men to the world conflict and the Tolland Roll of Honor for World War II contains the following names:

Aborn, Christian C.	Jakopsic, John Jr.	Prucha, Emil
Aborn, Clarence E.	Jarzynski, John R.	Prucha, Joe
Aborn, John J.	Kellum, Lawerence	Prucha, William Jr.
Ayers, Alfred D.	Kibbe, Richard O.	Prucha, John
Anderson, John D.	Kibbe, Robert C.	Putz, Leopold F.
Bell, Robert B.	Kibbe, Wallace D.	Raisch, Charles
Bodnar, Ladislaus	Kibbe, William B.	Regan, Joseph F.
Bodnar, Stephen J.	Knybel, Joseph	Regan, William R.
Caldwell, George E.	Knybel, Frank	Rudansky, Francis
Caldwell, William	Knybel, Michel	Rudansky, John S.

Campbell, Clarence
Chorches, Leon J.
Clough, Warren E.
Colombaro, Gino
Colombaro, Max
Crandall, George A.
Crandall, Howard
Dimmock, Ernest L.
Dirgo, John Jr.
Downes, John R.
Eimbath, John
Einsiedel, Elwin
Farnham, Woodrow
Fargo, Kenneth
Ferris, Walter M.
Forgette, Frank J.
Frachey, Nathan M.
Frank, Joseph
Giacomini, Leslie
Giacomini, Sylvester
Gilbert, Siegfried
Gessay, Anthony
Goetz, Clarence H.
Gordon, George Jr.
Gorky, Herman
Gottier, Albert
Gottier, Alfred
Gottier, Bernard
Hanko, Michael
Hansen, Robert E.
Husar, Joachim A.
Jachim, William

Knybel, Tony
Koehler, Leon R.
Kollar, Viera E.
Kollar, Vladimir
Kolodczak, Nicholas
Krechko, Henry
Kollar, Bohumil
Lathrop, John R.
Lemek, Joseph J.
Luginbuhl, Roy E.
Lynch, Edmund
Markham, Douglas
Magnuson, Roger
Meacham, James W.
Meacham, Maurice
Metcalf, Harold J.
Miffitt, Elmer
Miffitt, Julius J.
Miller, Lewis J.
Miller, Richard E.
Mitchell, Erwin Jr.
Meacham, Raymond
Morganson, Donald
Morganson, Harold
Morganson, Richard
Nedwied, Joseph A.
Nussdorf, Samuel
Ott, Frank P.
Ott, William J.
Pariseal, Richard
Prentiss, Elmer W.
Prucha, Arthur

Rudansky, Andrew
Schultz, William J.
Silverman, Ralph
Sunega, Edward
Szemreylo, Charles
Szemreylo, Stanley
Tobiassen, Alex
Triska, Ernest J.
Tureck, Henry
Usher, Richard
Usher, Robert H.
Ursin, Andrew C.
Ursin, John S.
Ursin, Herbert W.
Walekus, Edward A.
Wanat, John T.
Webber, William E.
Weingartner, Richard
West, Byron H.
White, William E.
Wolfe, Herman A.
Young, William
Zanghi, Concetto
Zaushny, Theodore
Zelinka, Nicholas

Gold Star List

William F. Caldwell
Herman Gorky
Robert E. Hansen
Sunega, Edward
Meacham, Raymond

THE ASIAN WARS

After the two world wars, which were supposed to end all wars, we are still embroiled in an undeclared war in Vietnam. Previous to this, in 1950-1953, our soldiers fought in Korea to keep the communists from taking over that country. This war ended in a truce, which established South Korea as a free country.

We are now trying to end an undeclared war in Vietnam, in which as many as 500,000 of our soldiers have taken part at one time. To date about 45,000 American soldiers have been killed to prevent the communist takeover of South Vietnam.

Again, many men from Tolland have taken part in these conflicts and some have made the supreme sacrifice for their country. Future history will record their brave deeds and properly place their names on the military honor rolls of Tolland.

In 1968, The Veterans of Foreign Wars, Post 241 of Tolland erected a beautiful monument on the Green in front of the Town Hall to honor all of the Tolland veterans who have fought in the wars of our Country. Our beautiful and great nation attests to the value of the sacrifices that these men have made. The monument was erected with the financial backing of residents and fund raising activities of the Post.

The Veterans Monument on Tolland Green.

The Tolland Courts and Jails

In writing about the Courts and Jails in Tolland, we must realize that these were not only concerned with the Town of Tolland, but were County functions, which took place in the Town of Tolland and were an integral part of its history. In order to properly relate the history of the Courts and Jails, we must go back and explore the formation of Tolland County and the reasons for the establishment of the courts and jails in the town of Tolland. Previous to the formation of Tolland County in 1785, Tolland town was a part of Hartford County and as such all of its legal affairs were attended to in Hartford.

The county of Tolland was established by the legislature of this State at its session in October, 1785. In May, 1785 a bill was introduced to make a new county in the northeast part of Hartford county, passed the lower house, but was dissented to in the upper house. A committee of conference was appointed, consisting of Mr. Holmes, Colonel Mott and General Parsons of the lower house, and Andrew Adams Esq., of the upper house, who made a report to the upper house, and that house, on re-consideration of their former vote, "voted to adhere to their first vote on this bill." The effect of this last vote in the upper house was to defeat the bill then under consideration.

At the following session in October, 1785, a bill was introduced in the lower house, entitled "An Act for erecting and establishing a new county." The first section of this bill provided that the towns of Tolland, Bolton, Coventry, Hebron, Somers, Stafford, Willington, Union, and the parish of Ellington in East Windsor, should be constituted a county by the name of the county of Tolland. The second section provided that there should be held annually in said county, two county courts; one on the third Tuesday in September in the town of Tolland, and one superior court in said Tolland on the last Tuesday in January. This bill was passed in the lower house but was dissented to in the upper house. Colonel Porter, Mr. Joseph Kingsbury and Colonel Thrall were appointed a committee of conference on the part of the lower house, and Oliver Wolcott, Esq., on the part of the upper house. Upon the report of this committee, and upon re-consideration the upper house "voted to adhere to their first vote on this bill." In the lower house the further consideration of the bill was referred to the general assembly to be holden at Hartford on the second Thursday in May then next. The upper house dissented to, the vote of the lower house continuing the bill; but upon further consideration, the upper house re-considered its former vote dissening to the bill, and concurred with the lower house in passing it, with alterations and additions in these words: "Exclusive of the town of Coventry named in the 7th line, and with an addition at the end of the bill, to wit, provided nevertheless that this act nor anything contained therein shall have any effect until a proper suitable court house and gaol, to be approved by this assembly shall, by voluntary subscription or otherwise, without taxing said county be erected and provided in said town of Tolland." The lower house, on re-consideration, concurred with the upper house in these alterations and additions. This completed the first act of legislation by which this county was established.

It does not appear why the Town of Coventry was excluded from the original bill, but it is certain the citizens of Coventry were early very much in favor of becoming a part of the new county. The town of Coventry then petitioned the General Assembly on May 9, 1786 that it be annexed to the county of Tolland. It was granted in the lower house, but was dissented to in the upper house. The two houses, however, finally concurred in granting the prayer of the petition, and Coventry was at that session annexed to the county of Tolland. But the difficulties attending the organization of Tolland county did not end here. The Town of Hebron was dissatisfied with the action of the General Assembly in establishing a new county, and on May 12, 1786 it petitioned the General Assembly to take the premises into consideration and grant relief to their distressed situation by re-annexing the Town of Hebron to the county of Hartford. This petition was granted, but immediately the town of Tolland presented a counter petition through its agent Colonel Samuel Chapman. His argument was, that the legislature had promised to constitute the towns named in the Act of October, 1785, a county with county privileges; and that the courts should be held in the town of Tolland, provided suitable buildings should be erected by voluntary subscription for the use of the county; that relying on the face of this promise, he and others had undertaken to build, and had nearly completed the necessary and proper buildings, and therefore he and his associates had a right to insist that the promise on the part of the legislature should be literally performed. The legislature listened to the arguments of the petitioners, and upon consideration re-considered their action upon the memorial of the town of Hebron; and by another act ratified and confirmed the act of October, 1785, accepted the buildings the citizens of Tolland had erected for the use of the county, and organization of the county of Tolland.

That portion of East Windsor included in the county of Tolland by the act of October, 1785, was incorporated into a town by the legislature, May session, 1786, and was called Ellington. At this time the county of Tolland consisted of nine towns, to wit: Tolland, Bolton, Coventry, Ellington, Hebron, Somers, Stafford, Union, and Willington. All of these towns except Coventry and Union before October, 1785, belonged to the county of Hartford. Coventry and Union were a part of the county of Windham. In October, 1808, the town of Bolton was divided, and the north society in Bolton was constituted a new town by the name of Vernon. Columbia and Mansfield were separated from Windham county and annexed to Tolland county, May session, A.D. 1827. The town of Andover, formed of contiguous portions of the towns of Hebron and Coventry, was incorporated, May session, 1848. These are all the towns included in the present limits of the county of Tolland. They were severally incorporated in the following chronological order, to wit: Mansfield, 1703; Hebron, 1707; Coventry, 1711; Somers, 1734; Union, 1734; Ellington, 1786; Columbia, 1804; Vernon, 1808; Andover, 1848.

The first county buildings, consisting of a court house and jail, were erected by the people of the town of Tolland. The town at first in its corporated capacity, assumed the responsibility of furnishing the necessary county buildings, but the funds were afterward raised by voluntary contributions.

The action of the town in this matter may be gathered from the following votes copied from the town records:

At legal town meeting held in Tolland on the 11th day of November, 1785, Captain Elijah Chapman, Moderator.

Mr. Medad Hunt, Captain Ichabod Hinckley, Captain Hope Lathrop, Mr. David Lathrop, Mr. Joseph West, Mr. Simon Chapman, were chosen a committee to inquire and see how, and on what terms the court house and gaol can be built in this town and make report to the next town meeting. The meeting adjourned to the 25th of November instant, one o'clock afternoon, Test, E. Steet, Town Clerk.

At an adjourned town meeting held in Tolland, November 25, 1785, Captain Elijah Chapman, Moderator:

Voted, that Captain Daniel Edgerton, Mr. Samuel Chapman, Captain John Hinckley, be a committee for that purpose, and to agree with Captain Hope Lathrop on his terms and proposals, or any other gentleman as they, the said committee shall think fit and proper, and also to collect the subscriptions made for that purpose.

Voted, to choose a committee in this town to affix the plan for said building. Test, E. Steet, Clerk.

It does not appear from the town record who was appointed on the committee raised by the last vote; but that a committee was appointed, that it was selected from the other towns in the county, and that it acted in the matter of locating the court house, is apparent from other votes, copies of which are given below. The town, at its annual meeting held on the 12th day of December, 1785, passed the following vote, to wit:

Captain Hope Lathrop and Ensign Medad Hunt, were chosen committee men, in addition to Captain Ichabod Hinckley, Captain Daniel Edgerton, and Simon Chapman, that was chosen a committee at the last town meeting for the purpose of building a court house and gaol in this town themselves, or by agreeing with any gentleman to erect said buildings as they should judge best.

The next and only other vote relating to this subject found upon the records of the town of Tolland is as follows:

At an adjourned town meeting held in Tolland on the 29th day of December, 1785, Captain Ichabod Hinckley was Moderator of said meeting.

Voted, in said meeting that the court house be built a due east point from the stake that was set by a committee chosen by this town to come from the several towns in this proposed county to set a stake for the court house and gaol, said house to be set near the middle of the highway where the committee appointed to build the court house shall think most convenient. Test. Benoni Shepherd, Town Clerk.

The court house was erected on the spot in the last vote indicated, which is a little south of the large elm tree near the hay scales, about where the small elm tree first south of the hay scales now stands. It stood east of the center of the Highway on the Green and a little to the north of a direct line drawn across the street from where the present Court House now stands. The lower story was unfinished except for an oak floor. The second story was used for a Court Room. There was a large outside door on each side and each end of the building. The court room had a raised platform on the west end about four feet high for the Judges.

In front of the Judges was a long table for the lawyers. South of this were raised seats for the Jurors. Farther to the east was a box five feet high and six feet square for the Sheriff, while back of the Sheriff were seats for the spectators. This building was taken down in 1822 and the present one erected by the county. The Probate Court of Tolland and Willington occupied the north end of the building. The whipping post and stocks stood at the southwest corner of the old Court House. They went out of use when the old building was torn down. The stocks were made to admit two persons.

Early Connecticut certainly could not be accused of coddling its criminals. Justice was stern and uncompromising. Public whipping posts were standard equipment in the market place, as were the stocks, where malefactors were placed for hours, or even days, to endure the scorn (and sometimes missiles) of righteous townsfolk.

For certain crimes, culprits were branded on the forehead and carried for life the letter designating their transgression — "A" for adultery, "B" for burglary, "C" for counterfeiting, and so on.

Horse thieves were compelled to ride on a wooden horse in the public square, an uncomfortable and humiliating experience. In Hartford in 1785, one such thief was placed on this steed but, far from being mortified, he seemed to enjoy himself hugely, laughing and joking with the spectators. He later received 15 lashes at the whipping post, a ten-pound fine, and three months in the workhouse.

The Tolland County Court House built in 1822 is still in its original location next to the bank. It was the only meeting place of the Superior Court and Court of Common Pleas for the county until 1888 when some of the sessions were transferred to Rockville and finally in 1892 when the last session was held in Tolland. It was also the seat of the County Court until 1955 when these courts were abolished throughout the State. The ground floor is now used as the town library but the second floor still houses most of the furnishings used by the court. The expenses of erecting this building were defrayed by a tax upon the county. The architects were Abner P. Davison and Harry Coggswell, then both of Tolland.

Until 1785, Tolland township was under the jurisdiction of the courts of Hartford County. During this time each town was given two or more justices of the peace who heard and determined without a jury, all civil cases under two pounds (one pound being valued at about $5.00, at that time). The courts of each county had five judges, who heard with a jury, all cases over two pounds. Five judges presided over the Superior Court. To this court were brought appeals from the County courts, when the verdict exceeded ten pounds, about $50.00.

The courts of probate were managed by a justice of the peace appointed by the general assembly. Each county has its sheriff and each town its constable. In 1724 the law requiring sheriffs to be appointed by the Governor and council was passed. Before this the sheriffs were annually appointed by county courts. This idea was borrowed from the law of England, where such a method was used.

The legislature provided that in the new County of Tolland, there should be held annually, two County courts; one on the third Tuesday in March, and one on the third Tuesday in September in the town of Tolland, and one superior court in said Tolland on the last Tuesday in January.

Elisha Steel was the first lawyer ever located in the town of Tolland. He was a son of the celebrated Rev. Stephen Steel of that town. He was graduated at Yale College in 1750, was educated for the bar and located in the town of Tolland, where he engaged in the practice of his profession. He was chosen a representative in the General Assembly in 1761, and was re-elected five times. He was one of two justices of the peace from 1761 to 1766, inclusive.

Other distinguished men of State-wide reputation who lived in Tolland were; Hon. Charles Joslyn, lawyer; Hon. Ratcliffe Hicks, lawyer; Hon. Alvin P. Hyde — one of the ablest lawyers of his time; Hon. Waldo Hyde, his son, lawyer and Mayor of Hartford, was born here; Solon Robinson, noted Agricultural writer and Agricultural

Editor of the *N. Y. Tribune*; Judge William Strong was Principal of the Academy; Judge Loren P. Waldo, member of Congress, Judge and lawyer; Hon. William W. Eaton, U. S. Senator; Hon. Calvin Willey, U. S. Senator; and Noah Grant, grandfather of Ulysses S. Grant, was born here.

THE TOLLAND JAILS

The first jail was built in 1785 of wood, and was located nearly on the spot of the present county prison. It was a small building and very insecure. At this time the law of Connecticut authorized imprisonment for debt; and if a debtor confined within the walls of the jail escaped through the insufficiency of the jail, the county was liable to pay the creditor the amount of his debt. The prisoners often escaped by burning holes through the walls of wood. By reason of this, and other causes, the county of Tolland was subjected to very considerable damages on account of the insufficiency of the jail. It was accordingly abandoned and taken down about the year 1805, and a new jail erected. This building was of stone and was placed to the south of the spot now occupied by the county house, with its west side in the line of the road, and was connected with the county house. This building was never satisfactory to the public, and was as insecure as the old jail. The jail windows were strongly protected by iron rods, but the door was of wood, which presented no serious obstacle to the escape of prisoners so disposed, and when this method of escape was not feasible, tunnelling was resorted to. It was therefore superseded by another stone building erected in the year 1824. This last building was located nearly on the site of the present county prison, and was the county jail until the year 1856. It was built under the superintendence and personal direction of Eliphalet Young and Arial Ladd, Esq; of Tolland, and Jabez S. White, Esq., of Bolton, a committee appointed by the county for that purpose. The principal idea that seemed to pervade the minds of this committee was to make a strong prison, and they paid but little attention to comeliness or comfort. It was built of large blocks of stone quarried from solid rocks, well doweled together, and was regarded as impregnable. It was two stories high, and contained six rooms — two large rooms and one small room in each story. It was indeed a strong prison, but was a most inconvenient place and wholly unfit as a place of confinement for human beings. Several unsuccessful attempts to obtain a better prison were made, and finally the feeling of humanity obtained the ascendency, and a more modern and much more convenient and comfortable prison was erected in the year 1856. One thousand dollars was paid by the State treasury toward the expense of this building, and the balance was met by a tax upon the county.

The present jail is of stone and iron. The total number prisoners received at the jail during 1884 was 85, and of this number two were females. A record is kept of the date received and discharged, together with a description of age, height, color, nationality, married or unmarried, sex, when received and from what court, offence committed, whether strictly temperate or not. On being received the prisoner is searched, and a record is kept of the articles found. These are kept, and returned at the expiration of the sentence. Keys, knives and like articles are taken from the prisoner and he is allowed to retain nothing except clothes and tobacco. After being searched the prisoner is conducted to the jail and locked in, for which operation the turnkey receives 50 cents. The jail contains two tiers of cells, seven in each tier, with two additional cells in an upper room for females. The floor and walls are stone, and heavy iron bars guard the windows. The doors are also iron, and at nine o'clock at night each prisoner is locked into a separate cell by the jailer, and released at 6:30 each morning into the large room, where they spend the day. The food given them is; for breakfast at 7:30, bread, coffee; dinner at noon, meat, potatoes and bread, with an occasional variation of pork and beans, and fish once per week. Supper varies from mush and milk to crackers and coffee. The food is well cooked and given in liberal quantities. The iron bedsteads in each cell are supplied with mattress, sheets, blankets and pillows, which are kept clean and together forming comfortable beds. The jail is washed two or three times each week by inmates, and every precaution taken to prevent sickness, but the sanitary conveniences are not too satisfactory.

The Tolland County Jails existed as a jail for about 183 years. In 1960, all of the county jails were taken over by the State and operated as State jails until the Tolland jail was officially closed on August 1, 1968. On August 13, 1969, the State of Connecticut turned over the deed of the property to the selectmen of Tolland. It was the first in the State to be turned over to the town in which it is located. It was a bill presented by Representative King, in the legislature, this term that made the transaction possible. Ernest E. Vlk, first selectman, made the following comment:

> We are a witness today of an end of an era for this prison complex. Its use as a retention facility is over by decree of our state government and its past is now legend and history. Its future is what we in Tolland make it, may it be used discreetly and maintained as the traditional landmark that it is.

THE HANGING IN TOLLAND

The only execution of the death penalty that ever occurred in Tolland county took place during the administration of Sheriff Johnson. At the April term of the Superior Court, in the year 1824, the grand jury for the county presented one George Henry Washington, a transient person, for the murder of his wife, Margery Washington, by beating her upon the head with a white oak stick. This indictment was tried before the Hon. Stephen T. Hosmer, chief judge, and the Hon. John T. Peters, one of the associate judges of the Supreme Court or Errors, The petit jurors were John Hall, Peleg Martin and Ebenezer Smith, of Ellington; Phineas Chapman, Francis Grant and Justus Talcott, of Vernon; Mantor Hammond, Joel W. White and Zenes Skinner, of Bolton; David Glazier, Chester Burnham and Horace Bicknall, of Willington.

George Henry Washington was a colored man, composed of a mixture of several races, in which the Indian predominated. He was an idle, vicious, dissolute person, of no character, and of no account so far as his being in this world was concerned. His wife was a colored woman, and a fit companion for such a husband. They were both addicted to habits of intemperance, and such was their indulgence in the use of strong drinks, that they were almost constantly under an unnatural excitement, and as constantly engaged in quarrels with and in beating each other. George had on these occasions frequently used threatening language toward his wife, and had even sworn he would take her life. On the day of the homicide, they called at the store of one of the magistrates of the County of Tolland, who was then in the business of selling intoxicating drinks, and procured a quart of rum. They united in drinking the rum, then quarrelled, and George struck his wife on the head with a cane he carried, causing almost instant death. He made no effort to escape, and was immediately arrested and carried before the very magistrate who sold him the rum, and was by him fully committed for trial. The late Mr. Barnes was then the attorney for the state, and he was assisted upon the trial by the Hon. Calvin Willey. The prisoner was defended by the late Judge Stearnes, of Tolland, and the late Judge Asa Willey, of Ellington. The trial was had in the meeting house of the Congregational Society, then standing at the south end of Tolland Street. The prisoner was convicted and was sentenced to be executed on the first Tuesday in June, 1824.

The counsel for the prisoner were of opinion, and not without some reason, that their client was not guilty of the crime of willful deliberate murder, and voluntarily undertook to procure a commutation of the severe sentence the court had pronounced upon the prisoner, to an imprisonment in the state prison for life. Mr. Stearnes drew up an application to the legislature in his usual felicitous style, and called upon the prisoner for his signature. After reading to him the writing he had made, George inquired how long he should have to stay in prison if he signed the paper. Mr. Stearnes told him he must expect to stay as long as he lived. "What!" said George, "must I stay there always?" "Yes," said Mr. Stearnes, "always." George spent a moment apparently in deep thought, when he looked up at Mr. Stearnes and said, "Massa, that is a great while. If I am hung it will be quick over. I guess we will let it be as it is." It is needless to say the application for a commutation was never presented to the legislature.

The execution was a memorable day for Tolland County. It happened at that season of the year when nature appears attired in all her lovliness, and the world looks too charming to be a place of violence and crime. The day was one of the lovliest of the season, and at an early hour hundreds of persons of both sexes and all descriptions, crowded the village of Tolland to witness the event. Sheriff Johnson was assisted by his deputies and attended by two military companies. The religious exercises were conducted by the Rev. Ansel Nash, then the pastor of the Congregational society in Tolland, in the open air, in front of the court house. They consisted simply of singing and prayer. The singing was led by Mr. Jarvis

Crandall. The tune was "Limehouse", the words — "Show pity, Lord, Oh Lord, forgive."

The prisoner was seated on his coffin in a wagon, clad in the habiliments of the grave, apparently unmoved through it all. The execution was between two and three o'clock of the afternoon. He was buried, it was said, close by the gallows. The hanging and burial was supposed to have taken place on Bald Hill.

The blacksmithing trade flourished from early colonial days until about 1920, when the work horse was entirely replaced by the automobile and the tractor.

The Tolland County Court House, built in 1822, is still in its original location next to the bank. It was the only meeting place of the Superior Court and Court of Common Pleas for the county until 1888 when some of the sessions were transferred to Rockville and, finally in 1892, the last session was held in Tolland.

The Tolland County Jail existed as a jail for about 183 years. The jail was officially closed on August 1, 1968. On August 13, 1969 the state of Connecticut turned over the deed of the property to the selectmen of Tolland. It is now used as an administration building for town offices and the jail part as a museum for the Historical Society.

In the early days of the settlement of Tolland there was no industry, where men could seek employment. The farm was a complete unit in its own and produced or made all the necessities of life.

The famous herd of Dutch belted cattle, that was raised by Mr. Oscar Leonard in 1891. This picture was taken in front of the Leonard homestead. If you look carefully you will see Charles riding the horse and Mary holding the cow in the center of the picture. Rufus is holding a calf on the very left and Florence is looking out of the milk wagon.

Industry in Tolland

In the early days of the settlement of Tolland there were only farms and there was no industry, where men could seek employment. The farm was a complete unit in its own and produced or made all the necessities of life. This the early settlers called "Making a living", and farms were graded as good or poor according to how one could make a living on them. In those days, the farmer had no thoughts of how to get rich, because his real problem was his day to day existence and how to make a comfortable living for his family.

The soil in Tolland, although quite stony, was found to be very fertile and well adapted to raising hay, corn, oats, and rye. Cattle, horses, sheep and hogs were also raised and butter and cheese were produced on all the farms. The farmers all had oxen to work their land and could plow their pastures and stony pieces of ground, where it would have been dangerous to plow and work with horses. Every farm raised young stock and the grain to feed them. Each Spring they planned to sell a pair of steers and a cow and other stock. Nearly every farmer's wife made all the cheese and butter for home consumption and then sold the surplus.

The home of the early settler was not only his home, but soon became his workshop, in which many of the articles needed for the home were made. By the light of the fireplace they began to manufacture various things. The women spun and wove; made clothes and bedding, knit mittens, scarfs, shawls and stockings; made candles and soap, and did all the cooking and baking. The men built and repaired. It took much skill to build good spinning wheels, chairs, cradles, tables, wooden spoons, bowls, farm tools and buildings. Men had very few conveniences with which to fashion these things.

This condition changed very slowly at first, but as the farms produced some surpluses, they were able to trade these for certain goods made by other people. At first they made their own shoes, but later a man skilled in shoe making toured the countryside and made shoes for the family in return for board and room and other produce. After a time, this man set up a shop in his own home and made shoes to sell. This gradual change also applied to other items, such as clothing, furniture, housewares, and tools.

Linen cloth was made in the families from flax and was used mostly for summer clothing. There was a man named Morey, who lived in the south end of the village street, in the present MacArthur home, and he bought up any surplus cloth made by families and made it into dresses with printed designs. The cloth was first whitened, and then impressed with figures engraved on a thin board, the impression being entirely done by hand. The only color used was a dark brown. The trimming and selling of ladies hats was first started by two sisters, Jane Underwood and Lydia Underwood. They had a small hat shop under the old Baptist Church.

In the early days, hoop skirts were worn to all fashionable affairs and it is said that the first one made in the homes were made by sewing grape vines into the hems of their cotton petticoats. Sargeant and Dresser had a store, where the present Clough store is, and they went into the business of making and selling hoop skirts. They also had a shoe shop and sold some other items and notions. Joseph Bishop also had a shoe shop near the Hicks Memorial School.

There was an attempt to manufacture molasses from green corn stalks, ground in a common cider mill and pressed like the pomace of apples. This mill stood just back of the former Mansion House.

During the Revolutionary War, there was a shortage of muskets; so two brothers, Titus and Joseph Baker, who lived in the southwest part of the town, decided to manufacture a number. Titus Baker was a blacksmith and he and his brother possessed great natural ingenuity in mechanical arts. The Muskets, being handmade, were clumsy and heavy, but were reputed to be very serviceable. The makers estimated that it took the labor of one man for two weeks to produce one musket.

The early settlers planted many apple trees, mostly Russet, Greening and Baldwin, and from the seeds of these apples many wild apple trees sprang up in the pastures. In those days there were no pests to spoil the apples and good crops were obtained without spraying. The surplus apples were made into cider, which was one of the first beverages for the early settlers. The cider, when kept over the winter, turned vinegar for the family use. Out of this also grew an industry of distilling the fermented or hard cider to obtain what was called cider brandy. Such a distillery was located just below the present jail. A story is told of a prominent gentleman, who lived in Tolland Street, going to the vat to sample its contents and as he bent over, his wig fell off and not until the brandy was drawn off, was he able to recover his wig. There was record of four distilleries in Tolland. One of them, however, was used to distill essence of peppermint. A Mr. Humphrey raised acres of peppermint, which he distilled and sold as essence of peppermint.

Tobacco was raised in Tolland extensively for over twenty years. More pounds per acre could be raised than in most places, but the quality was not as fine, because the soil was too heavy. Theodore Julow carried on cigar manufacturing in the south part of the town for several years; selling his cigars in nearby cities and New York. Fuller and Sons used to pack tobacco in yellow packages for market. Their factory was on the road below the present jail. Afterward it was made into a silk factory operated by James Tourtalette and his sons Henry, George and Chester. Later their factory was used by the Mortons for a furniture and carriage shop.

We usually think of silk as coming from Japan or China, but in 1770, Tolland residents received two shillings for each one hundred mulberry trees planted and three pence for an ounce of raw silk. The production of silk was at its height in the early 1800's to about 1844. These trees were raised in great numbers and commanded high prices. The leaves being used to feed the silk worms, which produced the cocoons from which the silk was reeled off on to a common hand reel or wheel and then sent to the mill. The Cheney Brothers of So. Manchester at first used only native raw silk. In 1844, a blight killed almost all of the mulberry trees in Connecticut and all of the silkworms died from lack of food. The silk industry in Tolland was then abandoned. At its height, the town of Mansfield produced over ten thousand pounds a year.

A silk mill was located on the pond at the foot of jail hill. In 1848, the silk mill was leased to Ebenezer Gurley and Phineas Turner. They were among the first in the country to engage in silk manufacture with power and machinery. The first silk mill was built in Mansfield and was known as Hanks Mill.

There was a thriving industry located "way down in Donkeyville", so called because donkeys were used to haul the raw materials and the finished goods. Donkeyville is on the Skungamaug River and is now owned by John Weigold, Jr. In 1847, it was known as Fuller's Thread Mill and in 1869 as Underwood and Hastings cotton mill. Here candle wicking and cotton and woolen goods, such as blankets were produced. The mill burnt down about 1875. A piece of very fine grade cotton cloth was in the possession of Mrs. Walter Anderson, who received it from her great-grandmother.

There were numerous other small shops during the 1800's. About 1820, Mr. Bliss manufactured blue ink. He was also a cloth dresser and bluer. There was a fulling mill at the foot of Grant's Hill. A tailor shop was on the site of the Baptist Church. A furniture factory and a harness shop were located on the site of the Congregational Church Parsonage. Charles Meacham ran a spool shop and saw mill at Meacham's Pond. Mr. Marvin had a wagon shop in the house, where the Bradshaws now live. Mr. James Clough had the first greenhouse in this vicinity. He supplied Rockville and Stafford Springs with flowers and plants, and had teams on the road peddling tomato, cabbage and pepper plants. Grains were milled at many locations. Cider and saw mills were numerous, among them were Anderson's and Crandall's mills. The Crandall cider mill just recently burned down in June of 1968.

The Tolland County Mutual Fire Insurance Company, chartered in 1828, had for its first president, the Hon. John Fitch of Mansfield, and Jeremiah Parish of Tolland was the first cashier. The first office was the southwest front room of the Jeremiah Parish house, now owned by Mr. McArthur. It remained there until the purchase of the first building south of the Congregational Church, where it remained until it retired from business in 1899, a period of nearly seventy-five years.

The blacksmithing trade flourished from early colonial days until about 1920, when the work horse was entirely replaced by the automobile and tractor. The blacksmith shop held the interest of both young and old, as they watched the brawny blacksmith work the red hot iron direct from the forge. He would hammer and shape horse shoes and wagon rims on an anvil, also make repairs to farm equipment. The shoeing of horses and oxen always was an interesting sight, especially, if the horses or oxen kicked and showed their resentment of the blacksmith's actions. A Mr. Price had a blacksmith shop for many years opposite the present Jewett home. A Mr. Hewlett also had a shop just north of the present Wilbur Cross highway on Cider Mill Road. In recent years a Mr. Nick Pivovarozuk operated a blacksmith shop near the old Grant's Hill school.

Many cattle and sheep were raised in Tolland and one of the prize herds was that of Mr. Oscar A. Leonard. He started raising Dutch Belted cattle in 1891 and developed a herd about 40 head, and was active in the raising of these special cattle until 1931.

These cattle were originally developed by the nobility in Holland, who kept the strain very pure. Dutch Belted cattle are mostly black, but have a broad white band all around their body, making a very beautiful and imposing contrast. They are above average size and their form is usually very fine. They are very productive as milkers, combining, as they do, beauty and utility in its highest development.

THE INNS AND TAVERNS

The position of Inn Keeper of the Town seems to have been an important one. Not only did he keep a public house where food and lodging might be obtained but also he was a source of information to residents and travellers alike. That Joseph Hatch, the first lieutenant of the "train band" (the military training group of Tolland, smaller than a company) was elected in January, 1718, as the first innkeeper indicates the high regard of the people of the time for the position.

In the 1790's Deacon Benoni Shepard kept a tavern in the house (where Elizabeth Hicks resides during the summer months), and also kept the post office in his house. Mr. Shepard was the innkeeper with the reputation of having been a good neighbor, a worthy citizen and a useful man. His tavern was known as "The sign of the yellow ball".

Col. Smith commenced keeping a public house, called the Mansion House in Tolland, soon after his first marriage, at the place now occupied by Ansel Barber and continued in that business until his death, — a period of about fifty years. To say that his house was excellent — that he was a model landlord, and his good lady a princess among landladies — would not be telling the whole story, and would give but a faint impression of the comfort afforded by his Mansion. His house was, indeed, the traveler's home, where a guest had every wish gratified without feeling that some extra effort had been put forth for his special benefit. The Colonel was always cheerful and familiar, without losing any of that dignity so essential to command the respect of others; and without seeming to exercise authority, he always kept his bar-room in such order that one would as soon think he was sitting in a gentleman's parlor as in a place of public resort. The whole establishment was managed upon the plan of having a place for everything, and everything in its place; and this general plan had few innovations. At this tavern, General Lafayette, in his tour in this country in 1824, halted and had an interview with some of his comrades in the Revolutionary War.

The old Steele House at the extreme southeast corner of the present schoolhouse yard, was the oldest hotel referred to in old histories. It was torn down after the school house was moved on the lot in 1863.

The County House, built and owned by the County, was connected with the jail. This was built especially for the jailer to live in and the Hotel part for the Court Attendants as well as for the traveling public. The first building must have been built about the time of the first jail and was probably torn down. The second one, as Judge Fuller remembered it was a two-story building with sloping roof and an ell. The sloping roof was later changed to a mansard with sleeping rooms in the third story and a large two-story veranda around the west side and south end of the building. It burned about 1893. The present building, erected in its place, is used to house administrative offices.

With the coming of railroads to the New England States, many of our neighbors from large cities and congested areas sought the "simple life" and came in the summer time to board with farmers' families and to special hotels in town. Two of these are well remembered — the Steele House of the 20th century, was on the west side of the village facing the junction of Rockville Road and Old Stafford Road. Mr. and Mrs. John H. Steele began to keep a record of their "Boarders" in January, 1914. They bought the house several years earlier and had guests before the above date. The first page of their register lists guests from New York City, Boulder, Colorado and Changli, China. People came from many places to live in Tolland for a vacation period and some stopped for years. The school teachers, during school terms, were residents of the Steele House for many years. Large sleigh ride parties and church groups from other towns in the area would come for oyster suppers, turkey dinners and chicken pie suppers. Folks from all walks of life were represented in those who came to Tolland to live for a while at the Steele House.

Lawyers, authors, doctors, professors and newspaper correspondents found in Tolland a relaxing atmosphere. Many would bring families to stay for the whole summer and commute for weekend visits. One professor of English, from neighboring Trinity College, has mentioned in a book his desire to visit this "familiar lodging." His description of Tolland is worthy of a bit of a pause. "Considering its station on a granite hill, Tolland is a remarkable streamy town — perhaps because I have so often gone there for April fishing — I never find myself in Tolland or ever hearing its name without giving thanks for its great store of water brooks." Later in the book he mentions "mine host of the Tolland Inn" who was John H. Steele. The elderly found a home with the Steeles and lived there for many years. Around the wood burning kitchen stove was often found a group seated in rocking chairs, visiting with their hostess as she prepared meals. 1942 finds the last registered staying guests as Mrs. Paul Meyer and her son. At the time Mr. Meyer was interned in China by the Japanese. The Meyers now own the Steele House.

The Tolland House of the 20th century was owned and operated by Mr. and Mrs. Chauncey Vinton, in the present Roman Catholic Rectory. There, too, came summer visitors, year after year. Many parties were held at the Tolland House for young people of the town.

THE UNDERWOOD BELTING COMPANY, as told by Mrs. Aaron Pratt, the grand-daughter of Charles Underwood

A prominent enterprise of the 19th century in Tolland was first the tanning of leather, then the manufacture of leather belting, then the invention of cotton-leather belting and the patenting of ten

The Mansion House, on the Tolland Green, was operated by Col. Smith for a period of about fifty years. In 1824, General Lafayette halted here to meet with some of his comrades in the Revolutionary War.

The County House was built and owned by the County. It first was a two story building with a sloping roof and an ell.

The sloping roof was later changed to a mansard roof with sleeping rooms in the third story. A veranda was also added on the west and south side of the building. It burned about 1893. The small picture was taken from a painting by James H. Clough.

The Steele House was operated by Mr. and Mrs. John H. Steele from 1914 until 1942. The house is now owned by Mr. and Mrs. Paul Meyer, who originally were guests in The Steele House.

*In 1878 the Underwood Belting Company needed and built what was always
called "the new factory," a plain, large four-story building situated where the
parking lot is now located directly in back of the Hicks School on Old Post Road.
In the next lot down, a four-tenement house was put up for workers in the factory.*

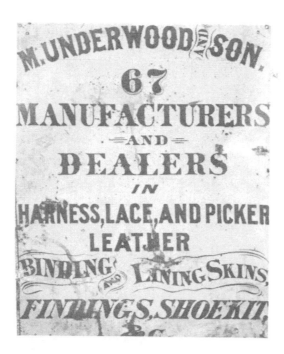

In 1836 Moses Underwood bought both the above house and factory from a Mr. George M. Hyde, who built the above factory in 1816. It is still standing but in very poor condition. When the new factory shown above was burned in 1897, the business was moved to the old factory, where they continued in the leather business until the mid 1920's.

or more types of belting, all by four successive generations of the Underwood family, from 1836 to 1893. One industrial historian late in the last century speaks of this Company as "the only extensive operators in the manufacturing line in the town". In 1893 the company was bought by William Sumner and operated by Mr. E. A. Agard and Mr. William Agard until the mid-1920's. Mr. E. S. Agard had been treasurer of the Underwood Company for a short time and thoroughly understood the business.

In 1816, a Mr. George M. Hyde moved to Tolland from Stafford Springs, conducted a "tan-works" and built the large "old factory" still standing but in poor condition (1969). He also owned the old home next to the factory on the Rockville Road, later called the Underwood Homestead for eighty-four or more years. Mr. Hyde moved back to Stafford Springs after selling the house and factory in two parcels, one in 1832 and the other in 1833, to James Crane.

Moses Underwood, a tanner in North Coventry, bought both of these parcels in 1836, as well as further adjoining land to a total of fourteen acres. Here he took over the "tan works" and developed with his growing sons the manufacture of leather belting. The early records are called first "M. Underwood Co.", "M. Underwood and Sons", and then "M. Underwood's Sons Co." Moses Underwood was said to be one of the first tanners in this country to tan leather from oak bark, white oak being preferred. For this purpose he and his sons, Charles and Henry, planted many acres of oak trees in different parts of this town, some of which, adjoining Route 15, are still referred to as "Underwood's Oaks."

In 1851, the factory and business were deeded to son Charles, the business head, then twenty-seven years old. His older brother, Henry, who was an inventor, carried on his work for the company on the second floor of the building now occupied by Mr. Harold Clough's store. Here Henry developed new types of belting and machinery for use in the factory. Several of these were patented and used for many years. In the Underwood Belting Company, at an early date, were made the round belts used for early sewing machines, the Wheeler and Wilson, The Elias Howe and the Willcox and Gibbs, as well as flat belting in all widths, for all kinds of machinery. Several other kinds of leather goods were in the inventory of early days, such as "picker leather" and "lace leather".

The "Belt Shop" gave employment to a number of men, some

of whom spent their whole working lives with the business. Among these there come to mind Mr. Frank Newman, Mr. Charles Newman, and Mr. John Bowers, all well-known residents of the town. Mr. John Steele traveled throughout the country for some years as the installer of belts in factories which purchased them from the Underwoods.

In the 1870's, Charles Underwood took his nephews Frank R. and J. Edward Underwood and his son-in-law G. Frank Uhler, into the business with him. About this time they perfected and patented a woven cotton-leather belting, the two fused together and considered stronger and more flexible for some machinery than leather alone.

By 1878, the Company needed and built what was always called "the new factory", a plain, large four-story building situated where the parking lot is now located directly in back of the Hicks School on Old Post Road. In the next lot down, a four-tenement house was put up for workers in the factory.

The greatest contribution to the development of belting at about this time was the Underwood Patent Angular Belting. After the Underwood patent on this type of belting ran out, the other companies, even from the far west, began to use it, one famous automobile manufacturer introducing it into cars. Today, angular belting which was started in Tolland, is almost universal. For this and various types of belts, agencies were established in New York, Boston, Chicago, Providence and Dayton, Ohio.

Not only were more people employed in the factory at this time but the products received a number of citations and medals. Among these were medals awarded at the World Exposition in Vienna in 1873, at the Centennial Exposition in Philadelphia in 1876, at the Massachusetts Mechanic Association Exhibition in 1878, and gold medals at the Association Exposition in Paris in 1878, to which two of the Underwood Company journeyed to personally display their products.

In 1881, the Company incorporated as the Underwood Manufacturing Company as other lines had been added, such as manufacturer's supplies, belt hooks and other small hardware, and stockinette. Corporators were four of the Underwoods, with three of their cousins, the Hawkins, and Mr. Frank P. Mack. All were residents of Tolland, but Mr. Mack soon became their agent in the Chicago Branch Office. The trade-mark continued to be that of the Underwood Belting Company as long as they were in Tolland.

In 1893, the younger Underwoods moved to Boston where they established the Underwood Manufacturing Company which was carried on until within the past decade, while here the factory continued with the Messrs. Agard operating for the William Sumner Belting Company.

The stockinette made at the "new factory" caused a great deal of lint and in this, sparks caused the disastrous fire which completely demolished the building on January 31, 1897. Very fortunately the wind was blowing from the East that Sunday evening which undoubtedly saved homes and buildings on the street from a great holocaust. The four tenements were also completely destroyed.

The "old factory" had been used as a warehouse for leather and other supplies and for small operations relating to the business. This building had been maintained in perfect repair and neat condition, so that the Messrs. Agard moved back at once to that location where they continued until the mid-1920's.

Memories remain in the minds of many people, such as the scraping the leather by hand; the huge vats in which the leather was tanned; the boiling fish glue pots and raw leathers with their unpleasant odors. Now the whole operation is a memory.

THE BASKET INDUSTRY IN TOLLAND

The basket industry flourished in Tolland for about forty years, from 1875 to 1915. It was mainly carried on by the Clough family and this description of basket making is related by Emery M. Clough:

There were two farms devoted exclusively to the work of producing fruits; such as strawberries, raspberries, currants, grapes, pears, peaches and apples. These farms required many thousand baskets, as most of the fruit was shipped to nearby markets, such as Hartford, Springfield, New Haven and Norwich.

The largest and latest shop was owned and operated by James H. Clough on property now owned by Francis Biehler on old Stafford Road. This shop was powered by a wood fired steam engine connected to a line of overhead shafting, which was belted to the various machines. One was a rip saw for sawing out boards which were later shaved into bands or blocks for the sides of the baskets, and one cutoff saw for cutting the blocks into the proper lengths.

One shave for shaving the boards and one shave for shaving the sides and one machine for cutting the round bottoms for peachbaskets. Native poplar trees from 6 inches to 15 inches in diameter were purchased by Mr. Clough and cut into logs 3 to 6 feet in length, or whatever could be used to advantage as these had to be cut into band boards or side blocks, depending on the type of basket for which they were to be used. It was necessary that these logs be cut and used while they were green before the wood had a chance to season.

Mr. Clough's shop consisted of four separate rooms; one an engine room, fire proofed from the rest of the shop; the main shop with the machinery; an assembly room and a storage room. The assembly room had benches, forms, etc., where five persons could work, mostly women. The work was mostly piece work, assembling pints, quarts, grape, peach, flower or fancy sewing baskets. Tacks were used to fasten the baskets together. Materials were also delivered to many homes, so that the women could assemble baskets in their spare time. They were paid $3.00 per 1000 baskets. To assemble 1000 baskets a person would be required to work about 20 hours. After Mr. Clough paid for the poplar logs, had them delivered to his mill and paid for the assembling and crating and delivery; he sold them for $10.00 to $12.00 per 1000, his profit was very small.

Another basket shop was operated by John E. Clough on old Stafford Road. This was a building adjoining the dwelling house and was operated only a few years, when it burned, including the dwelling house. Mr. Clough rebuilt the house and confined his efforts to the raising of fruits; strawberry, raspberry, peaches, apples, pears and grapes. The farm is now owned by Edward Gottier.

A third basket shop was operated by Earle S. Clough. This was a partly hand operated operation, as no power was available. Mr. Clough would cut the logs from poplar trees into 8 to 12 foot lengths from his woods, take them to the Anderson saw mill on Anderson road and have them cut into boards three fourths inch thick or into blocks three inches thick from which he would later cut into the proper lengths for bands or sides of the baskets. He then shaved the bands with a draw shave, using a guide for thickness, holding the board in a vise. The blocks were shaped into sides on a hand operated shave.

Each morning enough material for the day's work was placed

into a tub of warm water, which made it pliable, so it could be assembled without breaking. A few baskets and the form on which they were assembled is at the Tolland Historical Society Museum in Tolland. The Cloughs sold their entire production of about 25,000 baskets in Springfield, Mass. at $6.00 to $8.00 per 1000, being delivered by horse and wagon. This was their cash crop, which was done mostly in the winter months from 1880 to 1893.

There was a fourth basket enterprise operated by one LeRoy Slater who lived on the Slater road in Tolland. Mr. Slater confined his operations to strawberry baskets, being assisted by his mother. He had some machinery which was powered by a portable steam engine. This was in operation only a few years.

A fifth basket industry was operated by William Raisch, Sr. on Paulk Hill. Mr. Raisch was a native of Germany, where he learned his skill as a boy. He manufactured clothes, market and picnic baskets, using native willow which he wove into very sturdy serviceable baskets. Many of which are still in use. The weaving had to be done by hand while the willow was small and pliable, after which all the bark had been peeled off.

THE ICE INDUSTRY

Before the use of electrically operated refrigerators, most everyone had an ice box for storing and preserving foodstuffs. An icebox was cooled by natural ice, which was delivered as required by various ice companies. The cutting, storage and delivery of ice was a sizable industry in Tolland. When the ponds were completely frozen over, the snow was plowed off to enable the ice to thicken. A power saw was used to cut through the ice and finished cutting with a handsaw. The cakes of ice, which were approximately 2 X 3 feet, were floated to an endless chain conveyor which carried the cakes to the desired level of the ice house. These cakes could weigh from twenty-five pounds to over a hundred pounds apiece. The ice then slid on runs to the storage rooms.

The ice house had double walls for insulation which were filled with sawdust. The ice was stacked, face down, and each cake was packed in hay. If they ran out of ice during the summer, depending on how hot it was, it was shipped in by rail.

Many farmers had their own ice houses and the cutting of ice was a community affair with much interest shown by the young people.

The Ludwig Ice Company and the Howard West Ice Company were the main ice dealers in Tolland.

CRANBERRY BOGS

There were about six cranberry bogs in Tolland, that were in production up until 1915. There was Kelly's on Mile Hill road, Reed's on Reed road, two Maxwell bogs — one on Gehring road and one on Baxter Street. There was also a bog just north of Grant's Hill school and one at Charters in Skungamaug. The bogs produced up to 2000 bushels a year and these sold at from $2.00 to $4.00 a bushel. A profitable operation depended on cheap labor, as the usual payment for picking a bushel was fifty cents. With rising labor costs the bogs could no longer operate.

The bogs required level swamp land with numerous drainage ditches and a small stream with a dam; so that the plot could be flooded in the winter time, to prevent freezing damage to the vines. The plots were covered with sand and small plants with small glossy leaves of heavy texture, were set about eight inches apart. The plants grow rapidly and by the second year, the beds are a mass of vines covered with red berries by early September. The bogs must be weeded once a year to assure a good crop. At first all berries were hand picked, but later a scoop was invented, which had the advantage of being quicker but did some damage to vines and did not get all of the berries.

Picking time pickers came from neighborhood and some walked several miles to reach the bog. A boss assigned a picker to a strip in the bed. Pickers stationed side by side so that no part was skipped. They either sat or kneeled and scooped berries by hand, but also had to pick up scatterings (berries that dropped when you scooped). At starting point were crates, rectangular boxes for each picker, with a capacity of one bushel. An average day's picking was one bushel. The pay fifty cents a bushel. The berries were taken to a shed and were sorted of foreign materials and poor berries and then barreled and sold.

There are no cranberry bogs left in Tolland now, however, many wild berries are still picked each year.

THE BURROUGHS CORPORATION

Tolland's newest and largest Industry is the Todd Division of Burroughs Corporation, a leading manufacturer of business equipment. The Corporation was founded in St. Louis, Mo., in 1886, with the invention of the first practical adding machine by William Seward Burroughs. Through the years, the basic Burroughs machine was joined at intervals by calculating machines, portable and fully-automatic bookkeeping machines, typewriter accounting machines, complex statistical and data processing equipment and electronic computer systems. Burroughs expansion equipment and electronic computer systems. Burroughs expansion in the broad field of computation and processing also led to development of special-purpose military computers, high-speed printers, fire control systems, navigation and communications systems, and a host of their products. Burroughs today, with world headquarters in Detroit, Michigan, is an international manufacturing and marketing complex, employing some 34,000 employees world-wide.

Todd Division is the forms and systems arm of Burroughs Corporation, employing 2,700 in nine branch printing plants (one of which is the Tolland plant), and a machine production facility. Pioneering in the protection and control of funds, the Todd Company, predecessor of Todd Division, marketed the world's first check protecting machine in 1899. Founded in Rochester, N. Y., the company was purchased in 1955 by Burroughs. The Division manufactures both printed and machine products, and is a recognized leader in Magnetic Ink printing. Magnetic Ink Character Recognition (MICR) encoding, introduced several years ago, is the official "machine language" which allows the electronic, high-speed processing of the billions of documents — such as checks, deposit slips, reorder and installment payment forms — which annually flow through the banking system. MICR systems, utilizing scientifically-designed digit characters printed with inks which can be magnetized, provide financial and other data on the various bank documents which can be read not only by humans, but by electronic processing equipment.

Through use of magnetic ink-encoded documents, banking processes have undergone a revolution; and Todd Division played an integral part.

The Northeastern plant in Tolland is a distribution point for forms storage equipment, such as posting trays, indexing systems, binders, etc.; and it also manufactures; standardized accounting forms; hand-posted "write-it-once" systems for payroll, accounts receivable and accounts payable; Burroughs multiple-part System Set forms; a complete line of forms for accounting machines; specialized systems for insurance brokers, dentists, doctors, attorneys, contractors, credit unions, etc.; custom-built systems for any accounting application; imprinted pocket checks, money orders and official bank documents; protected and warranted safety paper products.

The Tolland plant, with an employment force of approximately 140, serves the New England area as well as Central New York, New York City and Long Island. It utilizes complete offset printing procedures, and is also equipped for complete direct printing operations. Equipment used includes; flat bed, cylinder and platen presses, plus a wide range of offset presses, collators and a graphic arts copy camera, etc.

The building, of approximately 60,000 square feet, is one-story masonry construction with a reinforced concrete slab. The entire plant production area is windowless, and is maintained at a temperature of 75° F, + 2°; and at a humidity of 50%, ± 5%, winter and summer, since rigid temperature and humidity control is particularly necessary to assure optimum conditions for the precision manufacture of Division Paper products, especially magnetically encoded forms.

The Division became interested in the local area as a plant site location as early as 1960, investigating sites in Ellington, Vernon, Tolland and Rockville under the guidance and assistance of the Industrial Committee of the Rockville Area Chamber of Commerce. The Greater Rockville area was chosen by Burroughs for a number of reasons; it is midway between Boston and New York, the two largest northeastern markets of Todd Division; it is near a major highway system; a wide choice of plant sites were available; there was exceptional interest by the community in having the type of industry which the Division could provide within the area.

It was in December 1962 that Burroughs Corporation Todd

Division, took an option on 13 acres of land known as the Gunther Farm, situated on Route 30 in Tolland, at the Vernon town line. Events moved forward rapidly in 1963, beginning with the Tolland Council vote for permission for a sanitary sewer hookup on January 3rd; a public hearing held on Jan. 7th by the Tolland Planning and Zoning Commission for the rezoning of the proposed plant site from rural residential and commercial to industry, at which no opposition was voiced and with the approval by Tolland voters on January 7th, of a bond issue for $100,000 to bring water and sewer lines to the site.

Ground-breaking ceremonies held on March 14, 1963 with Frank Merrill, First Selectman; Herman Olson, President of the Chamber of Commerce; and Jack Friedman and Robert Carter of the Todd Division participating. Construction commenced on March 20th, and on June 18th, Howard Wolfanger was named Plant Manager of the new facility.

On September 30, 1963, a half-year after construction began, the plant was completed and operations begun. Training programs for new employees were accomplished concurrently with the build up of production. In February, 1964 full production was reached.

BURGUNDY HILLS QUARRIES AND GARNET MINES, by Mrs. Bruce Cramer

Tolland never had a mine opened until the 1930's. The discovery was made by the late Bruce Cramer while traveling from New York on Route 30 near Mountain Spring Rd. A mining engineer and geologist, he stopped to examine a small stone, at the side of the road which caught his attention. Realizing that it had eroded off of the Mother vein, he later returned and, obtaining permission of the owners, prospected through the hills of Mountain Spring Rd., discovered the vein and leased the property. He began further prospecting and finding what he considered worthy of development, leased the property and then purchased it. It took a specialist to discover a beautiful product which had been hidden from people for the 200 years and more that Tolland had been settled. This was the beginning of Tolland's Garnet Mine.

Burgundy Hills is 170 acres, situated within the town limits of the Town of Tolland, on Mountain Spring Rd. It contains valuable mineral deposits, abundant woodland of hardwood; — oak, maple, ash and hickory, with several living springs with abundant water for mining and milling purposes.

Various open cuts were made upon the surface of the land for the purpose of drilling holes in the outcrop of mica and garnet veins and blasting holes with dynamite along the parallel strike. The garnet mine is a large open cut 35 ft. wide and 135 ft. long which encountered the mica deposits at a depth of 62 ft. Two tunnels were driven following the mica and garnet vein in its general direction for a distance of 145 feet.

The commercial value of garnet is found in the abrasive field for grinding and polishing metals and wood. The garnet here, on this property, is almandite, harder than quartz. It is used as bearings in watches, meters and scientific apparatus and for garnet paper, similar to sandpaper. Garnet hardness ranges from 6.5 to 7.5 in Moh's scale.

One discovery leads to another, during the development work along with much laboratory experimental work, a very hard micaceous quartz rock formation, beautifully studded with red and purple garnets, was opened up. This was the beginning of the Burgundy Hills Quarries. From these quarries comes the Jewel Building Stone (trade name) which has gone out all over the country for homes of magnificent beauty, for Churches, highway bridges, memorials and other buildings of importance.

The physical structure of the quarries, which are openings along the strike of this deposit, resembles the leaves of a book as the whole mass is in stratified form. Each line of stratification is an average of one-quarter inch thick. These seams are filled with soft white muscovite (mica) and small garnets, purplish in color. Steel wedges are driven into these mica filled seams, forcing them apart. The great slabs of stone vary in thickness from one to one-half inches up to twenty-two inches which can be further separated. They can be had in sizes up to 18 ft. wide and 25 ft. in lengths and are used for veneer stones, terrace stone, mantles, hearth stones, risers, windowsills, wall stones, etc. Colors range from silver and neutral gray through golden to bronze and red and brown. In another section mica is found and Nature has ground this mica so fine that a separate particle of it cannot be seen without a microscope. The mica is a silver white, resembling powdered aluminum and can be used in the paint field.

The first order after the quarries were opened for business was the War Memorial for Veterans of Wars on Fox Hill in Rockville. Dedicated in 1939, it has 1800 tons of this stone. Architect Walter Chambers of New York designed the memorial along lines of a tower in Europe. Stone was sent to the Eisenhower Farm in Gettysburg and the late Eleanor Roosevelt had a specimen sent to the Smithsonian Institute in Washington, D.C. and had an analysis sent to Mr. Cramer. M.I.T. wrote a report of the geology. Visitors come from all over the country, students, professors, rock hounds and builders seeking rock information, for collections, or a new product for commercial uses. Mr. and Mrs. Cramer have conducted them around the "park" pointing out many of the interesting geological formations.

MANUFACTURING BLACK POWDER

In the 1800's and the early 1900's, before dynamite was invented, the main explosive that was used was black powder. Black powder was invented many centuries ago by the Chinese and was used in all of the wars before about 1900.

There was a black powder mill in Hazardville, Conn., that produced black powder many years. The main ingredient of black powder was charcoal. It seems that the most desirable charcoal was produced from a small tree that usually grew in swampy places and was called the Alder tree.

Many of the farmers in Tolland cut Alder wood for the black powder mill. After the wood was cut in four foot lengths, it was beaten with a wooden mallet to remove all of the bark. It was then hauled, usually with oxen, to the mill in Hazardville, Conn. In return, the farmers were quite well paid for the Alder wood and usually returned with a can of black powder for use in loading shot gun shells and for blasting purposes.

THE PRESS IN TOLLAND

The National Examiner was the first newspaper published in Tolland County. The first number was issued from the printing press of Clapp and Robbins, at Tolland on Tuesday, February 10, 1830. It was four page six column paper ably edited and well filled with advertising matter. The paper was published at $2.00 per annum.

The business enterprise of Tolland village at this time was good and the paper was well patronized. The place was the center of trade for Tolland County. There were not only stores and shops and factories, but here was a prosperous bank, the home office of a flourishing insurance company and a well known Academy. In 1830, the prospects of the village, judging from the advertisements in the paper, were particularly encouraging.

The Examiner flourished but one year. In 1831, Mr. Clapp started on his second venture, The Free Press, which survived only a short time, and this was the end of newspaper enterprises in the village of Tolland, as far as we know, until recent times.

In June, 1928, Frank J. Kalas established a printing business, The Clinton Press, in a shop next to his home, on Route 74, in the Skungamaug section of Tolland. For several years the printing business was conducted in a small wooden structure, which had formerly been a chicken-house. At that time the business was small and equipment was hand-operated. As the business grew, a 20 X 30 foot one-story brick building, with a small basement and attic, was erected in 1938. Equipment was added little by little, and by the time of World War II consisted of machine-operated type setter and automatic printing presses.

On January 5, 1945, the "Rural Record", Tolland's third newspaper was published. This weekly paper carried items of local interest and news of Tolland residents serving their country around the world. As servicemen returned to their homes, the publication disappeared from the Tolland scene less than two years after its debut, except for a brief period in the 1950's.

In 1952 a 20 X 38 foot L addition with full basement, two stories and an attic were added to the existing building, making the shop look as it appears today. At present the shop consists of Letterpress, Offset, Bindery, Addressing, Hot Stamping, and Silk Screen Departments. Types of work done include designing labels, wrappers and programs, printing election forms, moderator's returns, town reports and other printing for neighboring towns as well as for Tolland. Work is done by the owner, three full-time employees and occasional part-time help.

THE MEACHAM FARM AND INDUSTRIES

In 1811 Enoch Meacham built an extensive home at the head of Snipsic Lake. The original house had 10 rooms and as the family increased and industries developed it finally became a residence consisting of nearly 30 rooms. This farm of 250 acres was known as the "Banner Farm" of the town, because of the excellent manner in which it was kept up and cultivated and because of its unusually beautiful location. A son, Enoch Giles Meacham, also devoted his mature years to farming, milling and carried on a butcher business as well. A dam was built over the Hockanum River which flowed through the property, which was reputedly "the strongest dam anywhere around." His son, Charles Meacham born in 1837 was engaged in the manufacture of spools made out of birch wood for the Willimantic Thread Company. The area known as the Meacham farm became an industrial center. A shop embracing mill stones for the making of rye flour, also machinery for the making of spools together with other mechanical equipment made the section an attractive center. A long railroad bridge at the foot of the dam connected the shop and a dry house, heated by a furnace and used for the purpose of seasoning of spools for market. These structures were part of the disasters of the not-to-be-forgotten Stafford Flood of 1869. The sawmill was badly damaged and the dry house and dam were swept away. Charles became agent for the "American Agriculturist" and his eldest son, Frederick Stoughton Meacham, operated the farm and sawmill, grist and shinglemill established by his grandfather. Thus four generations lived and worked here before a mysterious fire of undetermined origin completely destroyed this extensive establishment. As quoted in Biographical Record of Tolland and Windham Counties of 1903, "the Meacham Family is one of the old and honored families of the town, and has had among its various representatives some of the best citizens of the place." On Feb. 8, 1902 the water rights and land was sold to the Rockville Water & Aqueduct Company and it is still in use today as the main source of water for the City of Rockville.

ELECTRICITY IN TOLLAND, by Barbara Cook

In September, 1925, librarian, Miss Lucille Agard, noted in her annual report to the Town, the most marked improvement we have made this year is that on December 16th, we turned on the electric lights. Such a world of difference the change makes: "Surely a light in a dark place."

The Rockville Gas Light Company had its Charter amended to make and sell electricity in 1883. The Company generated electricity for the Rockville area with a steam engine. In Stafford Springs, power was generated by a waterwheel in the Willimantic River and a steam engine was later added. In those days power was generated only from dusk until midnight, when the lights went out. A line was run connecting Rockville to Stafford and Willimantic, and after 1908 most of the power for the area was supplied through Stafford by a Massachusetts company. The Rockville Company merged in 1914 with the Rockville-Willimantic Lighting Company, and that Company made power available to Tolland center late in 1924.

In 1935, The Rockville-Willimantic Company merged with the Connecticut Light & Power Company. Extensions were made over the years to provide service to every part of the Town.

In 1962, the Company constructed a service building on Route 74. This building provides for consolidation, in a central location, of personnel and equipment providing service to the Rockville and Stafford areas. About thirty-five employees are based at this service center.

Because of the increased construction of new homes and the additional use of electricity in Tolland, the company converted a major portion of the town to a higher voltage in 1962, and an additional area in 1964. Work is planned for the future to continue to meet the needs of this rapidly growing town.

NEW INDUSTRY IN TOLLAND

The highlights of the fiscal year for the Industrial Commission was the completion of the construction on three sites in the Industrial Parks.

The first and largest to be completed was the 58,000 square foot plant of the Kingfisher Corporation.

A subsidiary of the Garcia Corporation, Kingfisher is the world leader in the manufacturing of fishing tackle. This plant will also have the repair and distribution on facilities for Fisher, Rosignal skis and equipment, for which the company holds a franchise.

The second building will house the John Olender Corporation's offices and garage.

The third plant is that of Zahner's Woodworking, Incorporated.

The town has acquired an additional 45 acre tract of land from James Buckley of Kingsbury Avenue. This tract is immediately adjacent to the present Industrial Park and will greatly add to its size.

Careful planning and zoning have guaranteed the preservation of Tolland's colonial charm. Its schools and churches have been built to meet the needs of the town's increasing population as well as to add to its beauty.

Within the last five years, Tolland has also acquired a Super Market - Barber Shop - Beauty Salon - Restaurant - Hardware Store - Liquor Store - Gas Stations.

Public Services in Tolland

THE POST OFFICE

Before the year 1795 or 1796 there was no Post Office in Tolland. In one of these years an office was established in this town, Deacon Benoni Shepard was appointed postmaster. Deacon Shepard kept a tavern in the house that is now owned by Miss Elizabeth Hicks, and kept the office in his house. At that time there was but one mail a week between Hartford and Boston, and that was sometimes carried on horseback, sometimes in a one horse sulkey. No stage coaches passed through Tolland until the year 1807, when a line of stages was established from Hartford to Boston, passing through this town. Within fifteen years after its first establishment, the mail route through Tolland became a great thoroughfare; there was a daily mail both ways, which was carried through Tolland in four horse post coaches. The route for the mail from New York City to the Eastern states was through this town, until the western railroad was completed to Springfield, after which the mail was placed upon that route. There was also a tri-weekly mail from Springfield to Norwich through Tolland, from 1828 to 1851, carried in post coaches, when it was placed upon the railroad by the way of Palmer. These principal mail routes have been turned from Tolland in consequence of the building of the railroads, so that while other places have been benefited by those improvements, this town has been a sufferer. In place of the mail accommodations with which the town used to be favored, it is now supplied specially with a daily mail from Hartford, Tolland being the end of the route.

Benoni Shepard, the first postmaster, was probably a son of Noah Shepard, whose deed of land in Tolland, dated April 8th,

1763, describes him as belonging in Coventry. Benoni Shepard married Desire West a daughter of Zebulon West, Esq., June 16th, 1774, at which date he is described of Tolland. In another record he is found to be of Tolland, May 25, 1772. His first wife, Desire, died July 20th, 1778, leaving one child, whose name was Pamela, born January 23rd, 1777. Mr. Shepard married for his second wife, Anna Alvord, of Bolton, daughter of Saul Alvord, Sr., February 15th, 1781.

Upon the resignation of Mr. Shepard, in 1807, Colonel Elijah Smith was appointed postmaster, and continued in office until the year 1812, when, for political reasons, he was removed and Calvin Willey was appointed in his place. Colonel Elijah Smith was a son of Moses Smith, of East Hartford, and was born January 16th, 1767. He was by trade a hatter and removed to Tolland, and began business in the Spring of the year 1788. He took a deed of a house and a piece of land in Tolland from James Wills, dated March 19th, 1788. He married Melicent, daughter of Colonel Solomon Wills, in October, 1792; she died May 22nd, 1810. He married for his second wife Lydia Curtis, July 16th, 1810. Colonel Smith commenced keeping public house in Tolland soon after his first marriage, and continued in that business until his death, a period of about fifty years.

The Post Office was also, at one time, kept in a wing (which has now been removed) of the Harvey Clough house, and later in the Pearsall House. It has been located for about sixty years in the home of Miss Bertha Place. In 1903 Charles Sterry succeeded Abiel Metcalf and was postmaster for thirty-two years after which Miss Place became Postmistress and remained in the position until her retirement in 1956. Miss Helen Clough was postmistrees since July 1957 until her death in 1968.

Until recent years, the postmistress had time and encouragement to keep a small store of candy, tobacco and small paper items. Now instead of a one man operation (with part time help) we have a postmistress, a clerk and two rural carriers. Crowded conditions have caused the Post Office to move to its new quarters on Route 74, on July 1, 1965, when it was rated as a First Class Post Office.

POSTMASTERS IN TOLLAND

1795 - 1807 Benoni Shepard, at his Tavern - the Hicks house.
1807 - 1812 Col. Elijah Smith, at his tavern.
1812 - 1820 Hon. Calvin Willey, at his home.
1820 - 1845 Hon. Luther Eaton, at his home.
1845 - 1850 Joseph Bishop, at his home.
1850 - 1853 Henry Underwood, at his home.
1853 - 1861 Obidiah P. Waldo, in the office, at his home.
1861 - 1866 William Keith, east store under Baptist church.
1867 - 1868 Jerome Tourtelette.
1868 - 1871 R. J. Finley.
1871 - 1877 Daniel E. Benton.
1877 - 1884 Joseph P. Root, where Clough's store is now.
1884 - 1888 John C. Lathrop, at his home.
1888 - 1888 Dwight Satterlee, at his home until the fire.
1888 - 1893 Frank T. Newcomb.
1894 - 1895 Arthur Patten.
1895 - 1898 Harry Doyle.
1900 - 1903 Abiel Metcalf.
1903 - 1935 Charles H. Sterry.
1935 - 1956 Bertha Place.
1957 - 1968 Helen Clough. Died on October 7, 1968.
1971 -   Burton H. Frazier.

CEMETERIES IN TOLLAND

The first record of any burial in Tolland was made in the year 1735, and is in these words:

> Ebenezer Eaton, a son of William Eaton, died in June the 27th day one thousand seven hundred and sixteen, (1716), in the nineteenth year of his age, and was the first that was laid in the burying-place of the above said Tolland.
>
> Daniel Eaton, the son of William Eaton, died July the twentieth day, in the year one thousand seven hundred and sixteen, (July 20, 1716), in the twenty-third year of his age, and was the second in the burying-place in the above said Tolland.

These young men were the sons of William Eaton, the first of that name in Tolland, as mentioned in the record. It would seem that the inhabitants of Tolland, by a kind of common consent, set apart a portion of land where these young men were buried, and now included in the South burying-ground, as a public or common place of burial. Whether this was the only spot then used for that

The Tolland Post Office has been located in many buildings in Tolland, but its longest stay has been in the home of Miss Bertha Place. In 1903 Charles Sterry succeeded Abile Metcalf and was postmaster for thirty-two years in this building, after which Miss Place became Postmistress and remained in the position until her retirement in 1956. Miss Helen Clough was also postmistress in this building from 1957 until 1965.

The Tolland Post Office moved to its new quarters on Route 74 on July 1, 1965. It was then rated as a first class post office.

The Tolland Stage Coach
carried the mail and also
passengers from Rockville
to Tolland for many years.
The driver in this picture is
Mr. John H. P. Rounds.

On Feb. 15, 1879, a committee was
appointed to see what could be done
about building a town hall. The
Committee consisted of William
Holman, Henry Rix, Charles
Hawkins and Ezra Chapman.
Another meeting was held and $2000
was appropriated for the cost of
building. The committee for the
arranging of construction was William
Holman, William Sumner, Edmund
Joslyn, Henry Rix and Nathan
Pierson. Calvin Whiton was given
the contract for the foundation and
Nathan Pierson the contract for the
wooden structure. It was completed
in the same year 1879.

purpose, does not distinctly appear, nor does it appear that there was any action of the town or proprietors of the land upon this subject before 1720. At a town meeting held and recorded under date of August 3, 1720, the following vote was passed:

> At a town meeting in Tolland adjourned to the 8th day of the same month it was voted: that there shall be burying-place where they did formerly bury in, about two acres.

This vote constituted the whole action of the town at that same time, and was deemed a sufficient appropriation and consecration of the ground for the purpose of burying the dead. This ground was then common land, and it was permitted to remain in common without being fenced, for about fourteen years. On the 11th day of December, 1734, the town passed the following vote:

> It is further agreed and voted at said meeting to fence the burying-place in Tolland with a decent five rail fence; that is to say - post and rail fence in some convenient time in the year ensuing: Also voted to choose a committee to complete the fencing of the burying-place as aforesaid, - Sergt. Ephraim Grant, Ichabod Hatch are chosen a committee for to do or see said work well done.

In order to have the foregoing vote carried into effect, it became necessary to locate this ground; accordingly a survey was then made by Jonathan Delano, a selectman, and Zebulon West, surveyor, as follows:

> Whereas it was voted by the town of Tolland at a meeting on the 8th of August, 1720, that there should be a burying-place where some dead had before been buried, viz.: about two acres of land, and there being no survey of the same to be found on record: We the subscribers have this first day of March A. D. 1735, surveyed, measured and laid out for the town, two acres of land a little southward of Skungamaug Pond, containing within the same all the graves that are thereabout; bounding the same as followeth: Beginning at a white oak tree, marked, for the southeast corner - standing in the west line of Doctor James Stimson's land; from thence run with six degrees to the west, twenty-two rods and a half to a stake and heap of stones; - from thence run west twelve degrees to the south, fifteen rods to a stake and a heap of stones; - thence run south, six degrees to the east twenty-two rods and a half to a stake, and a heap of stones; - thence a straight line fifteen rods to the first mentioned white oak tree; - abutting east on said Doctor James Stimson, and west on Daniel Benton; south on the heirs of Barnabas Hinsdale. The above written recorded March 30, 1735. Signed by Jonathan Delano, selectman, Zebulon West, surveyor.

On the same day Daniel Benton gave a path one rod wide across his land to this burying-place.

On the 16th day of March, 1761, the town passed the following vote:

> Voted to procure two pieces of land of about one acre in each in the northward part of the town for bury-places. Also voted that Timothy Benton, Capt. Isaac Hubbard and Mr. Stephen Steel be a committee to procure such pieces of land by their discretion.

On the fifth day of January, 1762, Timothy Benton gave the town of Tolland a deed of one acre of land for burying-ground, to be used for that purpose, for the consideration of five pounds, lawful money. This is the burying-ground in the north-west part of the town. Jonathan Ladd, son of Jonathan Ladd, Jr., and Anna his wife, died August 25, 1762, aged two months and ten days, and was the first person laid in this burying-ground. The child was a brother of Elias Ladd, father of Ariel Ladd, Esq., now of Tolland.

On the seventh of February, 1762, Nathan Flynt, for the consideration of five pounds lawful money, gave the town of Tolland a deed of one acre of land for a burying ground, which is now the ground in Skungamaug village.

On the ninth day of April, 1859, the town voted to purchase land to enlarge the South burying-ground and grade and drain the one at Skungamaug. On the thirteenth of April, 1859, the town procured a deed of land lying between the South burying-ground and the highway, which was graded and prepared at the expense of the town, and the town also drained and graded the ground at Skungamaug, and erected a substantial stone fence on the side next the road, during the same year.

The South Cemetery was enlarged November 21, 1955 with the land purchased from Luther Barnard. According to the document stamps, the price was between $1001.00 and $1500.00.

THE MEDICAL PROFESSION IN TOLLAND

The early history of medicine in Tolland County has never been written, unless biographical sketches of such physicians as may be gathered from town and family histories and tradition may be considered such. Town records show the names of men bearing the title of doctor in almost every town, commencing soon after the date of their incorporation. Most of the obstetrical business was in the hands of midwives until some time after the close of the Revolutionary War. The clergy in the early colonial times gave attention to medicine and disease and were of much service to the early settlers. The general court sometimes granted licenses to practice medicine and surgery to such as they supposed were qualified, but as no one was obliged to have a license to practice, most commenced riding with some doctor for a time, longer or shorter, and when they thought they could ride alone, struck out for themselves, trusting to luck, pleasing manners and professional skill for success. Secret remedies were in use by doctors; sometimes the doctor and his wonderful secret knowledge shared the same grave, and the world never noticed the loss.

Doctor James Stimson was the first physician who settled in Tolland. He came from Lyme, Essex County, Mass., in 1716. He married Hannah Stearns, March 21st, 1710. He had an allotment of lands made to him June 21st, 1720. His attainments were fair, probably, for that period. Doctor James Stimson died March 10, 1758.

Doctor Thomas Barnard came from Hadley, Hampshire County, Mass., in 1734. He had four sons, one of whom was in the ill-fated expedition that went to Cuba in 1762, and died there. Moses, another son, died in the revolutionary army in October, 1776, at New Rochelle. Doctor Barnard died in 1780, aged 73, bearing the reputation of a good physician, a very respectable gentleman and good citizen.

Doctor Samuel Cobb settled in Tolland in 1743. He was born in Barnstable, Mass. in 1716 and was graduated from Harvard in 1737. His great grandfather, Henry Cobb, came from Kent, England to Plymouth in 1630, and settled in Scituate. He married first, Mary Hinckley, of Tolland, by whom he had one son and one daughter. His wife died December 9th, 1746. He married second, Hannah Bicknell, of Ashford, April 11th, 1749, and had seven sons and five daughters. The descendants of Doctor Cobb are quite numerous. Charles H. Leonard is one of his direct descendants.

It is not too much to say that Doctor Cobb was one of the most prominent citizens that ever resided in Tolland. He is reputed as having stood high in his profession, and as having possessed the entire confidence of the community. His practice was very general and extended into other towns. He was often consulted by neighboring physicians in cases of peculiar interest, and was considered the highest authority in all cases of difficulty and doubt. He was elected a Justice of the Peace for thirteen years, when there were but two magistrates in town; and most of the time he was the sole acting magistrate. In this sphere of duty he gave very general satisfaction. His moral influence in society was very effective in restraining vice and dishonesty, and in encouraging sobriety and virtue. While living he was greatly respected, and his memory will long be cherished as the conscientious, upright citizen and honest man. The following epitaph is copied from the tablet placed over his grave; "in Memory of Samuel Cobb, Esq., a Gentleman of Public Education and distinguished abilities, who, having served his generation as a Physician and Minister of Justice to great acceptance, and in his life and death was an example of sobriety and virtue, and evidenced the influences and consolations of Religion, lived much esteemed and died universally lamented on the 6th day of April, 1781, anno autatis 65.

Jeremiah West, M. D., son of Hon. Zebulon West, was born in Tolland, July 20th, 1753, and was graduated at Yale College in 1774. It is not certain with whom he studied, nor by whom he was licensed. He married Amelia Ely of Bolton, daughter of Captain Joel White's third wife, February 8th, 1781. He probably commenced business in Bolton, as his first child was born there. Mrs. Amelia West died April 28th, 1786. Doctor West married second, Patty Williams, of Deerfield, Mass., February 28th, 1787, by whom he had five children - two sons and three daughters. Mrs. Patty West died December 22, 1804. Doctor West married third, Mrs. Lucy Baker, of Brooklyn, January 1st, 1806, who survived him. Doctor West was practicing in Tolland before May 18th, 1784. He took an active part in the establishment of the State Medical Society, of which he was treasurer in 1794, vice president in 1803, and president from 1804 to 1807. He took a leading part in the organization of the Tolland County Medical Society, of which he was president six years, nine times one of its fellows, and for many years clerk. He had a large practice, was skillful and successful, and was regarded as the head of his profession in the county. He received the Honorary degree of M. D. from Yale College in 1804.

He was much in public life. He was fourteen times elected a

member of the general assembly, and was a member of the state convention in 1788 which ratified the Constitution of the United States. He was many years a Justice of the Peace, and fourteen years a Justice of the Quorum. "In stature, Doctor West was full six feet, with a large and well proportioned frame. He became exceedingly corpulent during the latter part of his life, and is represented as being unusually large and heavy. Tradition says that he weighed about three hundred and fifty pounds, and that his step as he walked seemed to shake the ground. In social life he was cheerful, humorous and pleasant. In his family he was peculiarly agreeable and companionable. He was an equal with the youngest member, and all were entirely free and easy in his presence. His death was sudden and singular. He had been from home during the day, and had returned just after the family had been to tea. He sat down to his supper and engaged in a conversation, unusually cheerful and gay. Suddenly he was seized with a fit of coughing, and moved his chair back from the table a short distance, and before any member of his family could get to him he had passed away.

Doctor William Grosvenor practiced medicine in Tolland from 1787 to 1798. He married Mary, the eldest daughter of the Rev. Dr. Williams of Tolland, October 4th, 1787. They had eight children, only three of whom survived their infancy. He was a member of the Tolland County Medical Society on its first organization, in September, 1792, was clerk of the Society one year, and one of its fellows in 1794 and 1797. "He had a fair reputation as a physician, and was reputed to be a conscientious man and worthy citizen." He died October 16th, 1798, age 84 years.

Doctor Gurdon Thompson, son of Samuel Thompson, of Mansfield, was born February 22nd, 1767. "He studied medicine with Doctor Roger Waldo, of Mansfield, Conn. He first located in Livingston Manor, N. Y., about 1790, and he resided in that place and in Brookfield, N. Y., until the death of Doctor Grosvenor, of Tolland, in the year 1798. Doctor Thompson then removed to and located in the town of Tolland, and was admitted a member of the Tolland County Medical Society, May 7, 1799. He married Elizabeth Steele, of Egremont, Mass., August 19th, 1790. They had eight children - five sons and three daughters. One of his sons, Horatio, was educated as a physician, stopped a short time in Tolland, and finally located in Belchertown, Mass., where he died. One other son,

Charles Steele, was educated as a physician, and located in Fair Haven, Conn. Doctor Thompson succeeded to a respectable practice, was rather popular with his patients, and regarded as very successful in treating insanity. He stood well with young men, and had a large number of students. He never took a very active part in public life outside of his profession; the only office he is known to have held being representative to the general assembly one session. He died in Tolland, May 28th, 1829, aged 62 years and 3 months."

Abijah Ladd, M. D., son of Abijah and Huldah (Fuller) Ladd, was born in Tolland, August 15th, 1788, and married Almy Cobb, daughter of William Cobb, and granddaughter of Doctor Samuel Cobb, January 20th, 1818. They had three sons, to wit; William Cobb, Charles Abijah and Theodore Stearns. Doctor Ladd studied medicine in the office of Doctor Judah Bliss, of Tolland, and received a license to practice in 1813, and settled in Tolland. He received the honorary degree of M. D. from Yale College in 1834. He was a member of the Tolland County Medical Society; admitted in 1814; was clerk six years, and was one of its fellows six times. "Dr. Ladd always had a respectable practice; in one or two branches he was decidedly superior; was reasonable in his charges, and very indulgent to his customers. He maintained a respectable position in society, and was a very useful man." He died July 17th, 1855, at the age of 67 years.

Gilbert H. Preston, M. D., was born in Eastford, Conn., in 1820, and graduated at Castleton Medical College, Vt. He was a member and clerk of the Tolland County Medical Society for thirty-five years, and was a member of the State Medical Society and one of its fellows fourteen years, and often a member of its committees. He was a member of the American Medical Association and frequently a delegate from the county and state society to the National conventions. His practice in Tolland and neighboring towns - 1873 - 1883 - was extensive and lucrative. He was trustee of the State Reform School from 1876 to 1883; representative from Tolland in 1880, and director and vice president of the Stafford National Bank. He settled in Tolland in 1848 and married Miss Sarah Cogswell, and left three sons who are active and successful business men, and one daughter.

Oliver K. Isham, M. D., was born in Tolland, Conn., on March 27th, 1797, received the degree of M. D., from Yale College in 1822, practiced in Coventry and Tolland, was a member of the Tolland County Medical Society and clerk of the same a number of years and received the appointment of fellow to the State convention of the State Medical Society, of which he was a member. He represented Tolland in the legislature in 1849, and was elected senator in the Twentieth district in 1858. He died in Tolland, March 10th, 1872.

William Henry Clark, M. D., was born in Tolland, Conn., July 14th, 1850, graduated from Colgate Academy, Hamilton, New York, in 1879, studied medicine with Doctor F. L. Dickinson, of Rockville, attended lectures at the Medical department of the University of the City of New York and received the degree of M. D. from that institution in 1882. He was married to Miss Olive J. Baker, of Tolland, July 3rd, 1882. Doctor Clark settled in Voluntown, Conn., in the summer of 1882 and remained there till December, when he removed to Tolland, where he has continued the practice of medicine. He is a member of the Tolland County Medical Society, of which he has been clerk for the last five years, also a member of the State Medical Society and medical examiner for the town of Tolland. He served as Tolland's physician until 1888.

Williard N. Simmons was Tolland's physician from 1890 to 1922. He was born in Coventry in 1860, the son of the late Nelson and Maria Simmons and spent his early life in Coventry. He was a graduate of the Medical College of Vermont from which he graduated with high honors. He was a practicing physician and surgeon in Tolland for many years until failing health made it necessary for him to give up his practice. In 1922, he sold his place in Tolland and purchased a place in Niantic, where he resided until his death June 6, 1925. He was 65 years old.

There are some other doctors that served Tolland at various times, who were; Dr. John Stearns, Dr. Jeduthan C. Eaton, Dr. Tilliston - homeopathic, and Dr. Isaac P. Fisk.

We now have two doctors located in Tolland and they are; Dr. Allyn B. Dambeck and Dr. Ames W. Lapan. They are both located in the same building on Route 30.

THE TOLLAND LIBRARY

When the Connecticut legislature in 1893 passed a statue giving the libraries established under certain conditions, an annual gift of books valued at $100, it was felt by some Tolland citizens that this should be one of the towns to receive these benefits. Proper steps were taken to arouse interest in a public library. In 1898, after meetings and speakers at the suggestion of Mrs. Hamilton R. Downing, the Tolland Public Library Association was formed for the purpose of starting a free library for the inhabitants of the town. Twenty-five women in the town were charter members.

Mrs. Downing gave her moral and financial support to the library through the early years. Money was raised by subscription with both residents and former residents contributing.

Through the kindness of the County Commissioners, three rooms were secured in the Tolland County Court House. These were furnished attractively through the generosity of a friend and book-cases were built to accommodate the books. The books in the library having been accessioned and catalogued were for public circulation January 1, 1899.

It is noted that the library opened with about 400 books and in 1948 had a selection of 5584, to give book enthusiasts of Tolland a variety of choice in its reading. The number of books has increased to 12,046 in 1970.

Retiring after 50 years' service as librarian of the Tolland Public Library from 1898 to 1948, Miss Lucille Agard, a resident of Tolland since her childhood, can count her years well spent and her work well done. She feels the work accomplished and the enthusiasm shown by Tolland residents and surrounding communities for library advantages have more than compensated her time and efforts. She feels the social contacts through her library hours have brightened her many years service and kept her happy.

The most important accomplishment, she emphasizes, has been with the children. It has been a satisfying pleasure to her to see youngsters brought to the library by either their teachers or their mothers and later to continue coming of their own volition. She believes the library habit should be acquired at an early age, not only to help in education, but assure many hours of pleasure in reading when one becomes an adult.

When the first annual report was published in 1899, C. D. Hine of the State Board of Education suggested the Tolland Public Library be given to the Town of Tolland so they might continue to obtain the $100 annual gift of books from the State. The town, at that time, voted to accept the gift in October of 1899 to make them legally a town library. Most of the books in this country library have been secured through the years from this yearly State grant.

Miss Agard proudly points to the library's part in the education of the children of Tolland County. In 1903, the library, of its own free will, undertook one of its most important duties. It decided to send eight cases of books containing 20 Books each to the eight school districts in the town for the use of teachers and pupils. From that time on, the books have proven both useful and appreciated.

In 1930, to be eligible for the State Grant of $100, it was necessary for the librarian to make a yearly report of relations with schools in the town to the State Board of Education. This had to show that the teachers and librarian were co-operating in providing books for the school children to read. The Tolland Library had long considered its obligation.

An historical event occurred for the library in 1930 when Mr. and Mrs. Samuel Simpson of Tolland presented the building housing the library to the Town Library Association. Mr. Simpson was in the Legislatue and had the right to buy it from the County Commissioners of Tolland who were enabled to sell it to him through an act of legislature. A part of the building housed the Probate Court for the Town of Tolland and the Town of Willington, as well as adequately providing library rooms.

At this time, Miss Agard remembers, a gift of $1000, from Miss Minnie Hicks was given for repairs which have been completed to make the library a beautiful old Colonial building any town might well boast, and an assured permanent home for the library.

In 1942, the principal of Hicks Memorial School and the librarian made arrangements to have Tuesday of each week reserved for the pupils to come to the library to get the "Library atmosphere." Children came from both upper and lower grades to fill the library to over-flowing. They were given talks by the librarian on "how to take out books and how to use the library." The pupils personally selected their own books.

The installation of an up-to-date oil burning furnace in 1936 made quite a transformation in the appearance of the library rooms as well as the atmosphere. After the old library coal stove was discarded, warmth and comfort greeted you upon entering the front door where before was coldness and chill. The whole surface of the lower floor of the building was warm, even in severe winter weather, for the first time in 38 years.

Many residents of Tolland have contributed time and money to the success of the library project. There are several bequest funds among them the Mary Theodosia Healy book fund. She left the library a substantial sum in her will and gave freely of her time in helping catalogue books.

Library teas are held every two months, weather and business permitting, and the women of the community welcome this opportunity. It stimulates interest in the library as well as pleasure in the social gatherings. There is always a good speaker and refreshments are served.

In 1948, the Board of Directors of the library were; Mrs. Helen A. Jewett, Mrs. Marion A. Baker, Mrs. Alice W. Steele, Mrs. Jennie J. Leonard, Mrs. Edith Simpson and Miss Elizabeth Hicks as well as William Anderson, I. Tilden Jewett and Samuel Simpson.

In 1971, The Board of Directors are as follows: Chairman, Mrs. Kenneth Kaynor; Secretary, Mrs. Alexander Tobiassen; Other members, Mrs. William Anderson, Mrs. John Tweet, Mrs. Irving Rau, Mrs. Robert McHutchison, Mrs. Wallace Lavoie, Mr. Robert Strout, Mr. Jean Auperin, Mr. Theodore Palmer, Mrs. Gerald Ralston, Mrs. Harold Garrity.

During the year 1969 there have been 19,426 books issued; adult 9672; juvenile 8925; magazines and pamphlets 829. The number of registered borrowers is now 2267. There were 267 new borrowers added and 19 removed. The library has purchased 510 new books and 233 received as gifts. Total books on hand, 12,046. There were 413 books borrowed from the State lending libraries.

The Tolland Public Library Association officers are as follows:

President	Mrs. Harold Garrity
Honorary Vice-president	Miss Elizabeth Hicks
Vice-president	Mrs. Robert McHutchison
Secretary-Treasurer	Mrs. William Summers

Librarian	Mrs. Francis Hodgins
Asst. Librarian	Mrs. Robert King
Program Chairman	Mrs. Kenneth White

THE TOLLAND GRANGE NO. 51

A great many people have little knowledge of the influence which, for more than 100 years, has been exerted by the Order of Patrons of Husbandry, more generally known as the Grange.

The basic purpose of the order was to serve the farm home, more than through merely increased dollars, by elevating its character and improving its spirit. To a marked degree, the Founders intended the Grange to be a social and educational Order, that should break up the isolation of farm life and open new channels of opportunity for country boys and girls; sensibly training them in early youth to grasp opportunities as they came along.

The original idea of the Grange was thought out by Oliver Hudson Kelley and he and six other men, known as the Seven Founders of the Order, worked out the plan for the Grange in Washington, D. C. in 1867. The Civil War left a divided nation with a prostrate agriculture, with its needs in the direction of efficiency, organization and cooperation. The Founders thought that only a well balanced farm fraternity could supply these needs. They set up an Order with its ritualistic ties — the impressive lessons of the degrees — the obligations taken before the open Bible on the altar — and the fine patriotic fervor marking every step. These, with non-sectarian religious background, were the substantials that could emanate from a Founder's dream — and they worked.

The principal factor stimulating farmers of Tolland to entertain the Grange idea was some exhibits by several Granges at Hyde Park, in Rockville at the Tolland County Fair in September, 1886.

The good impressions this obtained were strengthened and materialized on the 24th of the following November, after a talk for an hour or two by J. H. Hale, then Connecticut State Master, in the organization of Tolland Grange. This organization took place at the Tolland Town Hall with nineteen charter members whose names follow; George W. Adams, Dr. and Mrs. William Clark, Mr. and Mrs. James N. Clough, Frank Clough, Charles W. Joslyn, Mr. and Mrs. William Durand Holman, Mr. and Mrs. Loren H. Reed, Rev.

B. J. Savage, Mr. and Mrs. Charles Meacham, and Miss Anna Meacham. After receiving instructions, officers were elected as follows:

Master	George W. Adams	Secretary	William Holman
Overseer	James H. Clough	Gate Keeper	Charles Bradley
Lecturer	Erwin O. Dimock	Pomona	Mrs. Wm. Nelson
Steward	William Clark	Flora	Mrs. J. H. Clough
Asst. Steward	Loran H. Reed	Ceres	Mrs. Ed. Joslyn
Chaplain	Rev. B. Savage	Lady Asst. St.	Mrs. Wm. Clark
Treasurer	Edmund Joslyn		

Throughout the years, the lectures on agriculture were always the main function of the meetings with instructive lectures with pictures on poultry raising, dairying, forest fire prevention, safety driving, birds and their value, and meeting with the Farm Bureau. The Grange exhibits at the fairs were most extensive to show to the community the results of training received in agricultural methods.

From the beginning a winning feature of the Order has been its social life, for in the Grange the family man enjoys its privileges and old and young are interested alike.

The literary programs feature the variety which helps to hold the various groups. Music, drama and other educational and entertaining features bring out talent which is strengthening to the producer, involving a wealth of thought and initiative. Not only is benefit derived from the preparation of the subject matter but the thoughts obtained from the worthwhile programs furnish subsequent entertainment for the mind. A mental reservation which is needful and wholesome.

The social life of the Grange also included spelling bees, picnics, debates and Grange socials where generous amounts of strawberries and cream and watermelon were served. They always supported the worthy activities of the Town and gave assistance to any worthy members in distress.

The first meetings of the Grange were held in the Town hall until about 1925, when for a year or so they were held in various members homes. In 1926 they started meeting in the Federated Church until 1932 when they started meeting in the old Methodist Church which they finally purchased in 1959.

The present Grange with its 94 members is still very active in the agricultural and social life of the Tolland Community.

The Grange officers for 1971 are as follows:

Master	Harry LaBonte
Overseer	Robert Smith
Lecturer	Elizabeth Robertson
Steward	Chester Magnani
Asst. Steward	Robert West
Chaplain	Ernest Smith
Treasurer	Sylvia Pokorny
Secretary	Helen Wilcox
Gate Keeper	Rupert West
Ceres	Florence Ayers
Pomona	Blanche Marks
Flora	Mabel Skelley
Lady Asst. Steward	Elsie LaBonte
Executive Committee	Chester Magnani
	Francis Bushnell
	Ruth Lojzim

THE TOLLAND FIRE DEPARTMENT

The Tolland Fire Department had its origin in the late 1920's. After a near serious fire in the jail house, Mr. William Ayers, Jr., who lived in the Hayden house, thought that it was time that Tolland had some form of fire protection. He approached Edward Wochomurka with the idea and convinced him that he should organize a volunteer fire department. This was done and an organization of 22 members was formed and the first piece of equipment was an hose cart, which was manually hauled to the fire by the members. It was housed in Miss Bertha Place's barn.

The next advancement in the Fire Department was the purchase of an old Pierce-Arrow car, which was converted into a truck. Special mention should be made of the work done by Joseph Franc on the motor and wiring and that of Capt. C. P. Meacham and A. Louis Kalas who have been untiring in their efforts at rebuilding. Much of the work on the truck has been done by local men.

On August 7, 1930, a celebration was held at Tolland in honor of the putting into operation of the first fire truck the town has ever had. William J. Ayers, Jr. was master of ceremonies. The Rev. J. A. Davidson, pastor of the Tolland Church was the principal speaker. A program of music and singing was also presented. Following the dedication of the equipment, a fire alarm was sounded and the new fire truck was tested out at a mock fire. The membership at that time consisted of the following men; William Ayers, Jr., Edward Wockomurka, C. Preston Meacham, A. Louis Kalas, Samuel Simpson, Garrett H. Siegel, Albert E. Schaffer. Peter Mekeat, Joseph N. Metcalf, Maurice Meacham, Herbert Keune, Frank J. Kalas, I. Tilden Jewett, Ralph Haun, L. D. Hall, John Duell, R. K. Doyle, Emery M. Clough, Howard Crandall, Arthur Bushnell, John M. Bowers, Howard W. Ayers, Joseph Franc, Nicholas Zelinka, John H. P. Rounds, William A. Newman, Wilfred P. Young, Simeon Luhrsen, and Henry Duell. Edward Wochomurka was the first chief and Howard Ayers was the Assistant chief. Preston Meacham was the Captain.

At about this time some dissention arose between some of the members over the methods of operation of the department. As a result 14 of the members broke away from the organization and formed their own fire department. They made a drive on membership and soon had enlisted many men on their side. The first group was known as the Tolland Truck Company and the new group as the Tolland Fire Department. The two groups tried to operate for a time, but eventually the first group agreed to drop out and the second group then formed the present Tolland Fire Department.

The present Fire Department has about 48 active members. During 1969, ten men completed a basic training school taught by the State, and 22 radio alerting moniters were purchased and placed in some of the firemen's homes to increase the speed and efficiency in responding to emergency calls. Also two federal portables were placed in service to assist their officers in controlling emergencies.

The Merrow Road Fire House is equipped with the following equipment: an 800 gallon Farrar firetruck with a 750 gallon per minute pump. This built on a 1967 Ford chassis and was purchased new. A Forest Firetruck - a 1947 four wheel drive Dodge Power Wagon purchased used in 1959.

The Leonard's Corner Fire House has a Pumper — a 500 gallon Farrar firetruck built on a 1962 Ford Chassis and purchased new in 1962. This has a 750 gallon per minute pump. A Tanker — 1965 Ford chassis, Farrar body and a 500 gallon per minute pump with a capacity of 1,500 gallons of water.

The new fire house on Merrow Road.

The White School Fire House.

THE FIRST FIRE DEPARTMENT.

Back row — left to right:
Nick Zelinka
Arthur Metcalf
Howard Ayers
John Rounds
Ed Wochomurka
Eldred Doyle
Esten Clough
Emery Clough

Front row — left to right:
Joseph Metcalf
Maurice Meacham
Howard Crandall
William Ayers
Harry Morgansen
Albert Schaeffer
George Metcalf
Simeon Luhrsen

The first fire truck — 1930.

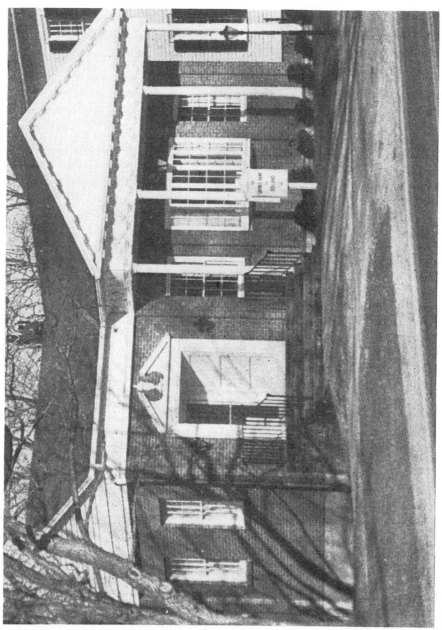

The Savings Bank of Tolland.

Land Grant of the Town of Tolland now on display in the Savings Bank of Tolland

The Center Fire House has a Pumper - A Farrar firetruck built on a 1967, 250 Ford four wheel drive chassis and purchased new. This truck is used as a combination pumper and forest fire truck since its 500 gallon per minute pump and small size give it a great deal of versatility. It has increased the Department's capabilities of getting to water holes that are not accessable to larger trucks.

Men of the Fire Department proudly display trophies won during the year, especially the grand trophy won for having the greatest number of points in a series of musters with other departments in the State. The fire department as now has obtained a new 1970 International Van which will be used as a service and rescue truck.

Each fireman has a dress uniform, which have been purchased by the Firemens Association supported by the Annual Ball and by contributions from the Woman's Auxilliary.

The Officers of the Fire Department in 1971 are as follows:

Fire Chief	Ronald Littell
Asst. Chief	Richard Symonds
Capt. Leonard's Corner	Arthur Kendall
Capt. Merrow Road	Cecil Evans
Capt. Center Fire House	Richard Dwire
Lieut. Merrow Road	Bruce Cropper
Lieut. Leonard's Corner	Robert Clough
Engineer, Leonard's	Fred Toms
Engineer, Merrow	Peter Piwoski
President	Find Peterson
Vice President	Erwin Stoetzner
Secretary	Brian Bishop
Treasurer	Richard Bean
Asst. Secry-Treas.	George Meacham

TOLLAND'S BANKS, by Mrs. George Cook

In the early years of the Eighteen Hundreds the village of Tolland called "Tolland Street", was in fact as well as in name the County-seat of Tolland County. This village was the center of population; here were held the County Courts; here were located a large number of flourishing industries. Of necessity there was an early need of some local banking institution.

The Tolland County Bank, a State chartered commercial

bank, was established August 4, 1826, when there assembled a few of the leading citizens of the County to consider a report of the Bank Commissioners as to the advisability of establishing a bank in the Town of Tolland. In this and two or three meetings following, the Charter having been obtained, the Bank was organized. The capital stock was $75,000 divided into 750 shares of $100 each. The Bank opened for business on March 18, 1929, and it is on that day that the first entry is made in day book No. 1-A. Business was conducted temporarily in the southwest chamber of the house of President Stearns and there the bank business was done for a year and a half. In 1829 work was begun on the new building. The building was completed and occupied by the Bank in 1830.

During those early years, commercial banks, such as the Tolland County Bank, catered primarily to the needs of business and commerce and made no special effort to provide thrift service for individuals. Mutual Savings Banks were established to fulfill this need for personal and family banking service.

On April 30, 1841, on petition of Jeremiah Parish and others, The Savings Bank of Tolland obtained a charter to establish a Mutual Savings Bank in the Town of Tolland. There are but four other savings banks now operating in Connecticut which antedate this charter. The records of the Savings Bank indicate that the men who became members of the Corporation and its officers were not all local men, but came from a wide range of the surrounding area. A definite number represented each town. Many of these men were associated with both the Savings Bank and the County Bank and held office in each bank at the same time. Yet each bank had its distinctive set of officers and board of directors. The Cashier of the Tolland County Bank and the Treasurer of The Savings Bank was always the same man. Both Banks conducted their business in the same building, with the Savings Bank occupying rented space in the County Bank building.

In 1865, the end of the Civil War and resulting legislation and economic conditions suggested some advantages could be gained for State chartered commercial banks by transferring to the National banking system.

On April 3, 1865, the stockholders of the Tolland County Bank met to consider converting the Bank to a National bank under banking laws of the United States. The change was approved and became effective June 6, 1865, when the Tolland County National

Bank obtained a twenty-year national charter. Upon expiration of this charter, the officers of the bank failed to get a two-thirds vote of the stockholders to take another charter, closed its business. In liquidating its assets, the Tolland County National Bank sold the bank premises including all its furniture and fixtures to The Savings Bank of Tolland on October 25, 1886.

After termination of The Tolland County National Bank in 1885, there were no regular checking accomodations for the community save as the Bank Commissioner allowed a small measure, but in 1894, after several banks in other towns had failed, even that restricted privilege was disallowed. In 1897, through the persistent efforts of Hon. Edward E. Fuller, an amendment to the charter of the Savings Bank of Tolland was passed by the General Assembly at its June session, permitting the bank to add checking deposits. Thus, The Savings Bank of Tolland became the only savings bank in the State of Connecticut having a Checking Department.

The security and protection offered to the patrons of the Bank were greatly increased in 1924 by the construction of a steel lined vault with a massive door weighing several tons. Safe deposit boxes of modern design were installed within the vault for the convenience of the bank's patrons.

The original building with the addition of the new vault in 1924 served the Savings Bank well until the population explosion following World War II increased the volume of business to such an extent that renovation and expansion became imperative.

In 1960 the Bank acquired additional land from Miss Elizabeth Hicks and The United Congregational Church of Tolland and engaged the Bank Building Corporation of America as architect to plan the new facilities which were completed in 1962.

The good old building was retained and is now the spacious lobby and tellers section. The vault installed in 1924 was not changed except for the installation of additional safe deposit boxes within its walls. New space was provided for the officers and for the accounting area on the main floor and a meeting room, storage space and employees' lounge at the basement level. The building is air conditioned and equipped with modern machines and facilities to assure the best possible service to customers and pleasant working conditions for the staff.

In reflecting upon the history of the Savings Bank since its origin in 1841, it is interesting to note its characteristic stability as indicated by its growth in assets and the fact that there have been but nine Presidents and eight Treasurers.

PRESIDENTS

George Kellogg	1841-1854
Rufus B. Chamberlain	1854-1866
Obadiah P. Waldo	1866-1879
Charles Underwood	1879-1902
William A. Agard	1902-1916
Perkins L. Lathrop	1916-1942
Lewis W. Philips	1942-1955
I. Tilden Jewett	1955-1965
Donald F. Morganson	1965-

TREASURERS

Jonathan Flint	1841-1854
George D. Hastings	1854-1868
Charles A. Hawkins	1868-1880
Arthur J. Morton	1880-1884
Frank T. Newcomb	1884-1919
I. Tilden Jewett	1919-1955
Donald F. Morganson	1955-

ASSETS

January 1, 1865	$ 349,622.02
January 1, 1875	280,431.38
January 1, 1885	82,241.26
January 1, 1895	174,994.18
January 1, 1905	258,155.95
January 1, 1915	491,837.34
January 1, 1925	2,145,016.56
January 1, 1935	3,452,794.60
January 1, 1945	3,826,405.36
January 1, 1955	5,371,706.39
January 1, 1965	9,865,885.34
January 1, 1970	14,424,184.09

The Bank has grown and prospered with the community even though called upon to endure three major wars, population fluctuation, panics and numerous recessions and international crises.

TOLLAND VOLUNTEER AMBULANCE ASSOCIATION

The Tolland Volunteer Ambulance Association, Inc. has successfully completed its seventh year of service to the residents of the Town of Tolland.

At the conclusion of the fiscal year, July 1, 1968 to June 30, 1969, we find that the emergency calls of the association have been increased considerably. The T.V.A.A. has responded to a total of 115 calls, administering first aid to 121 victims. This is a 28% increase in calls over the preceding year, and a 21% increase in victims treated.

This was accomplished only thru the sacrificial efforts expended by the membership of the T.V.A.A.

The T.V.A.A. membership consists of thirty-four technicians. Each holds an Advanced First Aid Card, a requirement of the association. Twelve of the thirty-four are First Aid instructors and are available to instruct First Aid classes.

The officers for 1971 of the T.V.A.A. are as follows:

President	David Hussey
Secretary	Beverly Trapp
Treasurer	Richard Lander
Records Officer	Gene Marquette
Schedules Officer	Donald Wheeler
Maintenance Officer	Ray Blanchette
Public Relations Officer	Omer Joly

POPULATION

Tolland population figures show a gradual decrease in population from 1830 to 1920, then a gradual increase until after World War II. The 1960 census is the first one to surpass the 1830 figure. In the year 1773, there were 1247 white and 15 black inhabitants; a census used for figuring how many men Tolland should send to the American Armies at Lexington and elsewhere.

Year	Population	Year	Population
1782	1362	1890	1037
1790	1538	1900	1036
1800	1638	1910	1126
1810	1610	1920	1040
1820	1617	1930	1064
1830	1698	1940	1192
1840	1566	1950	1659
1850	1406	1960	2950
1870	1216	1965	6000
1880	1169	1970	8500 (est.)

Town Government in Tolland

Tolland still has a town meeting form of government where the legislative branch is the town meeting, and the administrative branch consists of the selectmen and other elected, or appointed, town officials.

The annual town meeting is required by statute to be held on the first Monday of October, then the annual budget is acted upon. If the budget is adopted, the meeting is adjourned to the first Monday of March, at which time the budget is adjusted and the tax rate is set.

At the present time, the meetings are held in the gym of the addition to the Ratcliffe Hicks Memorial School. Previously, when the population and attendance were smaller, town meetings were held in the Town Hall.

Town meetings are called by the Board of Selectmen, opened by the First Selectman who is Chairman until a moderator is elected. Mr. Furlonge H. Flynn has been the most popular moderator for many years. The Town Clerk serves as the clerk of the meeting. If absent, a clerk pro tempore may be elected to take the clerk's place.

The meeting may act only on those matters that are specified in the warning of the meeting. Any person who has been admitted an elector in the town may vote on any matter. Any citizen of another town, twenty-one years old, or more, who is assessed for at least $1,000 on the last completed grand list, may vote on expenditure of funds, only. Decisions are carried by a majority vote.

Elections are held every Fall. Those for town officials are held the first Monday of October in odd-numbered years. State and National elections are held the first Tuesday after the first Monday in November in even-numbered years, those for President being in years, divisible by four, and those for Governor in the other even-numbered years. Voting is done by machines, of which the town has three.

The chief administrative official of the Town is the First Selectman, who heads the three-man Board of Selectmen.

The only full-time elected official is the Town Clerk, who maintains all town records. All others held regular meetings or set special hours for transacting specific business, such as collecting taxes, declaring property, reviewing taxes, etc.

TOWN - CLERKS

We have seen that a petition was presented to the General Assembly in May, 1716, praying for "the privilege to choose a town-clerk and other town officers," which was negatived. Whether any other petition was ever presented for this object does not appear; but in the year 1717 the town was permitted to choose town officers, and in December of that year commenced the exercise of that privilege. The town clerks are:

Joseph Benton	1717 - 1720
Shubail Stearns	1720 - 1722
John Huntington	1722 - 1723
Shubael Stearns	1723 - 1724
Jonathan Delano	1724 - 1736
Zebulon West	1736 - 1770
Nathaniel West	1770 -1776
Eleazar Steel	1776 - 1785
Benoni Shepard	1785 - 1803
Ephraim Grant	1803 - 1807
Samuel Ladd	1807 - 1808
Daniel Kellogg	1808 - 1810
Samuel Ladd	1810 - 1815
Eliakim Williams	1815 - 1816
Luther Eaton	1816 - 1820
Joseph Howard	1820 - 1836
Oliver Isham	1836 - 1846
Samuel Kent	1846 - 1848
William W. Brace	1848 - 1852
Joseph Bishop	1852 - 1852
Gurdon Isham	1852 - 1854
Oliver Isham	1854 - 1856
Gurdon Isham	1856 - 1857
Joseph Bishop	1857 - 1860
Joseph Dresser	1860 - 1861

Obidiah Waldo	1861 - 1868
Edgar N. Lull	1868 - 1869
Obidiah Waldo	1869 - 1870
Joseph Bishop	1870 - 1875
Erwin O. Dimock	1875 - 1876
Charles Lathrop	1876 - 1880
Edwin S. Agard	1880 - 1887
Frank T. Newcomb	1887 - 1919
Frank A. Luhrsen	1919 - 1930
Louis L. Barton	1930 - 1935
Harold M. Clough	1935 - 1943
Caroline Metcalf	1943 - 1948
Florence C. Ayers	1948 - 1953
Caroline Metcalf	1953 - 1966
Gloria M. Meurant	1966 - 1971
Elaine Bugbee	1971 -

MEMBERS OF THE HOUSE OF REPRESENTATIVES

It was not the policy of the Colony to impose any taxes upon new towns constituted by the General Court, until they had acquired stability and wealth, and those towns were never represented in the General Court until they were required to pay taxes to the treasury of the Colony. But so inseparable were taxation and representation connected in the minds of our forefathers, that just as soon as the government imposed a tax upon a town, their representatives would immediately be sent to the General Court. The following is the first act of the General Court requiring the town of Tolland to pay taxes, and was passed May Session, 1747, "Resolved by this Assembly, that the town of Tolland send into this assembly in October next the sum total of their List as the law directs." The town sent to the General Court in October, 1747, the sum total of its list, amounting to the sum of £7478, 19s, 0d., equal to $24,929.83. A tax of two pence on the pound was laid on this list at the October Session, 1747, and at the next October Session the town was first represented in the General Court. The following is a list of the representatives in the General Assembly, from October, 1748, to 1970, inclusive:

1748	Oct.	Zebulon West
		John Lathrop
1749	May	Same.
	Oct.	Zebulon West
		Joshua Wills
1750	May	Zebulon West
		John Lathrop
	Oct.	Same.
1751	May	Same.
	Oct.	Zebulon West
		Joshua Wills
1752	May	Ebenezer Nye
		Zebulon West
	Oct.	Zebulon West
		Joshua Wills
1754	May	Same.
	Oct.	Zebulon West
		Samuel Cobb
1755	Mch.	Same.
	May	Samuel Chapman
		Ichabod Hinckley
	Aug.	Same.
	Oct.	Zebulon West
		Samuel Chapman
1756	Jan.	Same.
	Mar.	Same.
	May	Zebulon West
	Sept.	Zebulon West
	Oct.	Zebulon West
		Samuel Chapman
1758	Mch.	Same.
	May	Zebulon West
		Samuel Cobb
	Oct.	Zebulon West
		Joshua Wills
1759	Feb.	Same.
	Mch.	Same.
	May	Same.
	Oct.	Same.
1760	Mch.	Same.
	May	Same.
	Oct.	Same.
1761	Mch.	Same.
	May	Zebulon West
		Elisha Steel
	Oct.	Same.
1762	Mch.	Same.
	May	Zebulon West
		Samuel Chapman
	Oct.	Same.

1763	May	Same.
	Oct.	Zebulon West
		Joshua Wills
1764	Mch.	Same.
	May	Zebulon West
		Samuel Chapman
	Oct.	Same.
1765	May	Zebulon West
		Samuel Chapman
	Oct.	Zebulon West
		Elijah Chapman
1766	May	Zebulon West
		Samuel Chapman
	Oct.	Same.
1767	Jan.	Same.
	May	Same.
	Oct.	Same.
1768	May	Zebulon West
		Samuel Cobb
	Oct.	Zebulon West
		Samuel Chapman
1769	Jan.	Same.
	May	Same.
	Oct.	Same.
1770	May	Same.
	Oct.	Samuel Chapman
		Samuel Cobb
1771	May	Same.
	Oct.	Same.
1772	May	Same.
	Oct.	Samuel Chapman
		Ichabod Griggs
1774	Jan.	Same.
	May	Samuel Chapman
		Samuel Cobb
	Oct.	Samuel Cobb
		Eleazar Steel
1775	Mch.	Same.
	May	Solomon Wills
		Samuel Chapman
	Oct.	Ichabod Griggs
		Jam. Chamberlain
1776	May	Samuel Chapman
		Solomon Wills
	Oct.	Ichabod Griggs
		Elijah Chapman
1777	May	Samuel Chapman
		Solomon Wills
	Oct.	Samuel Chapman
		Ichabod Griggs

1778	May	Solomon Wills		1793	May	Same.
		Samuel Chapman			Oct.	Jeremiah West
	Oct.	Same.				Daniel Edgerton
1779	May	Same.		1794	May	Same.
	Oct.	Elijah Robinson			Oct.	Daniel Edgerton
		Samuel Cobb				Elijah Chapman
1780	May	Samuel Chapman		1795	May	Daniel Edgerton
		Hope Lathrop				Samuel Ladd
	Oct.	Same.			Oct.	Same.
1781	May	Solomon Wills		1796	May	Same.
		Hope Lathrop			Oct.	Daniel Edgerton
	Oct.	Hope Lathrop				Solomon Wills
		Elijah Chapman		1797	May	Daniel Edgerton
1782	May	Elijah Chapman				Samuel Ladd
		Solomon Wills			Oct.	Daniel Edgerton
	Oct.	Solomon Wills				Elijah Chapman
		Elijah Chapman		1798	May	Daniel Edgerton
1783	May	Samuel Chapman				Samuel Ladd
		Solomon Wills			Oct.	Jeremiah West
	Oct.	Solomon Wills				Jonathan Barnes
		Eleazar Steel		1799	May	Daniel Edgerton
1784	May	Samuel Chapman				Jonathan Barnes
		Solomon Wills		1799	May	Daniel Edgerton
	Oct.	Solomon Wills				Jonathan Barnes
		Ichabod Hinckley			Oct.	Same.
1785	May	Same.		1800	May	Jonathan Barnes
	Oct.	Solomon Wills				Daniel Edgerton
	Oct.	Solomon Wills		1801	May	Same.
		Samuel Chapman			Oct.	Same.
1787	May	Same.		1802	May	Same.
	Oct.	Samuel Chapman			Oct.	Same.
1788	Jan.	Samuel Chapman		1803	May	Same.
		Jeremiah West			Oct.	Same.
	May	Same.		1804	May	Samuel Whittlesey
	Oct.	Solomon Wills				Jeremiah West
		Samuel Chapman			Oct.	Jeremiah West
1789	May	Same.				Jonathan Barnes
	Oct.	Same.		1805	May	Samuel Whittlesey
1790	May	Jeremiah West				Samuel Ladd
		Solomon Wills			Oct.	Jonathan Barnes
	Oct.	Solomon Wills				Daniel Edgerton
		Samuel Ladd		1806	May	Same.
1791	May	Jeremiah West			Oct.	Same.
		Solomon Wills		1807	May	Jeduthan Cobb
	Oct.	Same.				Samuel Ladd
1792	May	Jeremiah West			Oct.	Jonathan Barnes
		Samuel Ladd				Jabez Kingsbury
	Oct.	Same.				

1808	May	Jeduthan Cobb	1822	Hezekiah Nye
		Ashbel Chapman		Ezra Chapman
	Oct.	Same.	1823	Eliphalet Young
1809	May	Jonathan Barnes		George M. Hyde
		Jabez Kingsbury	1824	George M. Hyde
	Oct.	Same.		Cordial Newcomb
1810	May	Jonathan Barnes	1825	Jeremiah Parish
		Samuel Ladd		George M. Hyde
	Oct.	Samuel Ladd	1826	Cordial Newcomb
		Calvin Willey		Jeremiah Parish
1811	May	Calvin Willey	1827	Same.
		Ashbel Chapman	1828	Elisha Stearns
	Oct.	Calvin Willey		Jeremiah Parish
		Ezra Chapman	1829	George M. Hyde
1812	May	Ashbel Chapman		Rowland Lathrop
		Calvin Willey	1830	Eli Baker
	Oct.	Jonathan Barnes		Rowland Lathrop
		Elisha Stearns	1831	Eli Baker
1813	May	Same.		George M. Hyde
	Oct.	Same.	1832	Loren P. Waldo
1814	May	Same.		Eli Baker
	Oct.	Eliakim Chapman	1833	Loren P. Waldo
		Elisha Stearns		Novatus Chapman
1815	May	Jonathan Barnes	1834	Loren P. Waldo
		Elisha Stearns		Eli Baker
1815	May	Jonathan Barnes	1835	Novatus Chapman
		Elisha Stearns		Cordial Newcomb
	Oct.	Ephraim West	1836	Carlos Chapman
		Elijah Smith		John Warren
1816	May	Jonathan Barnes	1837	Same.
		Ephraim West	1838	Elisha Stearns
	Oct.	Eliphalet Young		Chauncey Griggs
		Jonathan Barnes	1839	Loren P. Waldo
1817	May	Eliphalet Young		Elisha Stearns
		Jonathan Barnes	1840	Ariel Ladd
	Oct.	Same.		Seth D. Griggs
1818	May	Eliphalet Young	1841	Ebenezer West
		Gurdon Thompson		Oliver Lord
	Aug.	Eliphalet Young	1842	Wm. C. Newcomb
		Ashbel Chapman		Luther Anderson
	Oct.	Eliphalet Young	1843	Wm. C. Newcomb
		Wm. Eldredge		Luther Anderson
1819		Wm. Eldredge	1844	Benjamin Young
		Hezekiah Nye		Talmon Cross
1820		Calvin Willey	1845	Benjamin Young
		Ashbel Chapman		Talmon Cross
1821		Calvin Willey	1846	Obidiah P. Waldo
		Hezekiah Nye		John P. Brigham

1847	Loren P. Waldo	1873	Edgar N. Lull
	William W. Eaton		Rufus J. Leonard
1848	Loren P. Waldo	1874	Lucius J. Phillips
	William W. Eaton		Henry E. Dimmock
1849	Joseph Clark	1875	Alden B. Crandall
	Oliver K. Isham		Charles M. Joslyn
1850	Ashbel Chapman	1876	Howard R. Rand
	Chauncey Griggs		Charles A. Hawkins
1851	Sherman Chapman	1878	John B. Fuller
	Ira K. Marvin		Ezra L. Chapman
1852	William Holman	1879	Henry Young
	Benjamin Fuller		George H. Olmsted
1853	Joseph A. Strait	1880	Gilbert Preston
	Orrin Ward		John W. Edgerton
1854	Alvin P. Hyde	1881	Edwin S. Agard
	Lucius S. Fuller		Spencer O. Grover
1855	Benj. D. Benton	1882	Henry E. Steele
	Abner Grover		Charles Young
1856	William Clark	1883	Henry E. Steele
	Daniel Grover		Charles Young
1857	Joseph Clark	1884	Thomas G. Root
	Joshua Griggs		Oscar A. Leonard
1858	Alvin P. Hyde	1885	Charles W. Bradley
	Elijah Ashley		Austin L. Edgerton
1859	Charles Lathrop	1886	Frank T. Newcomb
	Alvin Kibbee		Henry H. Doyle
1860	William C. Ladd	1887-88	Daniel B. Chapman
	Orson Richardson		William H. Buel
1861	Joseph Bishop	1889-90	Edwin O. Dimock
	Jabez West		William H. Buel
1862	Joseph Bishop	1889-90	Edwin O. Dimock
	Jabez West		John B. Walbridge
1863	Alvin P. Hyde	1891-92	Edwin J. Crandall
	Edmund Joslin		John B. Walbridge
1864	Nathan Pierson	1893-94	Ratcliffe Hicks
	Henry Ashley		Phillip Doyle
1865	Smith H. Brown	1895-96	William Sumner
	James J. Andrews		Ratcliffe Hicks
1866	George Hastings	1897-98	Edwin S. Agard
	William S. Moore		John S. Usher
1867	William Holman	1899-00	Albert D. Stedman
	Ratcliffe Hicks		Frank A. Newman
1868	Edgar N. Lull	1901-02	John H. Steele
	Edward Kellogg		Gideon Brown
1869	Joseph Webster	1903-04	David A. Brown
	Loren Newcomb		John J. Dunn
1870	George Kingsbury	1905-06	William A. Agard
	C. B. Pomeroy		Charles Hurlburt
1871	William Baker	1907-08	Cornell Green
	Joseph Bishop		Charles E. Usher
1872	Selden Hare	1909-10	Edward E. Fuller
	Charles R. Hicks		Joseph M. Metcalf

1911-12	Harry Wood	1937-38	James D. Burke
	Frank A. Luhrsen		Alfred F. Ludwig
1913-14	John Johnson	1939-40	Same.
	Edwin R. Dimock	1941-42	Irving Campbell
1915-16	Harry Bartlett		Burt C. Hallock
	Peter Morgensen	1943-44	Harwood Skelley
1917-18	Jesse Dearden		Rupert B. West
	Henry Martin	1945-46	Same.
1919-20	Nathan O. Ward	1947-48	Same.
	Oscar A. Leonard	1949-50	Harold M. Clough
1921-22	Edward E. Fuller		Mabel F. Cook
	Helen A. Jewett	1951-52	Harold M. Clough
1923-24	George D. Neff		Paul deMacarte
	Elizabeth Green	1953-54	Same.
1925-26	Samuel Johnson	1955-56	Stephen Ketcham
	Frank A. Newman		James W. Metcalf
1927-28	George Metcalf	1957-58	Harold M. Clough
	John M. Bowers		James W. Metcalf
1929-30	Samuel Simpson	1959-60	Charles Leonard
	Garrett Siegel		Ruth E. Lojzim
1931-32	Alfred F. Ludwig	1961-62	Harold M. Clough
	James W. Galavin		Ruth E. Lojzim
1933-34	Same.	1963-64	Robert D. King
1935-36	Same.		Ruth E. Lojzim
1937-38	James D. Burke	1967-68-69-70	Robert D. King
	Alfred F. Ludwig		

SELECTMEN

Towns were authorized by the act of 1672 "to choose a convenient number not exceeding seven of their inhabitants, able, discreet and of good conversation, to be selectmen or townsmen, to take care and order the prudential affairs of their town." By the Constitution of the State adopted in 1818, it is made "the duty of each town to elect annually selectmen and such officers of local police as the laws may prescribe."

By the provision of the statutes of 1821, towns were annually to choose and appoint a convenient number, not exceeding seven, to be selectmen, and by the statutes of 1852 they are to be chosen by ballot.

The first selectmen chosen in the town of Tolland were chosen in the year 1717. The following named persons have held the office of selectmen in the town of Tolland, during the year prefixed to the names of each respectively:

1718	William Eaton, Jonathan Wills, Daniel Benton.
1719	William Eaton, Jonathan Wills, Nathaniel Taylor.
1720	William Eaton, Joseph Benton, Nathaniel Taylor.
1721	John Yeomans, Francis West, Ebenezer Nye, John Stiles, Daniel Benton.
1722	Daniel Eaton, Joseph Hatch, Joseph Park, Shubael Stearns, John Stiles.
1723	Francis West, John Huntington, Noah Grant.
1724	Daniel Eaton, Shubael Stearns, Peter Emmons.
1725	Jonathan Delano, Samuel Benton, Noah Grant.
1726	Jonathan Delano, Samuel Benton, Noah Grant.
1727	Hope Lathrop, Jonathan Delano, Peter Emmons.
1728	Josiah Goodrich, Hope Lathrop, Peter Emmons, Samuel Benton, Jonathan Delano.
1729	Jonathan Delano, Josiah Goodrich, Samuel Benton, Joseph Baker.
1730	No record to be found.
1731	Josiah Goodrich, Jonathan Delano, Ebenezer Nye.
1732	Jonathan Delano, Ebenezer Nye, Samuel Chapman.
1733	Jonathan Delano, James Chapman, Ebenezer Nye.
1734	Jonathan Delano, Ebenezer Nye, Samuel Chapman.
1735	Jonathan Delano, Ichabod Hinckley, Samuel Chapman.
1736	Jonathan Delano, Samuel Chapman, Ichabod Hinckley.
1737	Samuel Chapman, John Huntington, Zebulon West.
1738	Samuel Chapman, Joseph Hatch, Zebulon West.
1739	Samuel Chapman, Zebulon West, Timothy Hatch.
1740	Joseph Baker, Ebenezer Nye, Samuel Chapman.
1741	Zebulon West, Ebenezer Nye, Samuel Chapman.
1742	Samuel Chapman, Ebenezer Nye, Zebulon West.
1743	Samuel Chapman, Ebenezer Nye, Zebulon West.
1744	Ebenezer Nye, John Lathrop, Zebulon West.
1745	Ebenezer Nye, John Lathrop, Zebulon West.
1746	Zebulon West, Ebenezer Nye, John Lathrop.
1747	John Tyler, John Lathrop, Zebulon West.
1748	Zebulon West, John Tyler, Joshua Wills.
1749	Zebulon West, John Tyler, Joshua Wills.
1750	Zebulon West, John Tyler, Joshua Wills.
1751	Zebulon West, John Tyler, Joshua Wills.
1752	Zebulon West, Joshua Wills, John Lathrop.
1753	Zebulon West, Joshua Wills, John Stearns.
1754	Ebenezer Nye, Joshua Wills, Zebulon West.
1755	Zebulon West, Ebenezer Nye, Joshua Wills.
1756	Ebenezer Nye, Joshua Wills, Joseph West.
1757	Ebenezer Nye, Joshua Wills, Joseph West.
1758	Joseph West, Joshua Wills, Samuel Chapman.
1759	Joshua Wills, Joseph West, Solomon Loomis.
1760	Joshua Wills, Joseph West, Solomon Loomis.
1761	Joseph West, Solomon Loomis, Ichabod Griggs.
1762	Joseph West, Solomon Loomis, Ichabod Griggs.
1763	Joseph West, Solomon Loomis, Ichabod Griggs.

1764   No record to be found.
1765   Ichabod Griggs, Elijah Chapman, Joseph Lathrop.
1766   Ichabod Griggs, Elijah Chapman, Joseph Lathrop.
1767   Ichabod Griggs, Elijah Chapman, Joseph Lathrop.
1768   Ichabod Griggs, Elijah Chapman, Joseph Lathrop.
1769   Ichabod Griggs, Elijah Chapman, Joseph Lathrop.
1770   Elijah Chapman, Joseph Lathrop, Stephen Steel.
1771   Elijah Chapman, Joseph Lathrop, Stephen Steel.
1772   Elijah Chapman, Joseph Lathrop, Stephen Steel.
1773   Joseph Lathrop, Stephen Steel, Samuel Chapman.
1774   Stephen Steel, Samuel Chapman, Solomon Wills.
1775   Solomon Wills, Caleb West, Samuel West.
1776   Samuel West, Jr., Samuel Chapman, Ichabod Hinckley.
1777   Samuel West, Jr., Samuel Chapman, David Lathrop, Ichabod Hinckley, James West.
1778   Samuel West, Jr., James Chamberlin, Solomon Wills.
1779   Samuel West, Jr., Jonathan Wills, Samuel Cobb, Jr.
1780   Joshua Wills, Samuel Cobb, Joseph West, Daniel Edgerton.
1781   Joseph West, Daniel Edgerton, Samuel Cobb, Ben. Shepherd.
1782   Joseph West, Daniel Edgerton, Samuel Cobb, Ben. Shepherd, Ichabod Hinckley.
1783   Ichabod Hinckley, Samuel Ladd, Joshua Griggs.
1784   Ichabod Hinckley, Samuel Ladd, Joshua Griggs.
1785   Ichabod Hinckley, Samuel Ladd, Joshua Griggs.
1786   Ichabod Hinckley, Samuel Ladd, Simon Chapman.
1787   Ichabod Hinckley, Samuel Ladd, Simon Chapman.
1788   Joshua Griggs, Daniel Edgerton, Samuel Ladd.
1789   Ichabod Hinckley, Elnathan Strong, Daniel Edgerton.
1790   Ichabod Hinckley, Daniel Edgerton, Elnathan Strong.
1791   Daniel Edgerton, Simon Chapman, John Steel.
1792   Daniel Edgerton, Simon Chapman, Samuel Ladd.
1793   Daniel Edgerton, Simon Chapman, Ichabod Hinckley.
1794   Daniel Edgerton, Ichabod Hinckley, Simon Chapman.
1795   Daniel Edgerton, Ichabod Hinckley, Simon Chapman.
1796   Daniel Edgerton, Samuel Ladd, Jonathan Barnes.
1797   Daniel Edgerton, Samuel Ladd, Jonathan Barnes.
1798   Daniel Edgerton, Samuel Ladd, Jonathan Barnes.
1799   Jonathan Barnes, Daniel Edgerton, Ichabod Hinckley.
1800   Jonathan Barnes, John Kingsbury, Jabez West.
1801   Jonathan Barnes, Jeduthan Cobb, Jabez Kingsbury.
1802   Jonathan Barnes, Jeduthan Cobb, Jabez Kingsbury.
1803   Jonathan Barnes, Jabez Kingsbury, Jeduthan Cobb.
1804   Jeduthan Cobb, Jonathan Barnes, Jabez Kingsbury.
1805   Jonathan Barnes, Jeduthan Cobb, Jabez Kingsbury.
1806   Jonathan Barnes, Jeduthan Cobb, Jabez Kingsbury.
1807   Jabez Kingsbury, Jeduthan Cobb, Simon Chapman, Jr.
1808   Simon Chapman, Jr., Jeduthan Cobb, Ashbel Chapman.
1809   Ashbel Chapman, Jeduthan Cobb, Ichabod Hinckley.
1810   Eliakim Chapman, Ephraim West, Jabez Kingsbury.
1811   Ashbel Chapman, Samuel Ladd, Ichabod Hinckley, John Warren, Ezra Chapman.

1812	Calvin Willey, John Warren, Ezra Chapman, Aaron Chapman, Thomas Howard.
1813	John Warren, Ezra Chapman, Aaron Chapman, Shubael Reed, John Stanley.
1814	Ephraim West, Eliakim Chapman, Shubael Reed.
1815	Ephraim West, Simon Chapman, Jr., Ashbel Steel.
1816	Ephraim West, Simon Chapman, Jr., Ashbel Steel.
1817	Hezekiah Nye, Ezra Chapman, Ichabod Hinckley.
1818	Hezekiah Nye, Sylvanus Haynes, Joseph Howard.
1819	Hezekiah Nye, Eliphalet Young, Ezra Chapman.
1820	Eliphalet Young, Ezra Chapman, Aaron Chapman.
1821	Stephen Griggs, Ephraim West, John Kingsbury.
1822	Ezra Chapman, William Tillinghast, George M. Hyde.
1823	George M. Hyde, Hezekiah Nye, Cordial Newcomb.
1824	George M. Hyde, Hezekiah Nye, Cordial Newcomb.
1825	George M. Hyde, Cordial Newcomb, William A. Sumner.
1826	George M. Hyde, Seymour Fuller, Solomon Howe.
1827	George M. Hyde, Seymout Fuller, Solomon Howe.
1828	George M. Hyde, Luther Eaton, Cordial Newcomb.
1829	Cordial Newcomb, Eli Baker, Solomon Howe.
1830	George M. Hyde, Eli Baker, Solomon Howe.
1831	Eli Baker, Hezekiah Nye, Samuel Kent.
1832	Samuel Kent, Cordial Newcomb, Loren P. Waldo.
1833	John Lyon, Loren P. Waldo, Ira K. Marvin.
1834	Loren P. Waldo, John Lyon, Ira K. Marvin.
1835	Loren P. Waldo, Novatus Chapman, Charles Fish.
1836	Loren P. Waldo, Novatus Chapman, Charles Fish.
1837	Oliver Lord, Carlos Chapman, Ebenezer West.
1838	Solomon L. Griggs, Warren Fitch, Joseph Burnham.
1839	Loren P. Waldo, Solomon L. Griggs, Joseph Burnham.
1840	Loren P. Waldo, Solomon L. Griggs, John Gager.
1841	Loren P. Waldo, Solomon L. Griggs, John Gager.
1842	Loren P. Waldo, Novatus Chapman, Luther C. Anderson.
1843	Luther C. Anderson, John W. Gager, Leve Drake.
1844	Luther C. Anderson, Sherman Chapman, Wm. C. Newcomb.
1845	Loren P. Waldo, Nathaniel K. Sibley, Lucius Fuller.
1846	Loren P. Waldo, Nathaniel K. Sibley, Lucius Fuller.
1847	Joseph Clark, Sheldon Eaton, Orrin Ward.
1848	Moses Underwood, John W. Gager, Samuel D. Merrick.
1849	William C. Newcomb, William Holman, Alvan Kibbe.
1850	William C. Newcomb, William Holman, Alvan Kibbe.
1851	John P. Brigham, Obadiah P. Waldo, Seth Brown.
1852	John P. Brigham, Obadiah P. Waldo, Seth Brown.
1853	Benjamin L. Young, Orson A. Richardson, Wm. Clark.
1854	Benjamin L. Young, Orson A. Richardson, Wm. Clark.
1855	Alvan P. Hyde, Charles Lathrop, Jabez West.
1856	Charles Underwood, Anthony M. Weaver, George Eaton.
1857	Lucius S. Fuller, Edward P. Kellogg, Edmund Joslin.
1858	Lucius S. Fuller, Edward P. Kellogg, Edmund Joslin.
1859	Sherman Chapman, Elijah S. Chapman, Porter Walbridge.
1860	Sherman Chapman, Elijah S. Chapman, Porter Walbridge.

1861	Charles Underwood, James Babcock, James Andrews.
1862	Chauncey Griggs, Orrin Ward, J. J. Andrews.
1863	Chauncey Griggs, James J. Andrews, Orrin Ward.
1864	Wm. C. Newcomb, Wm. Baker, Wm. C. Ladd.
1865	Sherman Chapman, Wm. Baker, Wm. C. Ladd.
1866	Sherman Chapman, Wm. Baker, Wm. C. Ladd.
1867	Wm. Holman, Smith H. Brown, Rufus J. Leonard.
1868	Wm. Holman, Smith H. Brown, Rufus J. Leonard.
1869	Smith H. Brown, Rufus J. Leonard, Samuel B. Slater.
1870	Charles B. Pomeroy, Nathan Pierson, Loren Newcomb.
1871	Nathan Pierson, Loren Newcomb, Wm. C. Ladd.
1872	Nathan Pierson, Loren Newcomb, Wm. C. Ladd.
1873	Charles Lathrop, John B. Kingsbury, H. F. Rand.
1874	Sherman Chapman, Howard F. Rand, Lucien W. Martin.
1875	Wm. Baker, Smith H. Brown, Lucius A. Kibbe.
1876	Wm. Baker, Smith H. Brown, Thomas G. Root.
1877	Wm. Baker, Smith H. Brown, Thomas G. Root.
1878	Edmund Joslyn, Lucius S. Fuller, Henry T. Rix.
1879	Edmund Joslyn, William Holman, Henry T. Rix.
1880	Smith H. Brown, Loren Newcomb, Ezra I. Chapman.
1881	Smith H. Brown, Henry Young, John W. Edgerton.
1882	Smith H. Brown, Henry Young, Spencer O. Grover.
1883	Smith H. Brown, Henry Young, Spencer O. Grover.
1884	Smith H. Brown, Henry Young, Dwight A. Satterlee.
1885	Wm. D. Holman, Dwight A. Satterlee, Gideon Brown.
1886	Wm. D. Holman, Gideon Brown, Loren A. Reed.
1887	Wm. D. Holman, Gideon Brown, Joseph P. Root.
1888	Bradley M. Sears, Gideon Brown, Joseph P. Root.
1889	Bradley M. Sears, John N. Walbridge, Loren H. Reed.
1890	Bradley M. Sears, John N. Walbridge, Loren H. Reed.
1891	Edmund Joslyn, Thomas G. Root, Andrew J. McCormick.
1892	Edmund Joslyn, Thomas G. Root, Andrew J. McCormick.
1893	Edmund Joslyn, David A. Brown, Loren H. Reed.
1894	David A. Brown, Oscar A. Leonard, Wm. T. Anderson.
1895	Wm. T. Anderson, Loren H. Reed, Edwin J. Crandall.
1896	George F. Kibbee, Henry Young, Lauritz Hansen.
1897	George F. Kibbee, Henry Young, Lauritz Hansen.
1898	Henry Young, William L. Ayers, Gilbert P. Babcock.
1899	Henry H. Doyle, William L. Ayers, Henry P. Rix.
1900	Edmund Joslyn, William L. Ayers, Henry P. Rix.
1901	Edmund Joslyn, Andrew J. McCormick, Albert Stedman.
1902	Edwin J. Crandall, Frank A. Newman, Andrew McCormick.
1903	Andrew McCormick, Frank A. Newman, John M. Bowers.
1904	Oscar A. Leonard, Frank A. Newman, A. Esten Clough.
1905	Oscar A. Leonard, Frank A. Newman, Lauritz Hansen.
1906	Oscar A. Leonard, Frank A. Newman, Lauritz Hansen.
1907	Oscar A. Leonard, Frank A. Newman, Lauritz Hansen.
1908	Oscar A. Leonard, Frank A. Newman, Lauritz Hansen.
1909	Oscar A. Leonard, Frank A. Newman, John W. Edgerton.
1910	Oscar A. Leonard, Frank A. Newman, John W. Edgerton.
1911	Oscar A. Leonard, Frank A. Newman, John W. Edgerton.

1912	Oscar A. Leonard, Frank A. Newman, Gilbert P. Babcock.
1913	Oscar A. Leonard, Frank A. Newman, Gilbert P. Babcock.
1914	Lorenzo Sparrow, Edwin Crandall, Robert Amidon.
1915	Lorenzo Sparrow, Edwin Crandall, Robert Amidon.
1916	Lorenzo Sparrow, Edwin Crandall, Peter Morgensen.
1917	Peter Morgensen, Joseph Metcalf, Lorenzo Sparrow.
1918	Cornell Green, Henry Martin, Peter Morgensen.
1919	Cornell Green, Frank A. Newman, Robert S. Amidon.
1920	Frank A. Newman, Joseph Metcalf, George Neff.
1921	Frank A. Newman, Joseph Metcalf, George Neff.
1922	Frank A. Newman, George Neff, Joseph Metcalf.
1923	Frank A. Newman, George Neff, Joseph Metcalf.
1924	Frank A. Newman.
1925	Frank A. Newman.
1926	Frank A. Newman.
1927	Harry Morgensen, Joseph Metcalf, George Neff.
1928	Frank A. Newman, George Neff.
1929	George D. Neff, Justin J. Lathrop, John M. Bowers.
1930	John M. Bowers.
1931	Frank A. Newman.
1932	L. Ernest Hall, George Neff, Rupert B. West.
1933	George D. Neff, L. Ernest Hall, Rupert B. West.
1934	George D. Neff, Burt C. Hallock, Robert E. Doyle.
1935	Burt C. Hallock, George E. Cook, George E. Neff.
1936	Burt C. Hallock, George E. Cook, John F. Lathrop.
1937	Burt C. Hallock, George E. Cook, Frank A. Denette.
1938	Burt C. Hallock, Charles Szemreylo, James D. Burke.
1939	Burt C. Hallock, Charles Szemreylo, James D. Burke.
1940	Burt C. Hallock, Charles Szemreylo, James D. Burke.
1941	Burt C. Hallock, George E. Cook, James D. Burke.
1942	Wilfred P. Young, George E. Cook, James D. Burke.
1943	Wilfred P. Young, George E. Cook, Simeon Luhrsen.
1944	Wilfred P. Young, George E. Cook, Simeon Luhrsen.
1945	Wilfred P. Young, George E. Cook, Simeon Luhrsen.
1946	Wilfred P. Young, George E. Cook, Simeon Luhrsen.
1947	Wilfred P. Young, George E. Cook, Simeon Luhrsen.
1948	Eugene I. Wanat, Valere Vasselet, George E. Cook.
1949	Eugene I. Wanat, Valere Vasselet, George E. Cook.
1950	Wilfred P. Young, Walter H. Anderson, George Cook.
1951	Wilfred P. Young, George E. Cook, Walter Anderson.
1952	Wilfred P. Young, George E. Cook, James D. Burke.
1953	Frank J. Kalas, George E. Cook, Walter Anderson.
1954	Carmelo Zanghi, Frank J. Kalas, Simeon H. Luhrsen.
1955	Carmelo Zanghi, Frank J. Kalas, Simeon H. Luhrsen.
1956	Carmelo Zanghi, Frank J. Kalas, Simeon H. Luhrsen.
1957	Carmelo Zanghi, Frank J. Kalas, Simeon H. Luhrsen.
1958	Carmelo Zanghi, Frank J. Kalas, Simeon H. Luhrsen.
1959	Carmelo Zanghi, Frank J. Kalas, Simeon H. Luhrsen.
1960	Carmelo Zanghi, Frank J. Kalas, Simeon H. Luhrsen.
1961	Carmelo Zanghi, Frank J. Kalas, Simeon H. Luhrsen.

1962	Frank P. Merrill, Loyde D. Barstow, Simeon H. Luhrsen.
1963	Frank P. Merrill, Loyde D. Barstow, Simeon H. Luhrsen.
1964	Carmelo J. Zanghi, Frank J. Kalas, John Burokas.
1965	Carmelo J. Zanghi, Frank J. Kalas, John Burokas.
1966	Carmelo J. Zanghi, Frank J. Kalas, Stuart Danforth.
1967	Carmelo J. Zanghi, Frank J. Kalas, Stuart Danforth.
1968	Ernest E. Vlk, Charles J. Luce, Eugene I. Wanat.
1969	Ernest E. Vlk, Charles J. Luce, Albert Morgansen.
1970	Chester Thifault, L. Robert Dumont, Charles Ramondo.

TOLLAND STATISTICS

YEAR	ASSESSMENT	TAX RATE	TOWN DEBT.
1747	$ 24,929		
1890	309,687	12.5 mills	$ 1,124.36
1900	380,537	15.0	6,103.43
1910	345,809	20.0	13,254.95
1920	596,555	20.0	32,014.26
1930	971,665	25.0	22,000.00
1940	1,028,932	20.5	40,000.00
1950	3,205,973	20.0	7,439.31
1960	6,509,207	33.0	372,000.00
1970	27,977,095	70.0	4,186,900.00

Tolland Historical Events

The steeple built by the town of Tolland in 1792, was just one hundred feet high, and was the first or nearly the first ever built in the County. It, of course, attracted great attention, and was scrutinized by people from other towns. One Oliver Arnold, happening in Tolland and knowing somewhat of the difficulties respecting the building of the steeple, stood gazing upon it, when a sort of inspiration came upon him, and he gave vent to his reflections in the following doggerel:

> "Poor Tolland; grand people!
> Old meeting house, and new steeple!"

This doggerel distich has more meaning than at first sight is apparent. It not only exhibits the envious feelings of the speaker toward the people of Tolland, but contains a sarcastic criticism upon their conduct. The term "poor Tolland" was intended to describe the pecuniary condition of the town, as exhibited in its barren hills and broken land. The term "grand people", was used to express the contempt which the speaker felt for the distinguishing characteristics of the town as the county metropolis. The people had just built a court house, jail, and a tall steeple. The other line is a biting criticism on the taste and judgment of the people in having an old building to meet in with a new steeple for ornament.

Another incident will illustrate this feeling more fully. It was formerly the practice of the profession to attend the Superior Court on its circuit, and remain until the court adjourned. Many leading members of the bar, in Windham and New London counties, were in the habit of attending the courts in Tolland, and were often engaged in the more important trials. On one occasion, after a session of some interest a gentleman from Norwich took occasion publicly to congratulate the people of Tolland on their recent improvements, and the brilliant prospects before them, and continuing his remarks with more of irony than truth, said he entertained no doubt Tolland would yet be a port of entry, and vessels would be seen unloading their cargoes upon the banks of the Skungamaug. A resident of Tolland, standing by, and not much relishing the sarcasm of the speaker, interrupted him by saying that the event of which he was speaking was, in his judgment, much nearer at hand than he, the speaker, anticipated; for, said he, the small craft from the city of Norwich have already found their way amongst us, and their larger vessels will doubtless follow in their wake.

SECRET SOCIETIES

Uriel Lodge, No. 24, A. F. and A. M., was instituted in Tolland in 1793. A sermon was given in the Congregational Church by Rev. Nathan Williams and a banquet held at "Shepard's Hotel", now the Hick's Homestead. The Lodge room occupied the entire front of the second story of the house now owned by Mr. Glenn Pfistner at the south end of Tolland Street. That Lodge is now in Merrow, Conn.

Nathan Hale Lodge, I.O.O.F., 1830 and 1840. It met in the rear room of the Court House, but is now out of existence.

A Lodge of Good Templars, instituted between 1860 and 1870 met in the basement of the Congregational Church, but is now out of existence.

In 1825 and 1826 the new Grand Council chartered three Councils in Connecticut, and Adoniram - meeting in Tolland - being one of these. Although all of the records of Adoniram Council were destroyed by fire in 1888, we do know that the Council met in Smith's Tavern on the Green in the center of Tolland Street near the old courthouse which now is the Library. In 1839, two of the Councils Chartered by the Grand Council lost their Charters and in 1840 Adoniram Council was compelled to relinquish its right to meet. For this reason the Council was dormant for 28 years, until 1868 when its Charter was restored allowing it to meet in Rockville.

STORMS IN TOLLAND

Tolland County suffered incalculable damage in most of the towns in the great freshet of 1869. It was terrible, overwhelming and general, nothing like it having been remembered by the oldest inhabitants. The waters poured with resistless force, sweeping down bridges and carrying off all movable property left along their banks. Railroad embankments were swept away, buildings near river banks were flooded and a general wholesale destruction of property caused. In the town of Tolland the highways suffered greatly. Paulk Hill, about a mile west of the village, became simply a succession of gullies from three to ten feet deep for more than a quarter of a mile. Charles Meacham's saw mill dam was swept away.

During the Hurricane of 1938, Connecticut suffered millions of dollars of damage. The eye of the hurricane passed directly over Connecticut and the wind first blew with terrific force from the east and then quieted down until the eye passed, when it blew with terrific force again from the west. Damage to houses on the seashore was very extensive and throughout Connecticut nearly half of the trees were blown down or suffered severe damage. A very similar hurricane passed through Connecticut in 1815.

In 1955, hurricane Donna dumped nine inches of rain on Connecticut within a space of 14 hours. As a result, most of the bridges were washed out and the damage to the roads was very extensive. Towns like Winsted, Putnam and Waterbury had torrential rivers flowing through their main streets, causing untold damage.

SLAVERY IN TOLLAND

Slavery was not abolished in Connecticut until 1848, although the importation of slaves into Connecticut was forbidden in 1771, while an Act declaring children of slaves thereafter born in Connecticut should become free on attaining the age of twenty-five years, was passed in 1784. There were a few family slaves in this town for a great many years. They had a separate place assigned to them in the Meeting House, when attending church.

Connecticut tolerated and protected slavery by its laws, and our Puritan fathers saw nothing wrong in slaveholding, nor even in the slave-trade itself, inconsistent with the Christian character.

It may here be stated that during the existence of slavery in Connecticut, several families in Tolland were in possession of the species of property, and that on the abolition of slavery by law, several slaves in Tolland gained their freedom.

One of the prominent slaveholders of Tolland was Mr. Zebulon West, who held one of the sable sons of Africa as property. The evidence for this assertion is found in the town's book of records of births, marriages and deaths, from which the following is copied: "Zebulon West's negroman Bristo, was married to Betty, Mulatto woman on the 21st day of September, A.D. 1757." This record is in the handwriting of Mr. West, and doubtless was made by him when Town-clerk. The name of this man was Bristo Harris, who lived until April 1, 1802.

BEARS IN TOLLAND

John Abbott, of Andover, Essex County, Mass., removed to Tolland in the year 1720, and purchased the place now owned by Mr. Steero on Grant's Hill, where he lived sixty years. It is said he never failed to attend meeting on a single Sabbath until the year of his death, and he usually went on foot. As he was going to meeting one Sunday, he discovered a bear on a Chestnut tree, by the side of the road, opposite the house then occupied by Capt. H. Cogswell, and called out "a bear! a bear! fetch a gun," in a voice that echoed through the forests and was distinctly heard by persons on their way to meeting, a mile north. A gun was brought and the bear was despatched. John Abbott lived until November 25, 1789.

CELEBRATIONS OF THE PAST IN TOLLAND

On the fourth of July, 1876, Tolland County celebrated on the Green of Tolland, the hundredth anniversary of the Nation's birth. At ten o'clock there was a parade and a grand procession under the marshalship of George M. Paulk of Stafford Springs and gaily decorated teams from Mansfield, Somers, Willington, Stafford and West Stafford. Many of those in the procession wore the costumes of a hundred years ago and the Somers delegation brought with them on wheels a representation of the Mayflower, on board which the pilgrims were still to be seen. At 10:30 the assemblage gathered in front of the Tolland National Bank at a grandstand which had been there erected and provided with a goddess of liberty, young ladies as States, and other paraphernalia of the glorious fourth.

After a prayer by the Reverend and Venerable Abram Marsh of Tolland, there were speeches by many of the prominent men of Tolland County.

The celebration of Independence Day on July 4, 1904 had a special feature called The Parade of Ancients and Horribles. The program was as follows:

> Ringing of Bells at daybreak.
> Parade of Ancients & Horribles at 10 o'clock.
> Athletic games and races.
> Ballgame about 3 o'clock.
> Fireworks at night.

Dinner was served in the Congregational Church parlors for 15 cents.

In July 1923, several anniversaries were celebrated; Town of Tolland 208th, Congregational Church, 200th, Methodist Church, 130th. On Saturday afternoon a Pageant entitled "Tolland Answers America's Call", written in three parts by Mrs. Charles H. Daniels, was presented. The story of the Pageant was told in three episodes, emphasizing Education, Industry and Religion. A great many Townspeople took part and many of the cast are active Tolland citizens today. The Rockville City Band favored throughout the afternoon with selections in keeping with the Pageant and was enjoyed by all. In the evening there was a concert and speeches by former clergymen and laymen. Among these was the Honorable Edward Fuller whose history brought up to that date several parts of the History of Tolland which was so ably collected by Judge Waldo in 1861.

On Sunday the exercises were of a religious nature. Special addresses were held in the Churches. Two addresses were given to the children by Mrs. Charles Daniels about the children of olden times in the Congregational Church and by Mrs. Ernest Hall about the children of the Methodist Church in olden times.

From June 27th to July 3, 1965, Tolland spent a full week in celebrating the 250th anniversary of the founding of Tolland. The celebration started with Commemorative Services in the churches and the Official Opening Ceremonies were held at the Hicks Memorial School grounds at 2:00 P.M. Numerous dignitaries participated including Governor John Dempsey, Senator Abraham Ribicoff, Former Ambassador John Lodge, and Congressman William St. Onge. Master of Ceremonies was Furlonge Flynn.

Each day had its program of contests, parades, athletic events, exhibitions, dances, displays and various shows. The week's celebration ended on Saturday, July 3rd with a large parade and the Anniversary Ball at 9:00 P.M.

The celebration was a huge success and much credit is deserved by the General Committee, who organized the whole affair. The General Committee, was composed of Frank J. Kalas, chairman; Mrs. Walter Anderson, secretary; Donald F. Morganson, treasurer. Their assistants were; Mrs. Donald Duncan, Mrs. Frank Kalas, Mrs. Theodore Palmer, John Burokas, Jerry N. Rojo, and Carmelo J. Zanghi.

Way back in 1824, a large celebration was planned, when Lafayette visited the United States and he passed through this town coming from Boston to Hartford. Expecting to see him, the militia was called out, which consisted of two companies with the addition of two heavy cannons. He was expected to make his appearance in the latter part of the day, but for some reason did not arrive until the next morning. From sunrise until past twelve in the night the guns kept up their continual roaring, for his presence was expected every moment. Runners on horses would often tell the troops he was near by until late in the night the story could be believed no longer. The militia remained at their posts past midnight, then disbanded and lost the pleasure of giving our nation's friend a grand salute. In the early morning he arrived, stopping long enough at E. Smith's tavern to give the people an opportunity to see him, then going on to the King's Stage House in Vernon, there stopping some little time. At that place he was met with kind remembrances and good wishes by many old soldiers who had fought with him in the revolution. One of the veterans was Solomon Eaton of Tolland, and he was well remembered by General Lafayette. After a short interview, hands were shaken. Mr. Eaton said: "I wish you health and a happy journey through this land of liberty and independence." In the old building in Vernon, known as King's Tavern, was a room in which General Lafayette slept. The room, which was papered and frescoed in anticipation of his arrival, remained intact until the building was recently torn down.

THE DANIEL BENTON HOMESTEAD

The house on Metcalf Road, known as the Bowering House, is actually the Daniel Benton homestead, the historical ancestral home of former U. S. Senator William Benton. The Benton homestead played an important part in local and national history. It is the oldest house in Tolland, lived in by Daniel Benton when British prisoners were captured in large numbers during the Revolutionary War. Daniel Benton housed 24 Hessian officers in the cellar. Huge rafters are carved with scrolls, now undecipherable, apparently done by the Hessians to while away months of confinement.

A grandson, Elisha Benton, in the first years of the Revolution was captured by the British in 1776 and held prisoner until a change was effected. When he returned home he contacted smallpox which proved fatal. The girl to whom he was engaged came to nurse him through his illness, but he died and his body was taken out through the window and buried in the front yard. Records show that the girl, broken hearted, died too and her body was buried "at a discreet distance" from her lover's. Incidentally the soldier's grave stone monument was removed through efforts of the DAR and relocated with honors in a nearby cemetery. A tiny headstone marks the girl's grave.

Miss Bowering came by the house in a rather unusual way. The auctioneer of household effects when the house was vacated by the Chapins, who were the last in the line of Bentons, told her that the house would be on the market. Miss Bowering, known for her "Mixing Bowl" programs over WTIC and later on WASN at Allentown, Pa., had asked him to be on the lookout for a Colonial home at least 150 years old and with original panelling.

One look convinced her this was her dream house. Some of the fine stone fireplaces had been plastered over and the gorgeous panelling had been painted or covered with wallpaper. But the floors were sound and so were walls and roof. There are 10 rooms in all and the cellar which once served to hold the captured Hessians has a flagstone floor and is cool as any air-conditioned room in a modern house.

Miss Bowering said she had "restored" but not "remodeled" the ancient house whose huge timbered beamed ceilings and delightful panelled walls bespeak early traditions. It has the original panelling and floors and Indian arrowhead hinges on the doors. The living room was at one time two rooms, one was used as a birth and death room. It now serves as a library.

Miss Bowering had furnished the house completely with antiques. Her bed was of Dutch origin, over 200 years old with massive hand-turned posts. She had hooked rugs, which adorn the living room. She used oil lamps and candles exclusively except in the kitchen where a modern electric stove and refrigerator are about the only concessions to modern living. The original door latches and hinges were all hammered out by a blacksmith. Timbers are held together with wooden pegs.

Prior to Miss Florrie Bishop Bowering's death on Christmas of 1968, the house was purchased by William A. Shocket of Buff Cap Road, Tolland, Conn. and Harrison, New York, together with his brother-in-law Charles Goodstein of Buff Cap Road in Tolland. They felt that the house represents a fine example of the 18th century architecture, which should be preserved for future generations to view and admire. They then considered donating it to the Tolland Historical Society for future restoration and preservation. Title to the property, house and valuable antique contents, was conveyed to the Tolland Historical Society on December 13, 1969.

THE TOLLAND FAIR

A Convention of the citizens of Tolland County was held at the County House, Tolland, August 22nd, 1853, to take into consideration the subject of forming an Agricultural society. The meeting was called to order by Jonathan R. Flynt, then treasurer of the county. Ephraim Dimmick was appointed president of the convention, and Leonard Loomis, secretary.

A resolution to form a society was unanimously passed and the committee who drew up the constitution consisted of John S.

Yeomans, Rufus B. Chamberlain, Justin Tilden, Marcus Woodward and Origin Dimock. There were fourteen appointed as chairmen of the awarding committees, whereas there are thirty-six to act at the coming Fair. A. C. Roberts was the first town committee from Vernon. It was voted to hold the first fair October 18th, 1853, which was done at Tolland Street. The following is the first premium list: Farms, $25; produce, $35; reclaimed lands, $25; domestic manufactures, $30; horses and colts, $20; plowing, $10; bulls, cows and heifers, $25; working oxen, $20; steers and fat cattle, $25; sheep and swine, $25; blood stock, $20; poultry, $5; arts and fine arts, $30; horticulture, $15; Total, $330. One week after the first Convention the committee reported the Constitution. The objects of the Society were declared to be the promotion and improvements of agriculture, manufactures and rural economy. It was voted that members and their families be admitted to the Fair, free.

The following are the officers elected for the first year: President, Ephraim Hyde, of Stafford; vice-presidents, Rufus B. Chamberlain, of Coventry, and John S. Yeomans, of Columbia; Secretary, William Sumner, of Tolland; Treasurer, Jonathan R. Flynt, of Tolland; Auditor, Marcus Woodward, of Somers.

The Fair the following year was again held at Tolland Street, and the amount paid for premiums was $412. There was a cattle show on the first day and an exhibition of horses and colts and a plowing match on the second day. Twelve and one-half cents was the price of admission to the exhibits. At this Fair the Vernon town team took first premium and received an unanimous vote of thanks for donating said premium to the society.

At the annual meeting following the Fair, the subject of trotting horses was discussed, and there was trotting the following year. The trotting was held on Tolland Street, up one side of the broad street and down the other. This was free and the admission was charged to the exhibits displayed in the Congregational Church. At this Fair, an address was delivered by one of the members, and this custom was carried out for several years. The address was delivered by Hon. Loren P. Waldo. In 1856, the secretary was granted a salary of $50 per annum and this year each member was entitled to a ticket, admitting five members of his family. Pasturage was given free for neat cattle, driven more than ten miles to the exhibition.

It was in April of 1858, that a proposal was received from the

Tolland County Association for the improvement of the breed and training horses that they would give the agricultural society the free use of their grounds in the western part of Tolland and the eastern part of Vernon, embracing eighteen acres and a graded half mile track, provided that the Agricultural society would enclose it with a good board fence. This was done and thereafter the Fair was held in Vernon and later was known as the Rockville Fair.

ENTERTAINMENT AND RECREATION

Entertainment was probably not a part of the early life. House raisings were held, quilting bees and similar work gatherings formed the principal group activities. As the years passed, the life became less severe, more time was allotted to play. Steamships sailed about on Snipsic Lake. Picnics were held at West's Landing. Music parties became the rule. Dances were for many years held regularly in the Town Hall and a dance hall was located in Buff Cap. Dances were also held in private homes, barns and even out-of-doors. In the autumn, parties of hunters would come to Tolland from New York. Bird hunting was the principal sport. Stylish horses were in vogue. The Tolland Agricultural Society conducted its Fairs on the Green. The distance around the Green was said to be a half-mile track.

In the 1800's a Lyceum was held in the church. This was a popular discussion group of the time. Also we hear of singing schools, and other singing groups. After the Second World War there was much interest in community recreation. Dances were held, plays and entertainments given and acreage obtained from the Bartlett family for a Community Center on Cider Mill Road. Many groups participated by furnishing labor and money. Tennis courts and softball fields were planned. The building was available to all, and used for business and good times by many social groups.

Across from the Community Center, Miss Lily Crandall had built a very popular beach where residents and others find recreation. Here many of the children of the town have learned to swim under the swimming program sponsored by the Tolland Parent Teacher Association. The Crandall pond and surrounding land was bought by the Town in 1967 and was further developed by the addition of a ball field into a new recreational center.

The Tolland Board of Recreation was established in March 1964, at the recommendation of a Recreation Study Committee which was appointed by the first Selectman, Carmelo Zanghi, in November 1963. The Board is made up of two women, four men and a representative of the Board of Education. Members are appointed by the Board of Selectmen for a three year term.

The Board of Recreation, with William A. Holley, Jr., Chairman; Mrs. Edward Jendrucek, Secretary; and Conrad L. Dwire, Treasurer; has been successful in establishing tennis facilities and instruction at Meadowbrook School, sponsoring the Tolland Boys' Basketball League, the Men's Softball League, and Adult Square Dance Instruction. It has also arranged a Teen Age Christmas Dance and a Block Dance Party for Teen Agers during the 250th Anniversary Celebration, a Track and Field Meet for boys and girls in Grades 4 - 8, and an Easter Egg Hunt for the 3 - 10 age group. During the winter, the Board initiated the construction of an ice skating rink by the Tolland Volunteer Fire Department on the property of St. Matthew's Church.

TOLLAND IN THE EARLY 1800'S

An old Gazateer states that Tolland had the following in the early 1800's:

One Furnace for casting iron; three Grain Mills; two Fulling Mills; three Distilleries; three Tanneries; four Stores; three Church Societies; one Social Library; thirteen Schools; two Clergymen; three Attorneys and four Physicians.

The Grand List was $37,335.

In 1810 Hartford had a population of 6,003, and Tolland had a population of 1,610, more than one-quarter the size of Hartford. Vernon had a population of only 827, being but a trifle more than half the size of Tolland.

In 1810 Hartford had 850 dwellings and Tolland had 300. In 1810 Hartford had 1,000 electors and Tolland had 300.

THE TOLLAND WATER SYSTEM

The Water system was organized in 1879, by a group of Citizens who contributed $25.00 per share for 100 shares of stock amounting to $2,500.00. John B. Fuller, being the representative that year introduced the act of incorporation and secured its passage, when the Charter was granted by the legislature in 1879. The system was installed immediately thereafter and the residents of Tolland Street have had water from the aqueduct on Burbank Road since that time.

The hydrants were not installed until the Fall of 1895 a few months after the Johnson building and the County House were burned. The County House was the wooden structure attached to the stone jail. The hydrants and the placing of them cost $550 of which Edward Fuller raised $400 by subscription from property owners in Tolland Street, paying the other $150 himself. He planned and engineered the installation. The hydrants demonstrated their usefulness as soon as they were installed, in saving the street from annihilation by confining the Tolland House fire to the one building which could not possibly have been done had not the hydrants been there. The old Post Office building and the Paul Meyer residence were so scorched by the fire that both had to be scraped before painting again. The hydrants were given to the Tolland Aqueduct Company with the stipulation being that they should be kept available and in good condition for fire purposes forever without charge for them or for the water used from them.

THE TOLLAND IMPROVEMENT SOCIETY

The Village Improvement Society was inaugerated sometime between 1870-80 and had an active existence for about 10 years. The actual date of its demise is probably not known, unless perhaps it is not really dead, but is in a comatose condition, and capable of being vitalized again into life and activity by injecting into it a sufficient amount of enthusiasm which is at the present time evidenced by the attempt being made to establish the Tolland Street area as an Historical District.

Lucius Fuller, the father of Edward Fuller, was the president of the Village Improvement Society. Some of the work accomplished by the Society was the grading of the steep bank in the street above the former Methodist Church, now the Grange Hall and the laying out of a little three cornered park at the north end of the street where Dunn Hill Road joins the Old Stafford Road. By vote of the Town, the Society took over the care of the roads of School District #1, which meant roughly speaking, all of the roads within a radius of one mile from Tolland Street and the street itself. The Town appropriated a certain sum each year for a certain number of years, the amount being each year the sum that the Town would have expected to spend on them had the Selectmen repaired them. The idea of the Society was to improve the roads by spending more money on them than the Town allowed, the extra money coming from the members. After the contract ran out and the roads reverted back to Town care, the brush was still kept mowed on the sides of the road for many years, being paid for wholly by William Sumner.

The Village Improvement Society having greatly improved the north end of Tolland Street did not possess quite enough vitality and enthusiasm to improve the south end of the street. At a later time Edward Fuller and William Sumner tackled having that done, they commenced around the Congregational Church, relaying the walks and steps, and returfing the lawn around the Church and as far north as the Courthouse, south to the Harvey Clough house. The gift of two horse-blocks installed near the front of the church was done at this time. They also cleaned out the stones from the center of the Green under the grass, none of them showing but lying so close to the turf that in times of drouth the grasses above them would turn brown. This was done from the Congregational Church to the Town Hall. They took out from under the turf fifty large two horse wagon loads of stone. These were dumped in a big hole on the west side of the street at the top of Cider Mill Road. Dirt was drawn in to cover them and the area was seeded to make a much nicer approach to the street from the south.

THE TOLLAND POUND

Each animal owner had a registered mark with which each animal was marked and every animal with that mark on it bore positive proof that it belonged to him.

There was a Hog-hayward who looked after stray animals and a Pound to imprison them till the fines were paid, and a Pound keeper to keep the Pound secure. The Pound is now just below the south end of the street, between it and Crandall's Pond.

November, 1853. Laws enacted to control the Pound.

Voted and enacted by the inhabitants of the Town of Tolland in lawful Town Meeting, warned for that purpose convened that no horse, neat cattle, swine or sheep shall by their owners be suffered to go at large on any of the highways, commons or uninclosed lands in said Tolland; and it shall be lawful for every freeholder and every person who rents a freehold, and it shall be the duty of the haywards of said Town to take up and impound any such creatures suffered to go at large as aforesaid in any of the Town pounds in said town; and the fee to be paid by the owner or owners of such horses, neat cattle, swine and sheep taken up and impounded as aforesaid shall be 12 cents for each or either of the horses, neat cattle and swine and 2 cents for each sheep whereof one half shall belong to the impounder and one-half to the keeper of the key and said creatures shall remain in the custody of the pound keeper till said fees are paid.

And be it further enacted, that if any horses, neat cattle, swine or sheep shall by their owners be suffered to go at large on any of the highways, commons or unenclosed lands in said Tolland on the Sabbath or Lords day, such owner or owners shall forfeit and pay to him who shall prosecute to effect a fine of 50 cents for each horse, neat cattle or swine so suffered to go at large and a fine of 12 cents for each sheep so suffered to go at large on the Sabbath or Lords day.

And be it further enacted that if any person or persons shall rescue any of said creatures taken up as aforesaid out of the hands of any person or persons or shall resist the driving or going to pound with them or shall break the pound, or by any improper means liberate such creatures from the pound when impounded as aforesaid the person or persons so offending shall for such rescue or resistance forfeit and pay a fine of Two Dollars and fifty cents and for such pound breach the sum of Three Dollars to him who shall prosecute to effect and also shall pay all damages to the person or persons wronged by such rescue resistance or pound breach.

TOLLAND DESERTED

Mention has been made of the westward movement of population after the War of the Revolution and after the War Between the States. After World War I Tolland Street was almost deserted in winter; their owners used these houses as summer homes. Mrs. Helen Needham wrote this poem in the 1930's.

Poor, forlorn houses in a row
Dreaming of days you used to know,
When there was life within your walls
And laughter echoed through your halls.
There is no path now to your door,
And friendly lights shine out no more.
Just piles of white unbroken snow
And sinister shadows crouching low.
The moaning winds their short breaths take
Like hired mourners at a wake.
Your smokeless chimneys testify
To everyone who passes by
No life is there, your hearths are cold,
Just empty houses, growing old.
It's hard, indeed, for me to know
Why those who love you treat you so.

Biographical Sketches
Tolland's Distinguished Citizens

SOLOMON WILLS, Captain of the volunteers from Tolland in 1775, was descended from Windsor Ancestry. In the latter part of the war of 1775, he was a subaltern, and was the lieutenant commanding in the expedition to Havana in 1762. He was also a Colonel of State troops temporary levies, etc., in the Revolution. He was a justice of the peace twelve years, and, on the organization of Tolland county, was appointed one of the judges of the county court. He was elected to the Assembly twenty-two times, semi-annually. The absence, or expected absence, of Col. Wills and Col. Chapman in the army, seems to have prevented their election several times each. Col. Solomon Wills died in 1807.

CAPT. SAMUEL CHAPMAN, born 1695, was a farmer in Windsor and after 1726, at Tolland, Conn., was Capt. of the 9th Conn. Co., at the Siege of Louisburg, 1745; was subsequently killed in the French War. In Tolland, he was a large landholder and justice of the peace. His home was about half a mile east of that of Sidney Stanley.

His son, Col. Samuel Chapman, born 1729, resided in the homestead until his death. He was Capt. of Militia in 1785; and before and during the Revolutionary War was a leader in the patriotic town of Tolland; was Col. of the 22nd Conn. Militia and as such made several campaigns; was at New York in 1776, with his entire regiment. On the evacuation of that city, his conduct was deemed peculiarly honorable by those who witnessed it. He was the wealthiest man in Tolland and the leading business man. He owned several slaves; was elected to the General Assembly at 45 annual elections, and is recorded as present at 15 special sessions; was a justice of the peace for 26 years, continuing in office until about 77 years of age; was retained command of his regiment until about 70, the business on field days being performed by an adjutant. He was a remarkable man, in hardihood as if made of iron. In the army he not only endured, but seemed to thrive upon food which the soldier ordinarily loathed. In the coldest weather he never used gloves or mittens, and walked outdoors barefoot in March, when above 80 years old. A neighbor who for 28 years resided near him never heard him laugh, and he seldom smiled.

JOSEPH HATCH. The name of Hatch is associated intimately with the settlement of the town. Joseph Hatch was one of the grantees in the first deed from the Windsor committee, and is one of the petitioners respecting the Coventry Lands in 1718. He probably lived in Windsor before 1713, but there is reason to believe he removed to Tolland in that year, and was one of the first two, if not the very first permanent settler in the town of Tolland. This Joseph Hatch was two years a selectman, and was the first tavern keeper in Tolland, being chosen a tavern keeper at a town meeting January 6th, 1718. He was the first military officer in Tolland, having been commissioned a lieutenant in October, 1722, and captain in May, 1725. He was the owner ot the land in the south part of Tolland, on Goose Lane, which always has been in the possession of the family for many years.

In the records of the marriages, birth and deaths in the town, are recorded several births in Tolland, prior to May, 1715. The earliest of them is that of Amy Hatch, a daughter of Joseph Hatch, who was born October 10, 1713. He also had a son, Joseph Hatch, and as tradition says, the first male child born in Tolland on September 12, 1715.

ZEBULON WEST probably came into town with his father, Dea. Francis West, about the year 1720. He was admitted an inhabitant, that is, a voter, September 21, 1725. He was first elected to a public office in the year 1736, and from that time to the day of his death, thirty-four years afterwards, he was always in the possession of some place of public trust; and no man could be found who served in more capacities, or rendered more acceptable service. He was for seventeen years one of the selectmen of the town; he was town-clerk thirty-four years, and a justice of the peace twenty-six. He was the first person ever chosen to represent the town in the General Assembly, and represented the town at forty-three regular sessions; being first chosen in September, 1748, and with one exception was re-elected at every session thereafter until his decease. He was Speaker of the House of Representatives several sessions. He was Judge of Probate for the district of Stafford, from its organization, in May, 1759, to his death. He was also one of the judges of Hartford County Court several years. All these offices, except those of selectman and speaker, and with the addition of member of the council or upper house, to which he had just been elected, he held at the time of his decease.

Mr. West was rather above medium size, was exceedingly popular with the masses, yet it is said he never associated with them nor was familiar in his carriage towards them. His personal appearance was imposing, and with his deportment, commanded the most profound respect. He was described as very sedate, inclined to talk but little, but was remarkable for his good temper.

In the petty prosecutions for violation of the moral law, so frequent in those times, Mr. West carefully distinguished between youthful thoughtlessness and confirmed depravity; and whenever such prosecutions arose from the disposition to annoy or revenge, he took care, as far as possible, to avoid making the law instrumental to gratify private malice under the mask of public virtue. It used to be said that "Zebulon West never did but one wrong thing," - and that was certainly a very unfortunate one for the harmony of the town. It was the procuring by his superior influence the location of the meeting-house contrary to the just and strenuous wishes of nearly, if not quite a majority of the inhabitants of the town, at a place south of the geographical center. But notwithstanding this momentary resentment, he always exercised an almost unbounded influence in the management of town affairs, and was, through an entire generation, the principal man in Tolland. He educated three sons at Yale College; Stephen, the eldest, was a clergyman, settled in the ministry at Stockbridge, Mass., and became one of the most distinguished theological writers in New England. Nathaniel, the second son, did not study a profession after graduating, but settled in Tolland as a farmer, was elected town-clerk after the death of his father, six years, then emigrated to Vermont. Jeremiah, the youngest son, settled as a physician in Tolland. He was a surgeon in the Revolutionary Army, was a representative in the General Assembly ten sessions. He was also a member of the convention in 1788, and voted for the adoption of the federal constitution, and he was justice of the quorum or Judge of Tolland County Court fourteen years.

Zebulon West lived upon the farm lately owned by Bilarky Snow, in the south part of Tolland on Goose Lane, and died on the 4th day of December, 1770, aged 65.

ELISHA STEARNS, the fifth presiding judge of the county court, was a son of Doctor John Stearns, and a descendant of John Stearns, one of the first settlers of the town of Tolland. Doctor Stearns married a Miss Wells of Tolland, and shortly afterward moved to Wilbraham, Mass., where his son Elisha was born on July 12th, 1776.

Elisha Stearns was favored with the advantages of an early education common to that day, and exhibiting uncommon aptness to learn. His elder brother (being a graduate himself) strongly insisted that Elisha should receive a collegiate education. He was accordingly placed under the care of Reverend Moses C. Welch, of North Mansfield, with whom he pursued his studies, preparatory to entering college. He entered Yale College at the age of sixteen years, and graduated, with credit to himself, in the year 1796. In college he was more particularly distinguished for his attainments in the languages and readiness and skill in compositions. He had the reputation of being industrious and moral, and his diligence and faithfulness secured for him general respect.

Mr. Stearns was admitted to the bar in the county of Tolland, in the month of September, 1798, immediately opened an office in the town of Tolland, and was soon in the enjoyment of a lucrative practice. He was never distinguished for his rhetorical powers, and his success before juries was never very marked. But he was a good technical lawyer, well versed in the principles of the science, a safe counsellor, a cautious practitioner, and remarkable for his skill in drawing legal instruments and special pleadings. His legal opinions were highly esteemed by his brethren, and never failed to be properly appreciated by the court. He received the appointment of clerk of the county court at the April adjourned term in 1814, and of the superior court at the September term thereof in the same year. He held the office of clerk of the county court until June, 1821, and that of clerk of the superior court until 1833, when, by an act of the General Assembly, the clerks of the county courts were made ex-officio clerks of the superior court. Mr. Stearns was not clerk of the superior court after 1835.

In May 1838, he was appointed Judge of the county court, which office he held by successive re-appointments for three years. Mr. Stearns was a very intelligent and acceptable judge of the county court. His reputation for integrity and honesty was above reproach, and none were found to doubt his learning or his capacity. Having the confidence of the public, his rulings and decisions were universally well received. He was judge of the court of probate for the district of Tolland four years. He represented the town of Tolland in the general assembly nine sessions, six of which were before the adoption of the present constitution. He represented the Twentieth Senatorial District in the senate of this state. He was very instrumental in procuring the charter of the Tolland County Bank, and as its first president, which office he held a period of nineteen years until October, 1847. He was first appointed a justice of the peace in 1806, and held the commission in all thirty-one years.

Mr. Stearns married Celinda Baker, a descendant of one of the first settlers in Tolland, November 4th, 1800. He had ten children, only five of whom survived their infancy. Mr. Stearns departed this life October 26th, 1850, in the seventy-fifth year of his age.

HON. CALVIN WILLEY was born in East Haddam, Conn., September 11th, 1776. His early advantages for education were very indifferent, being nothing more than the benefits of the common schools as they then existed. He commenced reading law in the office of the late Hon. John Thompson Peters, afterward one of the judges of the supreme court of errors, in June 1795. Mr. Peters was then a resident of Hebron, in Tolland county. Mr. Willey was admitted to the bar in Tolland county, in February 1798, and first opened an office in Chatham, in the county of Middlesex, but in 1800 he removed to Stafford, in Tolland county, where he resided until the year 1808. While in Stafford he was twice chosen a representative to the general assembly and was postmaster in that town from 1806 to 1808, when he removed to Tolland. He was judge of probate for the district of Stafford, then including the town of Tolland, from 1818 to 1825 - seven years; was six times elected a representative to the general assembly from Tolland, and twice to the State senate, upon a general ticket, before the state was districted for the choice of senators. He was a candidate for the office of representative in Congress in the year 1821, but was defeated by his own party because he had, in 1820, suffered his name to remain on a union ticket for state senators, consisting of an equal number of federalists and democrats. Mr. Willey was identified with the democratic party. In 1824, his friends brought him forward for the United States senate, when the same objection was urged against him. There had always been some rivalry and a little ill feeling between Mr. Willey and some of the prominent politicians in the south part of the county; and hence the strong opposition to Mr. Willey whenever he was a candidate for an office that called for their suffrages. He was defeated as representative to Congress by Hon. Daniel Burrows, a resident of Hebron.

In 1825, Mr. Willey was elected senator of the United States for six years. Mr. Willey entered upon and discharged the duties of the appointment, and retired from public life at the close of his term, in 1831, and at the age of fifty-five years.

Mr. Willey was a man of more than ordinary intellect, and his attainments as a lawyer were very fair. At one time he stood at the head of the bar in Tolland county. He was devotedly attached to his profession, entertained strong views of the ennobling and elevating effect its practice has upon the mind of the honest practitioner, and maintained that in its benefits to the community it stood second to none. He was very successful before a jury.

Mr. Willey was twice married. His first wife was Sally Brainard. They were married October 22nd, 1798. She died on February 25th, 1827, age 44. He married Nabby Brainard, a sister of his first wife, April 25th, 1827. Mr. Willey was postmaster in Tolland from 1812 to 1820. He moved to Stafford in 1854, and died on August 23rd, 1858, aged 82.

LOREN PINCKNEY WALDO. About the year 1796, Ebenezer Waldo, a man of strong mind and scholarly tastes, relinquished his purpose of entering the Christian ministry and settled in his native county in the eastern part of the State of Connecticut, in the school district embracing a portion of the town of Canterbury, and devoted himself to the work of teaching. Loren Pinckney, the secone son of this Ebenezer Waldo, and of Cynthia Parish, his wife, was born at Canterbury, February 2nd, 1802. Of French descent in his paternal line and as his name betokens, of Waldensian blood, he inherited the indomitable energy and resolution, the ardent love of civic and religious freedom, and the inflexible honesty of purpose which ever characterized his career. The example and counsel of a pious father and the judicious training of a noble minded and godly mother conspired to make him thus rich by inheritance, richer still in the faithful development of it. His education, so far as it was obtained from schools, was completed when he was fourteen years of age. From that time until he was twenty-one he taught school in winter and the remainder of the year labored on the farm to aid in the support of the family. Meanwhile he employed every leisure hour in study, and in this way mastered the higher branches of mathematics and acquired a good knowledge of the Latin language.

When twenty-one years of age, the farm having been sold, he entered upon the study of law with his uncle in the town of Tolland, at the same time earning his living until his admission to the bar in 1825, at the age of twenty-three. He married in Tolland on the 22nd of November, of the same year, Frances Elizabeth, daughter of William Eldridge, Esq., and soon after removed to Somers where his professional career was begun. The history of his brave struggles for an education and his sterling integrity recommended him to public confidence, and brought him a good degree of prosperity in business. In 1830 he returned to Tolland where he resided until his removal to Hartford in 1863. He was postmaster in Somers for two years and also one of the superintendents of public schools. He was a member of the board of visitors of Common schools in Tolland, of the board of commissioners of common schools of Connecticut, and chairman of the committee of education in the House of Representatives. He reported the authorizing the holding of normal schools in Connecticut. After returning to Tolland he was elected to represent that town in the general assembly of Connecticut in 1832-33-34-39-47-48, and in 1833 was clerk of the House of Representatives. Judge Waldo was attorney for the state for Tolland county from 1837 to 1849 and judge of probate for the district of Tolland in the years 1842 and 1843. In 1847, he was appointed one of a committee to revise the statutes of the state and in 1864 was again chosen to make the revision of 1866. In 1849 Judge Waldo was elected to represent his district in the 31st Congress of the United States and was chairman of the committee on revolutionary pensions. At the expiration of his term he was appointed to serve as ministration of President Pierce, he was appointed to serve as commissioner of the school fund of Connecticut. During the administration of President Pierce he was appointed commissioner of pensions at Washington, in which office he continued until elected Judge of the Supreme Court of the state for a period of eight years. In 1863 he removed to Hartford and engaged actively in the practice of his profession.

Throughout his entire life, Judge Waldo was politically united with the democratic party and gave the candidates his generous support. At an early age he stood at the head of the bar of his county and among the first lawyers of the state. Though not a brilliant advocate, he was successful by virtue of qualities of mind and character more solid than showy. His clear comprehension of the points at issue, his lucid and simple method of presenting his case and his manifest simplicity and honesty of character were elements of large success. In religion, Judge Waldo found a congenial atmosphere in the Unitarian fold, though most active in his support of the Congregational church, both in Tolland and in Hartford, where he was a devout worshipper and greatly beloved. The death of Judge Waldo occurred September 8th, 1881.

HON. LUCIUS SEYMOUR FULLER, son of Seymour Fuller, was born March 27, 1812, in Hampton, Connecticut, whence when four years old he removed with his parents to Tolland. There he received an excellent education in the common schools, which was supplemented by attendance at the Academy at Monson, Mass., after which until the spring of 1846, he taught school during the winters and worked on the home farm during the summer seasons. In 1846, he became landlord of the County House, in Tolland, which he conducted for two years, and then for three years conducted the stage route from Tolland to North Woodstock, Conn. At the end of that time he purchased a farm in Tolland, and thereafter divided his attention between agricultural pursuits, insurance and his various other public duties, up to the time of his decease, Nov. 14, 1890. In his insurance work, he was agent for various companies, and in June, 1872, was elected President of the Tolland County Mutual Fire Insurance Company, a position which he held up to the time of his death.

In 1869, Mr. Fuller became associated as director with the Tolland County National Bank, of which he was in 1871 elected vice-president, and president in 1878, a position which he filled with characteristic ability and fidelity. He was also a director and vice-president of the Savings Bank of Tolland. Mr. Fuller was also prominently identified with every public enterprise of his town. He was a Republican in politics, a chosen counselor and advisor, and for many years one of the most influential representatives of that party, representing his county as delegate to the Republican National Convention held at Philadelphia in 1872, while for over twenty years he was a member of the Republican State Central Committee. In addition to all these, he held many of the town offices with credit to himself and to the satisfaction of his fellow citizens. At one time he served as judge of probate of his district, was deputy sheriff of the county, and was offered the position of high sheriff, but declined that honor. In 1854 he represented the town of Tolland in the State Legislature, and during that time served on important committees. In the year 1863, and again in 1864, he served as State Senator from the 20th Senatorial district, serving on several of the leading committees. In 1869 he was appointed by the Senate as one of the first trustees of the Connecticut Hospital for the insane, at Middletown, Conn., and was serving in that capacity at the time of his death.

On July 4, 1838, Mr. Fuller was married to Miss Mary Eliza, daughter of John and Sally (Abbott) Bliss, of Tolland, Conn., and children as follows, all born in Tolland, came of this union, besides four children that died very young; there was John Bliss, 1845-1883; Lucius Henry, 1849; and Edward Eugene, 1853.

Lucius Seymour and Mary Eliza (Bliss) Fuller celebrated their golden wedding in 1888, on which occasion, which was a most enjoyable one, their children and relatives, as well as many friends, gathered about the venerable couple to give expressions of esteem, and many golden tributes testified to the regard and affection in which they were justly held. Mrs. Fuller passed away Sept. 25, 1899, highly esteemed and beloved by all who knew her. She was a devoted and loving wife and mother, and is most missed by those who knew her best. Mr. and Mrs. Fuller were consistent members of the Congregational Church, to the principles of which they were firm adherants. Mrs. Fuller was possessed of considerable poetical talent, which was frequently called into requisition by her friends and neighbors throughout her long life, her last poem being written less than a month previous to her death.

HON. EDWARD EUGENE FULLER, youngest son of Lucius Seymour and Mary Eliza (Bliss) Fuller, was born May 13, 1853, and passed his early boyhood on the home farm in Tolland. He received his education in part at the public school in the neighborhood of his home, in part at Woodstock Academy, afterward taking a course at Bryant & Stratton's Business College, in Philadelphia, from which latter institution he was graduated in 1871. On December 19th, of that year, he entered the office of the Aetna Fire Insurance Company, at Hartford, as a clerk, and remained with that company until January 1, 1882, when he was obliged to resign on account of impaired health, caused by too close application to his duties in the office. In June 1883, having regained his health, and his brother John B. having died, he was appointed the latter's successor as secretary of Tolland County Mutual Fire Insurance Company, which office he has since filled with the highest efficiency. This insurance company is one of the oldest and most conservative of the local insurance companies, having been founded in 1828. Senator Fuller has also been a director in several financial institutions, among which may be mentioned the Tolland County National Bank, in which he was a director for several years, having been elected a corporator in June, 1883, of the Savings Bank of Tolland. A staunch Republican in politics, Senator Fuller is a prominent and active figure in the ranks of the party, and has served his constituents in several offices of trust and responsibility. In 1894, he was elected Senator from the 24th Senatorial district, and during his term served as chairman of the committee on Insurance and the committee on Manual and Roll. In 1900, he was appointed by Gov. George E. Lounsbury, commissioner on Building &

Loan Associations of Connecticut. In town affairs he has been particularly interested, having served his town as auditor and member of the local school board, a part of which time he was acting school visitor and chairman of the board, filling the position for several years, until the pressure of other matters obliged him to resign.

Senator Fuller is a zealous advocate and champion of the principles of fraternal organization, and is a member of several, including the Masonic, in which he has attained to the thirty-second degree. He was a member of Fayette Lodge, No. 69 and served as Worshipful Master, and as Grand Master of Connecticut in 1908. He is also a member of the I.O.O.F., being Past Noble Grand of Rising Star Lodge, No. 49, of Rockville, and having served also as District Deputy of the Order for two years; he has also been Past Master Workman of Rockville Lodge, A.O.U.W.; he was a member of the Tolland Grange, No. 51, P. of H.; is a veteran of the Connecticut National Guard, being a charter member of Co. K. First Regiment; and belongs to the Sons of the American Revolution.

One cannot fail to notice in the foregoing sketches of a remarkably intelligent family, the rare instance of a father and three sons all intrusted with legislative office, each filling his position with credit and honor to himself and to his constituency, the father and two sons having served as Senators. The entire family have, in each generation, earned the respect and esteem of the entire community in which they bore.

Senator Edward E. Fuller never was married, but was one of Tolland's most revered citizens and he led his very active life in this town, where he was buried on August 22, 1932.

These remarks were made by Edward E. Fuller at the Two Hundredth Anniversary of the Congregational Church:

"Grateful indeed as we are for the priceless heritage bequeathed to us by our fathers; happy as we must be for the countless blessings which have come down to us with that heritage; Thankful as we should be for all the splendid if comparatively uneventful history which their lives have written for us; and proud as we well can be of the fine and glorious traditions and high ideals which they have transmitted to us; let us show our appreciation by being willing to make sacrifices for the general good, and by giving of ourselves for the common cause; that through that sacrifice and service we may contribute our mite to that glorious heritage.

Let us here today, and tomorrow and each succeeding day pledge to those high ideals and sacrifice and service, our unswerving loyalty; our regard for law, and for all that stands for the best in out community life, that our Town's good name, its fame and its history shall not suffer at our hands that its lustre shall not become dimmed or tarnished, but that it shall grow steadily, brighter and brighter as we and each succeeding generation pass it on to the one that is to follow."

RATCLIFFE HICKS. - Ratcliffe Hicks, the grandfather of the subject of this biographical sketch, was a celebrated sea captain of Providence, R. I. His father was Charles T. Hicks, a native of Providence, R. I. and for many years a successful dry foods merchant in New York City. He married Maria A., daughter of Judge Elisha Stearns of Tolland county. The children of this marriage are: Ratcliffe, Emma H., wife of H. F. Downing of Springfield, Mass., Richard S. and Minnie H.

The eldest of these sons, Ratcliffe Hicks, was born in Tolland, October 3rd, 1843, and pursued his preparatory studies at the Munson Academy and the Williston Seminary, after which he entered Brown University in 1860, and was graduated from that institution in 1864. Deciding upon the law as a profession he entered the office of Judge Waldo, of Tolland, as a student, and was admitted to the bar in 1866. Mr. Hicks, the same year, began practice with the present United States Senator Platt of Meriden, and continued this business relation for three years, the ten succeeding years having been spent alone. From 1879 to 1881 he pursued his profession in the City of Hartford.

He was married in 1879 to Mrs. Wilbur F. Parker, daughter of Jared H. Canfield, of Meriden, Conn., their only child being a daughter, Elizabeth. Mr. Hicks speedily attained both success and distinction in his profession. His practice was large and caused him to be identified with many of the most important cases in the New England courts, notably the celebrated Sprague suit in Rhode Island, where a fee of ten thousand dollars was received, doubtless the largest on record in that state.

Mr. Hicks in 1881 made the tour of Europe and on his return the following year was made executor of the estate of his father-in-law, lately deceased. Abandoning the law, where a career of brilliant distinction awaited him, he has since devoted his energies to commercial life.

Continuing in business he organized a joint stock company, known as the Canfield Rubber Company, with a capital of ten thousand dollars, which under his judicious management, was a great success. He has made twenty voyages to Europe, chiefly in the interest of his business, and established large foreign connections, with a corresponding demand for the products of his factory.

Mr. Hicks, has on one or more occasions, been diverted from his regular pursuits to enter the arena of politics. He represented his constituents in the Connecticut legislature in 1866, was from 1868 to 1874 attorney for the City of Meriden, and for three years attorney for the county of New Haven.

Mr. Hicks started a movement to repair and restyle the Church in Tolland in 1893. He served on the committee and contributed generously. In November 1894, Mr. Hicks was honored at a political gathering in Tolland. When called upon to speak, he said, "If there is any spot in this wide, wide world that I feel I can, and that I have a right to call my home, it is this little town of Tolland, nestled up here among the rock-ribbed hills of Tolland County". Recalling his family and friends who had passed to final rewards, Mr. Hicks was reminded of these lines:

"Dear Soul, who left us lonely here,
    Bound on their last, long voyage, to whom
We day by day, are drawing near
    When every bark has sailing room.

And now, in bidding you all a very good night, I pray that Heaven will shower upon you, and upon all the homes in goodly Tolland, its sweetest, and its choicest blessings - health, happiness and prosperity."

His legacy to the town included the Ratcliffe Hicks Memorial School, built in 1908. The quality of this building was unsurpassed and it was for many years considered one of Connecticut's finest schools.

Miss Elizabeth Hicks, only child of Ratcliffe and Lizzie Canfield Hicks, maintains the family residence on Tolland Green. She has created here an example of transitional architecture, furnished with family heirlooms, and accented with reminders of her world travels. Miss Hicks has keen interest in the local schools and in education generally. She is Consultant to the Ratcliffe Hicks School of Agriculture at the University of Connecticut, and has established there scholarships in Music and Agriculture, and prizes in Literature.

Miss Elizabeth Hicks has made major contributions of time, knowledge, and finances to Tolland. She was proposed as a candidate for the legislature, but did not wish to enter party politics. She has worked with the school and library for sixty years, and has helped many boards and committees steer a steady course. Unfortunately her aid to the town is such that few of the residents are aware of it, and her own nature forbids revelation. The Hicks Trust Fund provides annually for the Hicks Memorial School. The Junior High School wing and the Meadowbrook School are built on the Minnie Helen Hicks Memorial Property, made possible by Miss Elizabeth Hicks.

FRANK TURNER NEWCOMB was born in Tolland in 1861 and received his education in the district school and in the Brockdale Academy, finishing in the Rockville High School. At the age of seventeen, he began teaching in the 7th and 9th districts, which were combined, where he was employed during the winter term of 1878. Then having opportunity to enter the Tolland County National Bank, he left the schoolroom to become the teller of the Bank. This was in 1878, and in 1884 he was made cashier of the Tolland County National Bank, and treasurer of the same building. Two years later, the Tolland County National Bank suspended business, and since that time Mr. Newcomb has continued to be the treasurer of the Savings Bank of Tolland, which was given by the legislature the privilege of doing a checking business, and is the only one in the State doing business on that basis. Mr. Newcomb has been an official of the bank for twenty-four years, acting first as teller and then as treasurer.

In 1887, Mr. Newcomb purchased the old Elijah Stearns homestead on Tolland Street, and here he made his home. The farm buildings and the family residence were greatly improved, and the acreage increased by purchase, until Mr. Newcomb owned 293 acres, having at his first purchase only thirty acres, but in 1902 he purchased all the real estate in Tolland formerly owned by Charles Underwood. He started a creamery in the Fall of 1898, in connection with his farm, keeping about forty cows and shipping his produce to the Vernon creamery. On his farm was transacted a general farming business of considerable magnitude, and it is said that he raised more corn than any two other men in Tolland; he had the largest herd in this section of the county, having in addition to the cows above mentioned about thirty-five head of other stock. With his family he attended the Congregational Church in Tolland.

Politically, Mr. Newcomb was a Democrat; and devoted to Jeffersonian principles as enunciated by that great leader. In 1884, he was appointed a notary public by Thomas M. Waller, Governor of the State. He was appointed county treasurer in 1887 by a board of Republican commissioners and has been reappointed each time by a like board, with an exception of the year 1895, when the board was Democratic. In 1887, he was appointed town clerk and treasurer to fill an unexpired term, and he was elected to that position continuously for 32 years. He has also acted as school visitor and has been treasurer of the school deposit fund since 1888. He was appointed postmaster of Tolland by President Cleveland, but resigned after three year's term on account of pressure of private business. In 1886 he represented the town in the State Legislature, where he served on the committee on Banking. Mr. Newcomb was chairman of the Democratic town committee since he was twenty-two years of age, or since 1883.

On January 27, 1886, Mr. Newcomb was married to Addie L. Millard, of Mansfield, Conn. They are the parents of the following children: Harry Arthur; Philip Trumbull; Pauline Louise; Lilla Adelaide and Phyllis. Mr. Newcomb was one of the most successful men of Tolland of later years, and he was in every sense self-made. He died in 1924 at the age of 63 years.

OSCAR A. LEONARD was born December 14, 1853 in Stafford, Connecticut, a son of Rufus Jenks Leonard of Ellington. He spent the first eight years of his life in his native town, and at that age was taken by his parents to Tolland, where he attended school, finishing his education, however, at the Rockville School. When he was sixteen years of age he returned to the home farm, and since that time has been engaged in farming. In all, Mr. Leonard owned about 200 acres in Tolland, and was a capable and industrious farmer. For about twenty-five years he ran a milk route in Rockville, dispensing in this way the milk of some twenty-five to forty cows, which belong to what is known as the "Dutch Belt" breed, which he exhibited throughout the United States.

He was a Democrat and served in the General Assembly in 1884 and was a member of the committee on labor and in 1919 when he was on the prisons committee. At home, he served as first selectman for ten years from 1903 to 1913, during which period he helped to obtain the first state road in Tolland, running from Rockville to Tolland. He served on the board of relief a term, assessor two terms, and collector of taxes two terms. For many years he had been registrar of voters and was instrumental in forming The Farm Bureau and in obtaining perpetual care for the cemeteries.

He was deputy jailer under George Forster for four years, from 1911 to 1915 and was named a trustee of the Mansfield Training School in 1919 under Governor Holcomb and served until 1939. He was vice president of the Savings Bank of Tolland and has held various offices in the bank since 1890. He was a member of the Rockville Fair Association and served officially as well as an exhibitor. His family are members of the Congregational Church, of which he has always been a liberal supporter. Socially he belonged to the Ancient Order of the United Workmen, and the Royal Arcanum, of Rockville.

On April 21, 1880, Mr. Leonard was married to Jennie Roxana Joslyn, a daughter of Edmund Joslyn of Tolland. Their children are: Charles Henry Leonard, who worked for the U.S. Envelop Co. for 54 years, serving many years as manager. He served one term in the General Assembly in 1959; Mary Roxana Leonard, a school teacher in both Tolland and Hartford; Florence Jennie Leonard, a teacher of English in the Orange, N.J. High School for 34 years; Rufus Joslyn Leonard, who operated the family farm until his death in 1930 at the age of 35.

Oscar A. Leonard died on June 30, 1939, at the age of 85. His wife, Jennie Joslyn Leonard died on June 17, 1952. Mr. Leonard served his town well and was one of the most successful farmers of the town of Tolland, and his farm showed the handiwork of a skilled and progressive agriculturist. He was a genial and whole-souled gentleman, who was very popular in the community, and whose home was very hospitable.

CHARLES UNDERWOOD - born in Thompson, Conn., in 1824, married Mary Anthony Hawkins in Tolland in 1850. He was the son of Moses Underwood and Clarissa Tourtelotte Underwood and came to Tolland as a young boy when his father bought the "Old Factory" and the old home next to it.

As a young man he bought much land in various sections of Tolland and North Coventry for agricultural and investment purposes. He developed a large leather belting business in the "Old Factory" where his father carried on a tannery of wide reputation. Processes for preparing the leather were developed and products were sold throughout the country, from sewing machine belts to large steam engine belts. Moses deeded the "Old Factory" and the belting business to Charles in 1851.

For many years before the Civil War and during it, Charles Underwood was in charge of drilling the Militia on the Green. He was President of the Tolland County Bank and later President of the Savings Bank of Tolland, for a total of 37 years. He was also a Director of the Tolland County Mutual Insurance Co. In 1868 and 1869 he was a State Senator. At this time he bought a home in Hartford for the winter months for a period of six years to get to the Capitol more easily and to put his children into High School. He went back and forth from there to Tolland to see to affairs there. He was appointed a Commissioner of Tolland County and was First Selectman of Tolland in 1855 and 1860.

In his older years, he took up a section of land in Florida and became interested in raising oranges. He died in 1908, at the home of his daughter, Mrs. Charles H. Daniels in Framingham, Mass.

Soren P Waldy

Elisha Stearns.

Edward E. Fuller

Ratliff Hicks

Charles Underwood

Frank G. Bryant

Oscar A. Leonard

Appendix

THE AGARD FAMILY

John Agard

John Agard came from England; first settler of the Agard family in America.

1683-*John Agard*

John, son of John, born in Boston. He moved to Mansfield. He had 7 children.

1716-*Benjamin Agard*

Benjamin, son of John born in Mansfield, Conn. He had four children.

1750-*Benjamin Agard*
1. Lydia Dawn
2. Sarah Hiscock

Benjamin, son of John born in Mansfield, settled in Stafford. He had 8 children by Sarah.

1778-*Nathan Agard*-1868
1783-Hannah Hall-1859

Nathan, son of Benjamin, born in Stafford, Conn. He was a farmer and an iron forger. He had five children.

1815-*Ransel Agard*-1889

Ransel, son of Nathan, born in Stafford, was a school teacher and then in grocery business. Came to Tolland.

1848-*Wm. A. Agard*-1935
1852-Cath. Bissell-1906

Hon. William A. Agard, son of Ransel, attended Hartford schools & E. Greenwich Academy. He was a bookkeeper for Wm. Sumner & Co. in Ohio, Gen. Mgr. of Capital City Gas Light Co., Des Moines, Secy. Staten Island Milling Co. Came to Conn. in 1889, became Mgr. of Underwood Mnfg. Co., later known as Wm. Sumner Belting Co., of which he was President in 1898. In House of Reps. in 1904-5. President of Tolland Savings Bank 1902-16. Their children were: Mary Lucile, William H., Katherine (Meacham) and Marian (Baker). Eleanor, the daughter of Katherine Agard Meacham married Robert Jenks and reside in the original Agard homestead.

1851-*Edwin S. Agard*-1936
1855-Sara Browning-1922

Hon. Edwin Sumner Agard, son of Ransel, born in Hartford. He was treasurer of the William Sumner Belting Co. and a lawyer of ability, a town clerk, in the state legislature, and director of the Savings Bank of Tolland. His children were: Harry B., Florence (Babcock), Lilla (Safford), and Elizabeth (Carpenter). He was a leading citizen of the town and an influential politician and representative man.

THE BABCOCK FAMILY

1612-*James Babcock*-1679
1. Sarah Vose
2. Elizabeth ---

James Babcock was born in Essex, Eng. He came to America at an early age and settled in Portsmouth, R.I. He had 4 children by his 1st wife and 8 by 2nd.

1644-*John Babcock*-1685
Mary Lawton-1711

John Babcock, son of James, lived in Westerly, R.I. Served in King Philips' War. He eloped with Mary Lawton and they had 10 children.

1663-*James Babcock*-1736
1661-Eliz. Babbit-1730

Capt. James Babcock, son of John, was born in Westerly, R.I. He had

1708-Content Maxon

1734-*James Babcock*-1781
1719-Sarah Stanton
1736-Joanna McDowel-1820

1758-*Simon Babcock*-1851
1763-Han. Champlin-1831

1793-*Stan. Babcock*-1826
    Mar. Robertson
1798-Almy Barrows-1847

1820-*Jaynes Babcock*-1895
1826-Lovisa Hovey-1857
    Julia Babcock

1850-*Gil. Babcock*-1924
1854-Inez Brown-1939

Inez Brown was the daughter of James Avery Brown and Francis Allen (Kimball) Brown. James Avery Brown was born in North Stonington, Conn. in 1828 and died in Philadelphia in 1874. This branch of the Brown family descended from Thomas, James, Simeon, James, James and Darius to James Avery Brown.

seven children by his 1st wife and 3 by 2nd.

Col. James Babcock, son of Capt. James, born in Westerly R.I. He graduated from Yale in 1752, was a soldier in the Revolution. He had 3 children by his first wife and 5 by his second.

Simon Babcock, son of Col. James was born in Westerly R.I. Was a soldier in the Revolution. He had 14 children.

Stanton Babcock, son of Simon, was buried in Nathan Hale cemetery in S. Coventry, Conn. He had 4 sons.

Jaynes Babcock, son of Stanton, born in Columbia, Conn. He died in Vernon. In 1858 he moved to Tolland, in 1870 to Vernon to raise tobacco. He served as selectman. His children were: Maryette, Gilbert P., Jennie, William and Irvin.

Gilbert Potter Babcock, son of Jaynes, born in Columbia, came to Tolland 1858. In 1881 he was an engineer in Scranton. He then operated a grain and lumber mill in Vernon. In 1895 he came to Grant's Hill to raise peaches. In 1899 he was jailor of the County Jail for 12 years. His children were: Frank Gilbert, Harry Jaynes, who married Florence E. Agard; and Elliott.

THE BENTON FAMILY

1658-*Samuel Benton*-1746
1661-Sarah Chatterton

Samuel Benton was one of the grantees of the committee to the first proprietors of Tolland. He came from Hartford.

1700-*Daniel Benton*
Mary Skinner

Daniel Benton, son of Samuel, bought the land in Tolland of his father, on Feb. 20, 1719. This land and house is now known as the Benton Homestead. Daniel and Mary's children were; Daniel, William and Elijah.

1723-*Daniel Benton*
Mary Wheeler

Daniel, son of Daniel, had seven sons: Elisha, Daniel, Azariah, Jacob, William, Nathan and Silas. Daniel, the second of these sons married Betty Richards in 1779. Their children were; Elisha, Betty, Eunice, Agnes and Phoebe. Eunice married M. Bliss Chapin who took over the old Benton Homestead and it remained in the Chapin family until sold to Mrs. Bowering.

1760-*Jacob Benton*-1843
Sarah Weston-1787
Sarah Ladd

Jacob Benton, the fourth son of Daniel, was a revolutionary soldier. With his first wife, he had 2 children, Anna and William. With second wife he had Azariah, Ruth, Daniel, Chester and Jacob. Azariah, born in 1790, married Precendia Ladd, had 2 sons: Azariah, Jr. and William Austin. Azariah, Jr., married Louise Alden, then Mary Smith. With Mary he had a daughter Ellen who married Hibbard West. Their children were: Edith, Rupert, Hazel and Lathrop. William Austin, was a missionary in Syria for 22 years. He married Loanza Goulding. Their son, Charles W. Benton, married Elma Hixon. Their son, William, was the U.S. Senator from Conn. in 1948 to 1953.

1794-*Daniel Benton*-1876
1797-Marcia Ladd-1880

Daniel Benton, son of Jacob, was a farmer in Tolland.

1831-*Randolph Benton*-1904
1836-Clara C. Usher-1915

Randolph Benton, son of Daniel, was a farmer and large land holder. He lived just below the cider mill.

1859-*Henry Benton*-1917
1861-Frank Rounds-1914

D. Henry Benton, son of Randolph, married Frank E. Rounds, daughter of Wm. Rounds of Grant's Hill. They had 8 children: William, Avis, Neal, Lester, Louis, Hazel, Almy and Rutherford.

THE CHAPMAN FAMILY

Edward Chapman-1675

Edward Chapman, the first American ancestor came about 1660 to Windsor from England. He settled in Simsbury than a part of Windsor, and lost his life at the storming of Narragansett Fort in December, 1675.

1669-*Simon Chapman*

Simon Chapman, son of Edward, born in Windsor but held lands in Tolland, of which town he was one of the proprietors. He married in 1692, had a son.

1696-*Samuel Chapman*-1746

Capt. Samuel Chapman, son of Simon was the progenitor of all the Chapmans in the western part of Tolland. He was the only justice of peace in Tolland for nine years, and was selectman for eleven years. He died in the service of his country in the French and Indian war in 1746. His children were: Samuel, Elijah, Simon, Ruth, Sarah, Hannah, Margaret and Mary.

1726-*Elijah Chapman*-1812
Sarah Steele

Elijah Chapman, son of Samuel, was a member of the General Assembly in 1765, 1776, 1781, and 1782. His children were: Johanna, Rueben, Elijah, Ashbel, Sarah, Ruth, Esther, Roxana, Aaron, Dorcas and Daniel.

1765-*Aaron Chapman*-1842

Aaron Chapman, son of Elijah, had two sons, Novatus and Daniel. He was a selectman for three years.

1803-*Daniel Chapman*-1887
Hannah Buell

Daniel Chapman, son of Aaron, was born in Tolland. He had two children: Annis and Daniel Buell.

1840-*Daniel Chapman*-1898
Amanda Lewis-1911

Daniel Buell Chapman, son of Daniel, was always known as Buell Chapman. He lived on the corner of Mountain Road and Old Post Road. His children were: 1868 Clifton, 1869 Norvall, 1871 Alice, 1873 Annie, 1876 Lottie, 1879 Frank, Harriet, 1887 Clarence.

1869-*Norvall Chapman*-1931
Gena Hansen-1951

Norvall Chapman, son of Daniel, lived on the corner of Mountain and Old Post Road. His children were: 1893 Nora (Carver), 1895 Carl, 1897 Daniel Buell, 1898 Annie May, 1908 Frank Henry.

THE CLOUGH FAMILY

1613-*John Clough*
  Jane -

John Clough came from England in 1635 to Boston. He had seven children.

1649-*John Clough*
  Mercy Page

John Clough, son of John, had twelve children.

1688-*Jonathan Clough*
  Hannah Gile-1727
  Mary Gile

Jonathan Clough, son of John, had nine children by Hannah and three by Mary.

1724-*Ephraim Clough*
  Mary Johnson

Ephraim Clough, son of Jonathan, had thirteen children.

1749-*Joseph Clough*
  Mary Ferry

Joseph Clough, son of Ephraim, had nine children.

1784-*James Clough*-1823
1784-Eliz. Popkin-1816

James Clough, son of Joseph, had four children.

1807-*James L. Clough*

James L. Clough, son of James, had eight children. Francis Wayland 1841, Abby Elizabeth 1842, James Hurdis 1845, Alfred Beecher 1849, Earl Fenelon 1850, Roger Minot 1852, John Eliot 1854, and Justin Edwards 1858.

James Hurdis Clough married Abby Jane Arnold and their children were: Frank James 1872, Burton Andrew 1873, Harvey Burnett 1881, and Grace Emeline 1883. Harvey Burnett Clough now lives in Tolland and has two children, William Clough and Doris Clough Tobiassen.

Earl Fenelon Clough married Nellie Arnold and their children were: Chester 1884, and Emery 1893. Emery Clough lives in Tolland and has three children.

John Elliot Clough married Sarah Tilden and their children were: A. Esten, Clayton and Walter. Esten married Maud Crandall and their children were: Florence, Harold, Wilma, Helen, Leon and Mildred.

THE CRANDALL FAMILY

1612-*John Crandall*-1676
1. Unknown-1670
1647-Han. Gaylord-1676

John Crandall, Colonial pioneer, First Baptist Elder, Deputy Commissioner, and Statesman of Newport and Westerly, R.I., the head of the Crandall Family in America, was born in Monmouthshire, Eng. Came to Boston in 1634, Salem in 1635, Providence in 1637 as associate of Roger Williams, Newport 1651, Westerly 1665 as First Baptist Elder.

1663-*Samuel Crandall*-1763
Sarah Colby

Samuel Crandall, son of John of Tiverton, and Newport R.I. Married in 1685 and had 7 children.

1697-*Peter Crandall*-1765
1700-Mary Richmond-1765

Peter Crandall, son of Samuel, of Tiverton, Little Compton, R. E. Peter and Mary had 11 children.

1725-*Giles Crandall*
Elizabeth -

Giles Crandall, son of Peter, born in Tiverton, R.I. Came to Tolland with brother Constant, who died on the Expedition to Cuba in 1762. He married Elizabeth in 1747, had 10 children.

1754-*Samuel Crandall*

Samuel Crandall, son of Giles, born in Tolland. He had 7 children.

1774-*Samuel Crandall*
1774-Roxana Rawdon-1792

Samuel Crandall, son of Samuel, born in Tolland, had 4 children. One son, Jarvis, was a celebrated singer.

1801-*Amos Crandall*-1862
1801-Eunice Day-1883

Amos Crandall, son of Samuel, born in Tolland, children: Luranna (Walker), Roxanna (Brown), Mary Ann, Maria (Brown) and Alden B.

1801-*Alden Crandall*-1904
1801-Rachel Usher-1904

Alden Bradford Crandall, son of Amos, was a farmer in Tolland. He served in the General Assembly and in the Civil War. In 1845 he married Rachel Usher and their children were: Mary (Usher), Ellen M. (Williams), Alden and Edwin.

1854-*Edwin Crandall*-1938
1858-Mary J. Rounds-1940

Edwin Crandall, son of Alden B. was a farmer in Tolland and also operated a grist and cider mill in Tolland Center. He served as selectman and in the Gen. Assembly. In 1873 he married Mary Jane Rounds and their children were: Harry, Harvey E., Rose (Smith), Elizabeth (Hughes), Clayton Howard, Luella Maud (Clough), Cora Melissa (Aborn), Ellen (Reed), Susan (Robinson), Herbert, Lillie, Henry and Carrie (Ayers).

THE FULLER FAMILY

Robert Fuller-1706
Sarah-1676

Robert Fuller, the founder of the American branch of the family, came to America in 1638 and made his home in Salem and Rehoboth, Mass. He was the first bricklayer in New England.

1640-*Jonathan Fuller*-1709
Eliz. Wilmarth

Jonathan Fuller, son of Robert, was born in Salem, where he served as selectman. On Dec. 14, 1664, he married Elizabeth Wilmarth.

1667-*David Fuller*
Mary Ormsby
Constance

Deacon David Fuller, son of Jonathan, was born in Attleboro, Mass. In 1716 he moved to Coventry, Conn., where in 1717 he served as selectman.

1710-*David Fuller*
1714-Hannah Fuller

David Fuller, son of Deacon David, was born in Attleboro, Mass. He died in Hampton, Conn.

1753-*Abijah Fuller*-1835
    Abigail Meacham-1840

Sergt. Abijah Fuller, son of David, born in Hampton, Conn. He served in the Revolutionary army under Gen. Putnam at Bunker Hill. He was a farmer and cooper and a highly honored citizen. He had seven children.

1787-*Seymour Fuller*-1862
1790-Louisa Butler-1876

Seymour Fuller, son of Abijah, born in Hampton, Conn. He moved to Tolland in 1816 and was a cooper and farmer. They had five children.

1812-*Lucius S. Fuller*-1890
    Mary E. Bliss-1899

Hon. Lucius Seymour Fuller, son of Seymour, born in Hampton, Mass. At age of four moved to Tolland. He taught school, drove a stage coach, and was a farmer. He was very active in the insurance business. He was a director of the Tolland County National Bank and vice-president of the Savings Bank. He served as State Senator. He had 7 children, 3 sons were prominent in public affairs.

1853-*Edward Fuller*-1932

Hon. Edward Eugene Fuller, son of Lucius, was born in Tolland. He was very active in the insurance and banking business. Served as State Senator and was very interested in town affairs. He belonged to many fraternal organizations. In this family we have the rare instance of father and three sons all intrusted in legislative office, the father and two sons having served as senators. A very respected and esteemed family.

THE GRANT FAMILY

1601-*Matthew Grant*-1681
 Priscilla-1644
 Susan Rockwell-1666

Matthew Grant was born in England. He arrived in Boston on May 30, 1630 from Plymouth, and settled in Dorchester, Mass. In 1635 he came to Windsor, Conn. He was a carpenter, town clerk and a selectman.

1631-*Samuel Grant*-1718
1638-Mary Porter

Samuel Grant, son of Matthew, was born in Dorchester, Mass., and died in E. Windsor Hill, Conn. Was a sawmill operator, surveyor and a carpenter.

1659-*Samuel Grant*-1710
1664-Anna Filley-1686
1670-Grace Minor-1753

Samuel Grant, son of Samuel, was born in Windsor, Conn. He owned a cider mill and kept a tavern.

1693-*Noah Grant*-1727
1696-Martha Huntington-1769

Noah Grant, son of Samuel and Grace, lived on Grant's Hill. He moved from Windsor to Tolland at 22 years old. He was surveyor and a selectman. He was one of the original proprietors of Tolland and was granted lot #6 on Grant's Hill.

1718-*Noah Grant*-1756
1724-Susan Delano-1806

Noah Grant, son of Noah, was born in Tolland. He served in the French and Indian Wars. When he was 9 years old, his father died and his mother married Lieut. Buell and moved to Coventry.

1748-*Noah Grant*-1819
1738-Anna Richardson-1787
 Rachel Kelly-1805

Noah Grant, son of Noah and Rachel, was born in Tolland and died in Maysville, Ky. He was a farmer and tanner and served in the Revolution.

1794-*Jesse R. Grant*-1873
1798-Hannah Simpson-1883

Jesse R. Grant, son of Noah and Rachel, born near Greensboro, Pa. He was a tanner and served as postmaster.

1822-*Ulysses S. Grant*-1885
1826-Julia Dent

Ulysses S. Grant, son of Jesse, was born in Point Pleasant, Ohio. He graduated from the Military Academy in 1843. Served in the army and rose to the rank of General in the Civil War. He served as Sect. of War in 1867-68. He was President in 1869-1877. He had four children: Frederick 1850, Ulysses 1852, Ellen 1855, and Jesse 1858.

The first Noah Grant came from Windsor and was granted lot #6 on Grant's Hill. He may have moved to Tolland prior to 1720, and lived in a rough cabin on lot # 6, as there is no trace of any house on this lot now. He bought the Reiske farm in 1724.

THE LATHROP FAMILY

Zebulon Lathrop

Zebulon Lathrop came from Lebanon and bought a farm in the southeast part of the town. He received a deed from Joshua Tilden, on Mar. 26, 1800. His ancestors came from Norwich.

John Lathrop
Miss Dimock

John Lathrop was a native of New London, Conn. He married a Miss Dimock of Willington, Conn., and each lived to a ripe old age. They made their home in the southern part of Tolland where he successfully engaged in farming. He had six children.

1802-*Justin Lathrop*-1875
1. Mary Isham
2. Ruth Kendall

Justin Lathrop, son of John, was born in Willington, and died in Tolland in April 1875. He attended school in Tolland and became a blacksmith, a trade he followed many years. In 1867 he purchased a farm in Tolland, on which he passed the remaining years of his life. He was twice married, first to Mary Isham, by whom he had three children. He then married Ruth P. Kendall, born in 1817. They had three children: 1. James A., a farmer in Tolland, married Emma Dunn and they had nine children; 2. Perkins L. and 3. Mary Angeline, wife of Eli Carver of Coventry.

1858-*Perkins Lathrop*-1941
1867-Fannie Walker-1931

Perkins Lloyd Lathrop, son of Justin, was born in Willington on June 11, 1858 and had his schooling in Tolland. When he was 16 years old, he taught his first winter school in the 7th and 9th districts. In December, 1880, he married Fannie E. Walker, and they had these children: Arthur Justin, born 1883, Everett Perkins, born 1884, and Ruth Lillian, born 1896.

Mr. Lathrop was selectman for two years, on the board of relief three years, town auditor four years, assessor in 1894 and served in the General Assembly. He also served as President of the Tolland Savings Bank from 1916 to 1942. He operated a large farm in North Coventry and carried on an extensive lumber trade.

THE LEONARD FAMILY

1620-*James Leonard*-1691
   Mary Martin
   Margaret (Ford)

James Leonard, son of Thomas of Great Britain, came from England and settled in Rayham near Taunton, Mass. in 1642. He and his brother built the first iron works in the old colony. He died in 1691 and was survived by his widow, Margaret, the stepmother of their 8 children.

1662-*Uriah Leonard*-1742
1664-Eliz. Caswell

Uriah Leonard, youngest son of James, born July 10, 1662, married Jan. 1, 1685, Elizabeth Caswell. They had five children.

1688-*William Leonard*-1772
   Annie Barney

William Leonard, son of Uriah, born in 1688. He was married to Annie Barney. He died in 1772.

1716-*Jacob Leonard*-1743
1737-Margaret Wild

Jacob Leonard, son of William, born in 1716. He was married to Margaret Wild and he died in 1743.

1742-*Jacob Leonard*-1815
1763-Rhoda Wheeler

Jacob Leonard, Jr., son of Jacob, born in 1742. He was married to Rhoda Wheeler.

Rufus Leonard-1837
   Jemima Hicks
   Silence Newell

Rufus Leonard was a farmer in Stafford, Conn., where he also worked at blacksmithing. He was Justice of the Peace for many years. He was married 1. to Jemima Hicks and 2. to Silence Newell. He had three children.

1802-*Jenks Leonard*-1836
   Lucy Pease

Jenks W. Leonard, son of Rufus, was born in Stafford, Conn., where he worked as a blacksmith and later as a butcher. He died at the age of 34 years. He was married to Lucy Pease. They had six children.

1828-*Rufus Leonard*
1830-Mary Howlett-1859
 Adelaide Davis-1890
 Lucy Pank

Rufus J., the oldest son of Jenks W. Leonard was born in Stafford, Conn. He spent many years as a school teacher and had a general store in Stafford. After this burned down, he worked in a lumber firm until he could buy a farm in Tolland. After 20 years, he bought a farm in Ellington in 1884.

1853-*Oscar Leonard*-1939
1851-Jennie Joslyn-1952

Oscar was the only son of Rufus J. and Mary Howlett. His children were: Charles Henry, Mary Roxana, Florence Jennie, and Rufus Joslyn Leonard. Mr. Leonard was very active in the town affairs. He was selectman 10 years.

THE METCALF FAMILY

Michael Metcalf

Michael Metcalf was the founder of the Metcalf Family in America. He came from Yorkshire, England, and arrived in Boston, June 17, 1637.

Michael Metcalf
Mary Fairbanks

Michael Metcalf, son of Michael, came from England with his father and in 1644 married Mary Fairbanks.

Jonathan Metcalf
Hannah Kendricks

Jonathan Metcalf, son of Michael, Jr. was married to Hannah Kendricks in 1674. They had ten children.

1680-*Ebenezer Metcalf*
 Hannah Abel

Ebenezer Metcalf, son of Jonathan, settled in Lebanon, Conn. in 1702.

 Timothy Metcalf
 Hannah Metcalf

Timothy Metcalf son of Ebenezer, was the first deacon of the Congregational Church in Mansfield, Conn. He owned large land tracts in Mansfield.

Ebenezer Metcalf
Silence Morey

Ebenezer Metcalf, son of Timothy, lived in Mansfield. He answered the Putnam alarm during the Revolutionary War. He had 8 children.

1804-*Joseph Metcalf*-1898
1808-Elmina Leonard-1871

Joseph Bonaparte Metcalf, son of Ebenezer, lived in Somerville and in Tolland. Possessed of great mechanical skill, he invented many types of machines. He was an expert weaver and a cabinet maker. He had 4 children: Charles 1831, twins Andrew Jackson and Martin Van Buren 1837, and Elizabeth.

1837-*Andrew Metcalf*
Jane Morrison

Andrew Metcalf, son of Joseph, lived in Tolland and his children were: Abial Leonard and Joseph Morrison.

1860-*Joseph Metcalf*-1941
1864-Anna Rounds-1954

Joseph Metcalf, son of Andrew, lived in Tolland where he worked as a farmer and carpenter. His children were: Mildred who died in World War I, serving as an army nurse, and George.

1896-*George Metcalf*-1961
Caroline Kimmel

George Metcalf, son of Joseph, farmed in Tolland. He had a son, Harold.

Abial Metcalf, son of Andrew and brother of Joseph was born in 1858 and died in 1948. He married first Amelia Miller in 1882, born in 1859 and died in 1894. Their children were, Fred, Elmer, Clarence, Leslie and Nellie. He married second, Minnie Booth, born 1879 and died in 1953. Their children were: Howard, Maud, Samuel, Leonard, Arthur and Murilla. Abial Metcalf was postmaster from 1900-1903. He also served as assessor and fire warden for many years. The family lived in Skungamaug.

THE NEWCOMB FAMILY

1618-*Andrew Newcomb*-1686
Unknown
Grace Hicks

Andrew Newcomb was born in England, came to America as captain of a sailing vessel.

1640-*Andrew Newcomb*-1706
Sarah -
Anna Bayes

Andrew Newcomb was born at the Isle of Shoals, N. H. He later lived on Martha's Vineyard. He had 7 children by Sarah and 8 by Anna.

1665-*Simon Newcomb*-1744
1664-Deborah -

Simon Newcomb was born at Kittery, Maine, and moved to Lebanon, Conn. He had 8 children.

1693-*Hezekiah Newcomb*-1772
1692-Jerusha Bradford-1739
1742-Hannah-1794

Hezekiah Newcomb was born on Martha's Vineyard, and moved to Lebanon Conn. He had 10 children.

1724-*Thomas Newcomb*-1753
1757-Ann Hibbard

Thomas Newcomb was born at Lebanon, Conn. He died at 29 years of age. He had one child.

1752-*Joseph Newcomb*-1812
1757-Rhoda Scripture-1828

Joseph Newcomb, born at Lebanon, moved to Willington, was a farmer. He had 11 children.

1783-*Cordial Newcomb*-1851
1786-Mary Deming-1863

Cordial Newcomb, born in Willington, and settled in Tolland. He was a selectman, assessor, member of school board, town agent, and member of house of Reps. He had 8 children.

1806-*William Newcomb*-1864
1807-Maria Merrick-1890

William Crocker Newcomb, born in Tolland. Was a farmer, selectman, Member of House of Reps., state senator, and Capt. of militia. He had 8 children.

1836-*Loren Newcomb*-1909
1838-Anna Turner-1904

Loren E. Newcomb, born in Tolland and a dairy farmer. Was selectman, assessor, board of relief, constable, justice of the peace and collector of taxes. He served in General Assembly and Constitutional Convention of 1902.

1861-*Frank T. Newcomb*-1924
1861-Addie Millard-1951

Frank Turner Newcomb was born in Tolland, Conn. At the age of 17 he began teaching at the 7 and 9 districts. He then joined the Tolland County National Bank, where he was cashier and also treasurer of the Savings Bank of Tolland. He was an Extensive farmer. He served as town treasurer and clerk, school visitor, and postmaster. He had the following children: Harry, Philip, Pauline (Grant), Lilla, and Phyllis.

THE PRESTON FAMILY

Medina Preston

Medina Preston lived in Ashford, Conn.

Zephaniah Preston
Mary Bishop

Zephaniah Preston, son of Medina, was born in Ashford, Conn. He was a farmer and a man of reliability and of ample means. He had five children.

1792-*Reuben Preston*-1884
1795-Lucy Howard-1876

Reuben Preston, son of Zephaniah, was born in Ashford, Conn. He was an extensive and successful farmer. His two children were: Gilbert H. and Newton Work Preston.

1820-*Gilbert Preston*-1883
1820-Sarah Cogswell

Dr. Gilbert Howard Preston, son of Reuben, was born in Eastford, Conn. He graduated from Castleton College, Vt. in medicine and practiced for 3 years in Westford. In 1845 he moved to Tolland and practiced medicine there for 40 years. He was very prominent in his profession and also took an active interest in public affairs. His four children were: Charles Henry 1849, Edward Howard, Sarah Cornelia 1854, and George Cogswell 1856. Charles and George Preston conducted a hardware business in Norwich, Conn. Edward H. was a very prominent business man in Rockville, Conn.

1854-*Sarah C. Preston*
Joseph Lathrop

Sarah Cornelia Preston, daughter of Dr. Gilbert, was born in Tolland and married Joseph Lathrop, a bookkeeper. Their only child, Edith Lucy 1879, married Edward Meacham of Tolland. Their children were Florence Meacham, who married Walter Anderson; and Preston Meacham, who married Marge Weismiller. They have two children: George and Margaret.

Edward Meacham and Edith Lucy had four more children as follows: Robert, Francis, Maurice and Helen Smith.

THE SUMNER FAMILY

Roger Sumner
Joane Franklin

Roger Sumner was a farmer of Bicester, Oxfordshire, England.

1605-*William Sumner*-1688
Mary West-1676

William Sumner, only child of Roger, was born in Bicester, England. In 1636 he came to New England to Dorchester, Mass. He had 6 children.

William Sumner-1675
Eliz. Clement-1685

William Sumner, son of William, was born in Dorchester, Mass. He moved to Boston, where he followed a seafaring life. He had ten children.

1671-*Clement Sumner*
Margaret Harris

Clement Sumner, son of William, was born in Boston. He had 7 children.

1699-*William Sumner*
Hannah Hunt

William Sumner, son of Clement, was born in Boston and later moved to Hebron, Conn., where he was a physician. He had 11 children.

1727-*Reuben Sumner*-1807
Elizabeth Mack-1805

Reuben Sumner, son of William, was born at Hebron, Conn., where he made his home. He had eleven children.

1761-*William Sumner*-1838
Jemima Tarbox-1837

William Sumner, son of Reuben, was born in Hebron, Conn., where he became prominent. He had ten children.

1792-*William Sumner*-1868
Anna Washburn

William A. Sumner, son of William, was born in Hebron. Later moved to Tolland. He had nine children.

1826-*William Sumner*-1897
Juliette Bishop

William Sumner, son of William A., was born in Tolland, Conn. He first became a lawyer for two years and then moved to Cincinnati, Ohio, where he became general agent of the Wheeler and Wilson Sewing

Machine Co. He sold out in 1874, and organized the Capitol City Gas Co. of Des Moines, Iowa. After 5 years he built a flouring mill on Staten Island. Returning to Tolland, to take an active interest in the Underwood Belting Co., which became the William Sumner Belting Co., with Mr. Sumner as president. He also served as judge of probate and in the General Assembly. He had 3 children, two of whom died young. His daughter, Edith Bishop Sumner born in 1871, married Rev. Samuel Simpson, of Centerville, Mich. They are the parents of William Sumner Simpson, who resided in Tolland and now lives in Litchfield, Conn.

THE UNDERWOOD FAMILY

1614-*Joseph Underwood*-1676
1. Mary Wilder
2. Mary How

Joseph Underwood of Watertown, Mass., came from England in 1637 and settled in Hingham, Mass. He and Mary Wilder had seven children.

1650-*Joseph Underwood*-1691

Joseph Underwood, son of Joseph, lived in Watertown, Mass. He married Elizabeth in 1672, had 9 children.

1685-*Jonathan Underwood*

Jonathan Underwood, son of Joseph of Watertown, Mass. He was a mariner and had five sons.

1721-*Nehemiah Underwood*-1772
Anna Marcy

Nehemiah Underwood, son of Jonathan, lived in Woodstock, as a farmer. Married in 1743 and had 10 children.

1769-*Samuel Underwood*
Susannah Richardson

Samuel Underwood, son of Nehemiah, was a shoemaker in Pomfret. Married in 1791 and had 9 children.

1799-*Moses Underwood*-1862
1799-Clarissa Tourtellote

Moses Underwood, son of Samuel, born in Pomfret, moved to Tolland in 1836 to establish a tannery business in the "old factory". He served as a State Senator. Married, 1820, and they had seven children.

1824-*Charles Underwood*-1908
1826-Mary Hawkins-1905

Charles Underwood, son of Moses, acquired much land and real estate as a young man. Was President of the Tolland County National Bank and later of the Savings Bank of Tolland for 23 years. He was a director of the Tolland Co. Mutual Fire Ins. Co. Married in 1850, children were: Jennie, Mary, Kate and Charles.
He built up the leather belting and tannery business of his father and was President of the Underwood Belting Company for many years.

1858-*Mary Underwood*-1933
1847-Charles Daniels-1914

Mary Louise Underwood, daughter of Charles and Mary, married the Rev. Charles H. Daniels, D. D. of Newton and Framingham, Mass. Their children were Margarette and Agnes Carter.

Agnes C. Daniels
1891-Aaron P. Pratt-1961

Agnes C. Daniels married Aaron Paul Pratt, M.D. They lived and he practiced in Windsor for about 40 years. Children are Aaron P., Jr. and Mary Agnes (Wine). Mrs. Pratt occupies the Charles Underwood home built in 1859.

THE WALDO FAMILY

1626-*Cornelius Waldo*-1700
1624-Hannah Cogswell-1704

Cornelius Waldo was born in England about 1624. He settled in Ipswich, and there married Hannah Cogswell, who came from England in 1635 and was wrecked on the shore at Pemaquid in the gale of Aug. 15, 1635, with loss of many of passengers and crew. They had 12 children.

John Waldo-1700
Rebecca Adams-1727

John Waldo, first son of Cornelius, born at Ipswich. He lived in Boston around 1695. In 1697 he bought a grist mill in Windham, Conn. He had 8 children.

1684-*Edward Waldo*-1767
1682-Thankful Dimock-1757
1695-Mary Paine-1764

Edward Waldo, son of John, born at Dunstable, Mass., moved to Windham in 1697. Served in General Assembly in 1725 and 1730. He had 10 children. He was the great great grandfather of Judge Loren P. Waldo, who wrote the *History of Tolland*.

1707-*Shubael Waldo*-1776
1712-Abigail Allen-1799

Shubael Waldo, oldest son of Edward, born at Windham. He first lived in Norwich, and in 1738 moved to Mansfield. In 1767 he moved to Alstead, N.H. He and Abigail had fifteen children.

1736-*Jesse Waldo*
1735-Briget Thompson-1805
1752-Hannah Welch

Jesse Waldo, son of Shubael, was born in Norwich. He served in the Revolutionary War. He and Hannah Welch had seven children.

1770-*Zacheus Waldo*
1776-Thankful Dunham
Anna Stewart

Zacheus Waldo, youngest son of Zacheus and Anna, born at Merrow. He worked in the quarries at Portland and then returned to Mansfield. He and Sarah had 8 children.

1847-*Wilbur F. Waldo*
1848-Martha Hale

Wilbur Fiske Waldo, son of Zacheus, born in Mansfield. He also lived at Willington, Mansfield Hollow and at Providence, R.I. Since 1888 he lived in Tolland. He was always employed in the thread business. He had three children: Harry D., Mabel Pearl who married Arthur Spicer, and Roy Kenneth Waldo.

THE WEBSTER FAMILY

1590-*John Webster*-1661

John Webster was born in England in 1590. He came to Hartford with the Rev. Thomas L. Hooker in 1636, an original proprietor. The Founders Monument, in the cemetery behind the Center Church, shows his name as the seventh in the list of 101 names of the original founders of Hartford. He was the fifth governor of Conn. in 1656-57, and also a magistrate and legal adviser in the colony. He died in Hadley, Mass. on April 5, 1661.

Thomas Webster-1686
Abigail Alexander

Thomas Webster, son of John, was married on June 16, 1663.

1670-*George Webster*-1721
1677-Sarah Bliss

George Webster, son of Thomas, moved to Lebanon in 1699 and the original proprietors gave a "name lot" to him.

1720-*Joseph Webster* .
Hannah -

Joseph Webster, son of George, was a shoemaker and sold real estate.

1760-*Simeon Webster*-1842
1762-Sybil Converse-1837

Simeon Webster, son of Joseph, married on Oct. 17, 1784. He first lived in Stafford then moved to Tolland, as a farmer. He was a Revolutionary War veteran with 3 years service, having served at Monmouth and Chestnut Hill. Was wounded in service.

1798-*Milton Webster*-1846
1798-Sarah Eddy-1866

Milton Webster, son of Simeon, was married to Sarah Eddy Nov. 22, 1822 in Stafford, Conn. He was a farmer.

1831-*Gardner Webster*-1910
1836-Martha Drake-1916

Gardner Webster, son of Milton, was married on March 15, 1855. He was a farmer and Yankee Peddler.

1860-*Alice Webster*-1958
1856-John H. Steele-1950

Alice Webster, daughter of Gardner, married on April 12, 1877. Their children were Leila and Raymond Steele. He married Maude Price and a son, Mason, has 2 children: Raymond and Nancy by Loretta Macfarlane.

1880-*Leila M. Steele*-1965
1876-L. Ernest Hall-1948

Leila Steele, daughter of Alice, was a school teacher and married to L. Ernest Hall, who ran a grocery store in Tolland for many years. Their children were: Bernice Adalena Hall, a librarian and Alice Ernestine Hall, a school teacher who married Ira E. Creelman on Aug. 9, 1947.

Bibliography

The following publications have contributed information for this book.

The History of Tolland - 1861 - by Loren P. Waldo. Meeting House Hill - Establishment of Tolland County - The Congregational Church and Ministers - Military History - Town Government - Cemeteries - Geneologies.

The History of Tolland County - 1888 - By J. R. Cole. Tolland Village in 1888 - Tolland Jail - The Hanging in Tolland - Biographies.

Commemerative Biographical Record of Tolland and Windham Counties - Biographies - Geneologies.

History of the Congregational Church - Mrs. Charles H. Daniels.

Personal Notes Concerning Tolland - Mrs. John H. Steele.

Two Hundred and Fiftieth Anniversary Book of Tolland.

The Early History of the Methodist Church - The Souvenir History of the New England Southern Conference by Reverend Rennets C. Miller in 1897.

Many other citizens of Tolland have helped to make this book possible by contributing sketches and photographs pertinent to the History of Tolland.